# AVRO
## THE HISTORY OF AN AIRCRAFT COMPANY

# AVRO
# THE HISTORY OF AN AIRCRAFT COMPANY

## Harry Holmes

**Airlife**

England

Copyright © 1994 by Harry Holmes

First published in the UK in 1994
by Airlife Publishing Ltd

**British Library Cataloguing in Publication Data**
A catalogue record for this book
is available at the British Library

ISBN 1 85310 531 7

Printed in Great Britain by Butler and Tanner Ltd. Frome and London.

# Airlife Publishing Ltd
101 Longden Road, Shrewsbury, SY3 9EB

# CONTENTS

# DEDICATION

To A.V. for starting it all and H.V. for helping him.

To Sir Roy Dobson for employing me.

To Roy Chadwick, arguably the world's greatest aircraft designer, who I would loved to have met, but never got the chance.

To Jimmy Orrell, a good friend and a true gentleman in every sense of the word.

To Stan Worrall, a little man with a big heart who loved everything about Avro until he died. At 82 years of age he was about to leave home to go to Woodford to work on restoring an Avro Anson when he passed away!

To my friends and colleagues and all ex-employees of Avro.

To aviators past and present who flew those magnificent Avro aeroplanes.

# AUTHOR'S INTRODUCTION

Writing the history of A.V. Roe & Company Limited is akin to fighting with one arm tied behind your back because the disastrous fire at the Chadderton factory in October 1959 destroyed all the company's historical records.

Chadderton was Avro headquarters and, unfortunately, the historical records for both the company and its aircraft were lost. However, in mid-1958 fellow enthusiast Derek Monk and I had received permission to copy historical material from the files and every lunchtime was spent at this task. After the blaze we were able to restore some of the records, but we had only scratched the surface of the wealth of the information which had been available.

Over the years the history has been pieced together and I have been fortunate, as public relations manager for the British Aerospace (ex Avro) factories at Chadderton and Woodford, to be able to receive as well as give information on the company.

It would be impossible to write any history which gave every small detail and this case is no exception, but I have endeavoured to produce a complete story which covers all the important periods and the various issues with which Avro had to contend. I have also tried to use as many unpublished photographs as possible, but a small number have been seen before and as they are the only ones available they are used for completeness.

In the research for this book I have used as many official records as are available and also some early notes of Humphrey Verdon Roe.

I am grateful to many people who have contributed in some way to the production of this book with some of the Avro stalwarts deserving much praise. Four who have now passed on, Jimmy Orrell, Teddy Fielding, 'Sandy' Jack and Stan Worrall, all of whom are still remembered with great affection. Stuart Davies and Alf Sewart are also to be thanked for their assistance.

Always willing to help in any Avro project are Roy Chadwick's two lovely daughters, Margaret Dove and Rosemary Lapham who, quite rightly, have done more than anyone to perpetuate their father's memory.

Historians who have assisted in a variety of ways over nearly four decades are, Eric Harlin, George Jenks, Derek Monk, Derek Tattersall, Chris Ashworth, Jack Bruce and Phil Jarrett.

I am greatly indebted to Brian Robinson for reading the manuscript and for his valuable comments. Brian, of course, is a fine historian and the leading authority on aviation in the Manchester area.

As we were chatting after the 1988 Avro 504 Club Annual Dinner, Jimmy Orrell said, 'Harry, you should write all of this before we go to that big hangar in the sky!' In fact, Jimmy's health was failing fast and he passed away just three months later. He left a space in the aviation scene which can never be filled and he is sadly missed. I hope that this book is the kind of thing he was looking for.

H.H.
Manchester
March 1994

RIGHT:
A twenty years old Edwin Alliott Verdon Roe. The surname of Verdon-Roe was adopted in 1933 in honour of his mother Sofia Verdon.

BELOW:
A. V. Roe, third from the left, with his helpers lifting the Roe 1 biplane from its shed through the railings which had been made detachable unknown to the Brooklands' management. The famous shed was the inspiration for the design of the Avro logo.

# CHAPTER 1

## The Early Years

The history of aeronautics has been the result of the foresight, courage and determination of a few individuals.

One such individual was Edwin Alliott Verdon Roe who was born in Patricroft, Manchester on 26 April 1877 and was the fourth child of Doctor Edwin Hodson Roe and his wife Sofia Verdon.

Doctor Roe, a well respected physician in the Patricroft and Eccles areas, wanted young Alliott to follow in his footsteps into the medical profession. However, the youngster had different ideas and at the age of just fourteen years and seven months he left school to join a civil engineering firm working in British Columbia, Canada. The job was ideal for Alliott, but a slump in the industry forced him to return to England in February 1893.

Roe then took up an apprenticeship at the Lancashire and Yorkshire Railway Company at Horwich near Bolton. During his five years of training he decided that working on locomotives was not for him, however, he did complete his apprenticeship before applying for a job at Portsmouth Dockyard. After studying marine engineering both at the dockyard and, later, at King's College, London, he fixed his sights on a career in the Royal Navy. His entry examinations to join the Navy proved to be unsuccessful, but it was not his engineering capability which caused him to fail.

His fascination for the sea remained unchanged and he was delighted when his application to join the African Royal Mail Company was accepted. He became fifth engineer of the SS *Inchanga* and it was during his many voyages to South Africa that he began to study the flight of birds with the albatross being of particular interest to him. After long spells in the engine room he would come up on deck and go to the stern of the vessel so that he could watch these giant birds as they followed in

the steamer's wake . . . the more he watched them, the more he loved their flight.

Roe began to ask himself if he could design wings so that he too could soar and he began to make a number of model flying machines.

In order to spend more time studying the problems of flight he left the sea in 1902 and became a draughtsman in the motor car industry at Brotherton and Crockers Limited. He continued to study the theory of flight and corresponded a number of times with the Wright brothers after their historic flight at Kittyhawk, North Carolina, USA, on 17 December 1903. In a letter to *The Times* which was published on 21 January 1906, Roe complained about the lack of progress in heavier-than-air flight to which the newspaper replied that artificial aviation was dangerous to human life and, as such, "was doomed to failure."

He had expected some enthusiasm, but the paper's reply made him even more determined with his efforts and he then resigned from his job to devote all his time to aviation. He soon applied for the position of Secretary to the Royal Aero Club, but after a few days in office he decided that the post did not offer the type of encouragement or assistance he had expected and so, once again, he resigned.

Roe heard that draughtsmen were required to work on a gyrocopter project which was being built by G.L.O. Davidson in Denver, Colorado, USA, and he soon joined the American, who was being sponsored at that time by Sir W.G. Armstrong Whitworth and Company, before that firm had begun to build aircraft. The Davidson gyrocopter had been originally designed in 1898 with two large revolving wings which looked like umbrellas with the power supplied by a steam engine. However, as the Wright brothers and others were proving successful with types of aeroplanes, Davidson's enthusiasm started to

The first Roe 1 triplane outside the railway arch 'hangar' at Lea Marshes. In 1984 one of the famous blue heritage plaques was placed on the arches to commemorate the pioneer's achievements.

wane. Roe sensed this and returned to England.

In July 1906 Roe took out a patent for the world's first control column for a flying machine. This had a combined movement which controlled an aeroplane laterally fore and aft with a forward elevator which could be warped as well as changing the angle of incidence. This patent, for a single control column instead of one for each hand which had been used by the Wright brothers, was given the British Patent Number 26099. Over one year later a French pioneer, Robert Esnault Pelterie, apparently unaware of Roe's patent, took out a patent of his own, but for a much cruder type of joy-stick. After World War One the Frenchman claimed damages of £1 million from Roe for infringement of his patent, but the Englishman produced the evidence of the earlier submission and Esnault Pelterie's case was dropped.

In August 1906 Lord Northcliffe, through the *Daily Mail* offered prizes totalling £250 for model aeroplanes capable of sustained mechanical flight. The competition was held at Alexandra Palace in April 1907 and Roe, who entered three models, flying against over two hundred competitors, carried off the first prize of £75.

His success encouraged him to build an aeroplane which would be able to carry him aloft. A half-used stable behind his brother, Dr Stephen Verdon Roe's surgery at Putney, was ideal for the construction of the flying machine.

The aeroplane was a scaled-up version of an earlier model and would be a front elevator biplane with a wing span of thirty-six feet for the upper wing and thirty feet for the lower. The elevator's span was twenty feet with the power plant being a 6hp J.A.P. motor-cycle engine and not the 9hp one as usually, but erroneously, quoted.

Construction of the aeroplane began in May 1907 and Roe received a great incentive when he heard that the management of the Brooklands motor racing track offered the magnificent prize of £2,500 for any aviator who could make the first flight around the track before the end of that year.

Roe immediately cycled all the way from Putney to Brooklands to discuss the offer with the manager of the track, Mr Radakowsky who, far from being in favour of the event, was extremely sceptical of the whole concept of flight. He did, however, agree to Roe erecting a shed at his own expense and within days he was building a wooden workshop which would be large enough to take his biplane, albeit sideways.

The aeroplane was completed early in September 1907 and Roe commenced his trials, but with only a 6hp engine, the machine was badly underpowered and could hardly move forward on the ground!

Despite many changes to the design it was still unsuccessful and New Year's Day 1908 arrived with great disappointment for Roe as his chance of winning the Brookland's prize disappeared. 'A.V.' as Roe was known to his friends, painted the name *Avroplane* above the door of his shed and was still confident that he could fly, but it was obvious that more power would be needed to get his biplane into the air.

He was promised the loan of a 25hp Antoinette engine and while he was waiting for its arrival, he tested the structure by being towed around the track by a car. Again changes had to be made as the aircraft lacked directional stability and on a number of occasions it weaved and pitched crazily before hitting the ground, usually causing damage.

The new engine duly arrived late in May, but as Roe was installing it, he was informed by Radakowsky that he would have to leave the place. A.V. pleaded with the manager arguing that he was there because of the prize, but Radakowsky pointed out that it was long past. However, he agreed that A.V. could stay at Brooklands providing that he moved his shed to the far end of the race paddock, painting it dark green and only operated during the evening so that he would not be seen.

On 8 June 1908 Alliott Verdon Roe succeeded in getting into the air in the Antoinette-powered biplane completing a flight of some seventy-five feet. However, because of Radakowsky's restriction on A.V.'s flying experiments there were no official observers to witness the event and this nor any other of his short flights were ever recognised by the Royal Aero Club and claims to

A. V. at the controls of his Roe 1 triplane at Wembley Park.

be the first Englishman to fly were always looked upon with some scepticism. The great honour of being the first British subject to make a flight within the British Isles went to J.T.C. Moore-Brabazon (later Lord Brabazon) who made such a flight at Shellbeach on Sunday 2 May 1909. The incontestable confirmation of the flight came from Oswald Short, of Short Brothers fame, who witnessed the event.

A.V. who had facetiously become known as 'Roe the Hopper' because of his inability to remain airborne for any length of time, was not discouraged by this, but was dissatisfied with his machine and began to look at other designs. His new type of aeroplane would have a tractor engine layout instead of the pusher-type being favoured by aviators at that time and it would be a triplane. The triplane would have a control column as patented by him in 1906, but because of an extremely light structure it could use the 9hp J.A.P. engine which he had planned for his Roe 1 biplane.

The engine manufacturer was Mr J.A. Prestwich who became A.V.'s first partner on 15 September 1908 when together they formed the JAP AVROPLANE COMPANY. The capital being £100 then in the bank. It was a strange arrangement and seemed unlikely to flourish with such a small investment even though Prestwich was providing the engine. However, much credit must go to Prestwich for supporting A.V. when no-one else had the courage.

Unfortunately, the partnership did not last long as Alliott wanted to build a small machine while Prestwich wanted a larger one. Both aeroplanes were started, but owing to the difference of opinion the partnership was dissolved amicably in November 1909. The larger machine in its complete condition, together with a number of other aeroplanes, was sold by auction in the sale room of Friswells, Albany Street, London. The sum received was £4. 19s. 0d.

---

OPPOSITE TOP:
The untested triplane crashed after its wing tip caught the race pylon during the 1910 Flying Meeting at Blackpool.

---

OPPOSITE BELOW:
Howard Pixton takes A. V.'s wife Mildred, seen in the front cockpit, for a flight in an Avro Type D at Brooklands in 1911.

In February 1909, A.V. had written to the War Office requesting the use of Farnborough Common for his flying experiments, but his request was refused even though the site was being used by 'Colonel' S.F. Cody, the American aviation pioneer.

Disappointed at the War Office refusal, he contacted London County Council for permission to use Hackney Marsh or any other suitable site, but again to no avail. He cycled many miles searching for an area of land and he finally found a half mile stretch of even ground at Lea Marshes in Essex. To his delight one side of the site had a railway embankment with two unused brick arches which were ideal for housing his machines. He contacted the Great Eastern Railway Company and was amazed by their rapid response confirming that he could use the arches at a nominal rent.

A.V. and his helpers soon boarded up the ends completely leaving the arches without any windows, but with removable panels for light and ventilation.

With the triplane complete A.V. began his attempts to fly, but early trials usually ended in failure with the smashed machine being pushed back to the arches for repair. It was a difficult task for he was attempting to do two different things at the same time. He was really learning to fly and at the same time, he was designing an aeroplane . . . each of these jobs being seriously handicapped by the lack of knowledge of the other.

Everything was against him, ·especially attempting to fly in a machine with so little power in the 9hp engine. When he was to attempt a flight he would hand over any keys, loose change and even his watch in order to reduce weight. Just to get off the ground was an achievement, but it enabled him to proceed with learning to fly. A.V.'s two main helpers were E.V.B. Fisher and R.L. Howard Flanders and one of their important tasks was to make sure that the triplane's three wheels were off the ground at the same time. These two gentlemen would lie on the ground and shout when the wheels were off as the machine was then actually flying.

As finance was always the greatest of A.V.'s troubles it was wonderful news to hear that his brother, Humphrey, was so impressed with the young pioneer's efforts that he decided to enter into a partnership initially with a view to assisting

A.V. in finding someone to finance his experiments.

Humphrey Verdon Roe, know to all as 'H.V.', had resigned his army commission to purchase the webbing manufacturer Everard and Company from one of his aunts in 1902. Just as A.V. had a natural instinct for inventing, Humphrey was a born organiser and excellent manager. Everards was a great challenge as the company was near to bankruptcy when he took over, but he completely turned it round making it into a highly successful business. An expansion programme and an energetic young manager by the name of John Lord gave H.V. more time to pursue other interests which included assisting his younger brother. After a meeting on 27 April 1909 a partnership was formed, but purely for H.V. to seek finance for Alliott. Doctor Roe and the rest of the family were overjoyed at the arrangement as the somewhat wayward son Alliott would now be supervised and guided by Humphrey.

On 29 June 1909 *Aero* magazine published a letter from A.V. in which he gave a very fair account of what he was doing and what he had accomplished so far. He was seeking a financial partner, but as usual, his letter brought no response.

Undaunted, A.V. continued his experiments with his triplane repaired and modified after two crashes in quick succession had caused extensive damage to the wings. With the knowledge of his mistakes firmly in his mind he was learning all the time and after every hop he would change the gear ratio between the engine and propeller and also experiment by changing the size and pitch of the propeller.

However, his activities were soon to be disturbed by Leyton Council who were increasingly concerned about their image by allowing A.V. to continue with his experiments while spectators who went to watch labelled him a crank. A bailiff set out to catch him in the act, but Alliott had been warned about this and changed his flying schedule so that he could make his attempts just after dawn.

His most encouraging hop had been made on 5 June and a flight of one hundred feet was achieved on 13 July, but on the following day the bailiff caught up with A.V. just as he was taxying the triplane back to the arches. Now that the summons had been served he decided to throw caution to the wind and fly as much as possible. On 23 July 1909 he made his most successful flight when the triplane was airborne for 900 feet at an altitude of some twenty feet before some rapidly approaching trees forced him to land as he had not yet learned how to turn the aeroplane! This flight was recognised and earned Alliott Verdon Roe the distinction of making the first flight in Britain of a British designed aircraft powered by a British engine. The power plant was the same J.A.P. 9 hp engine which was later used on his biplane, but that aeroplane was vastly underpowered. However, his experience in design had enabled him to build the triplane structure much lighter with an excellent power-to-weight ratio. This machine became known as the Roe 1 Triplane and besides the trade name 'Avroplane' painted on the fuselage it also bore the name 'Bulls Eye' to advertise that particular type of men's braces produced by his sponsoring company Everards.

The first triplane took part in the Blackpool Air Meeting of 18–24 October 1909 with A.V. also taking a second engine-less triplane with him. The latter was awaiting a J.A.P. engine of some 20 hp, and this arrived in Blackpool on 20 October with the aeroplane being made ready to fly on the following morning, but storms cancelled out the flying for the rest of the meeting.

After eviction from Lea Marshes A.V. and his small band of helpers moved to Old Deer Park in Richmond, Surrey, but this site was found to be unsuitable and in November 1909 he moved to Wembley Park, Middlesex; in fact, to the site on which the Stadium now stands.

Despite the successes of other pioneer aviators besides A.V. himself, the public was still sceptical about flying and this was brought home to Humphrey when he went to place an order with Burtinshaw, Metal Stampers, of Ancoats, Manchester. When H.V. told his requirements were for aeroplanes Mr Burtinshaw was adamant that he would have nothing to do with it. He commented,' Aeroplanes will never be more than a toy', to which Humphrey replied, ' I will see you in five years time and see what you have to say then'. The date was 16 September 1909 and H.V. did see Burtinshaw just over five years later when production of the aircraft for the First World War was in full swing and, needless to say, his reception was much different that time.

# CHAPTER 2

## The Company is Formed

Early in December 1909 Humphrey and Alliott had serious talks on the direction they should be taking. H.V. felt that he must do something more than just look for someone to be a partner for his brother and it was agreed that a company should be formed.

On New Year's Day 1910 the brothers established A.V. Roe and Company, the world's first company ever to be registered as an aeroplane manufacturer. As A.V. and most of the family were living in the London area it was felt that the new company should be based in that location, but Humphrey argued that his business was in Manchester and if he was to continue with his own company as well as the new one then aeroplanes would have to be built in the north. In fact H.V.'s company Everards, in Brownsfield Mill, Ancoats had a basement which was ideal for the new company.

Realistically, A.V. did not have much choice as Humphrey was the only one prepared to help him and if the aeroplane manufacturing was not

One of the world's first aviation advertisements was for 'The Aviator's Storehouse' operated by Avro from Brownsfield Mill.

undertaken in Manchester he would have to give up the idea and find himself another job! The brothers' father had already stated that he would not lend Alliott any more money and if the company was to go ahead Humphrey would be solely responsible for the finance, organisation and management of the new venture. He also guaranteed that if the company failed he would be personally responsible for all debts. Such was H.V.'s faith in Alliott's ideals.

As the company was coming together, A.V. had collected a few youngsters who wanted to join the aeroplane industry. One of these was Reginald J.

RIGHT:
Howard Pixton, left, discussing the day's flying with Freddy Raynham who is busy wiping the oil from his hands after an early meeting.

BELOW:
An Avro Type E under construction at Brownsfield Mill in 1912

Parrott who had just completed his apprenticeship at a firm of boiler makers, but he was eager to learn about aeroplanes and impressed the brothers so much that Parrott was made works manager.

Production at Brownsfield Mill got underway and more good news came with the notification that Brooklands was to be made into an aerodrome. Flying at Wembley Park had been excellent, but the owners made it known that aviators could come to fly there free of charge and the arrival of a French pilot with his Blériot-type monoplane and the prospect of others appearing made Alliott feel that he must look elsewhere.

A new and sympathetic manager, Major Lindsay Lloyd was now in charge at Brooklands and it was at his instigation that a flying area was established with the backing of the owners, the Locke-Kings and the enthusiasm of a wealthy gentleman by the name of George Holt Thomas. The whole area would be a permanent aerodrome surrounded by the motor racing track with twelve hangars being built and hired out at a rent of £100 per annum each. On 1 March 1910, A.V. moved back into Brooklands.

The triplane design now had a 20 hp J.A.P. engine and the Brooklands facilities together with the enthusiasm of other aviators now using the aerodrome gave Alliott great encouragement. Telegrams of his achievements were always sent back to Manchester and one of these was of special delight to Humphrey and the small band of workers as it reported that A.V. had been aloft for nineteen minutes and twenty seconds. Soon he was flying three triplanes, each of twenty feet wingspan, but using engines of 9 hp, 20 hp and 35hp. The 9 hp version was later sold to the Rangie Cycle Company.

Another new triplane was designed, known as the Roe II. This aircraft had a twenty-six feet wingspan and was powered by a 35 hp Green engine. This aeroplane was given the name 'Mercury' in a ceremony at the White City Stadium in Manchester on 4 March 1910. One week later the Roe II was on display at London's Olympia where the Aero Show was taking place between 11–19 March. The triplane was in advance of anything on show for it retained the triangular fuselage favoured by A.V. for a lighter structure and with both a design and structure input from Parrott, the aeroplane was voted the finest in the

exhibition. A firm order was received from Captain Walter Windham, who had earlier been approached to invest in A.V. Roe and Co., but declined, plus an option from another buyer, which later did not materialise.

The company frequently advertised in *Flight* with one such advertisement declaring 'Aeroplanes from £450, with five mile flight guaranteed. Adjustable blade propellers, six feet diameter, seven guineas and guaranteed not to burst'.

At Brooklands, Avro as the company became known, had started a flying school along with the experimental flying which was being undertaken. There was a standard fee for tuition, but many of the students had a great enthusiasm for flying, but not much money. If A.V. considered a pupil likely to make a good pilot and was prepared to work as well, he would allow him to pay for the lessons by the work he did. Another method was for gifted pilots to defer their payments until they had, hopefully, won prizes at a later date. These prizes were offered by Brooklands management for various feats of flying during weekend air displays. One would-be student who was later to become a famous pilot was C. Howard Pixton, who wrote to the firm asking if they could teach him to fly. He was taken on by Humphrey as a 'Ground Engineer', but this was for no pay. Pixton had to pay a £30 deposit to the company. 'to be returned when flying lessons complete, less the cost of any repairs to the aeroplane'. Pixton recalled that the £30 was greatly exceeded!

The 'Mercury' was proving to be a great success and on June 2 1910 this machine completed six circuits of Brooklands at an altitude of twenty feet.

Alliott received his Aviator's Certificate on 26 July 1910 after passing a stringent test for the Royal Aero Club. His certificate was number 18 which was a great source of annoyance to A.V. as many thought he should have held Number One! The tests were devised by the RAeC with the first one going to Alliott's great rival J.T.C. Moore-Brabazon on 8 March 1910, who passed his test in a Farman biplane. Alliott was well down the list of certificate holders and always maintained that he was too busy experimenting and could never find the time to sit such a test when they were originally established.

In addition to his experimenting and running

The Type E being transported through the streets of Ancoats, Manchester to London Road (now Piccadilly) Station for the train journey to Brooklands.

the flying school at Brooklands, A.V. would journey to Manchester once a week to oversee the production of the aeroplanes. However, he always returned south before the weekend to drum up business during the flying displays which, by now, were attracting good sized crowds.

As sales of aeroplanes were still few and far between, H.V. invested more money to keep the company on an even keel and he was always seeking new ways of bringing in the vital finance. More and more people were building and experimenting with their own aeroplanes and Humphrey hit upon the idea of selling spare parts which otherwise the aviators would have to manufacture themselves. Advertised as 'The Aviator's Storehouse' the venture was an outstanding success selling everything from bolts, screws, wire, wheels, propellers to engines.

The greatest success for 'The Storehouse' was the Avro wire-strainer which was designed by Alliott himself. Early aviators found them difficult to find as few were manufactured and those that were located were so expensive that flyers often went without meals to buy them. Later known as the turnbuckle, it was a device to change the tension on bracing wires and the Avro strainer was the first to be patented. When the First World War came, aircraft production was delayed through lack of suitable strainers and the Avro type became the standard equipment. The company received orders

OPPOSITE TOP:
The world's first enclosed cabin aeroplane was the Avro Type F.

OPPOSITE BOTTOM:
A rare photograph of the Avro 500 at the Eccles Cricket Ground in July 1912. The aircraft had landed there during a series of demonstration flights operated from Trafford Park, Manchester.

The Trafford Park demonstration flights were piloted by Lieutenant Wilfred Park, R.N., seen here preparing to take-off.

for tens of thousands and it was also manufactured under licence by Chobert in France where it was used by every aircraft builder. A.V. Roe and Company made an average £40,000 per year profit from the strainers alone for several years during and after the war.

By mid-July 1910 the Roe III triplane had successfully flown and this machine, together with the Roe II, were carefully dismantled and on 28 July were loaded onto railway wagons for transporting to Blackpool to take part in the Flying Meeting to be held there. Recent successful flights had made Avro confident of achieving sales at the meeting, but hopes were soon dashed by a nasty quirk of fate. The two machines together with spare parts, a couple of bicycles and practically all the contents of the Brooklands' hangar were on open wagons under tarpaulin sheets as no covered vans were available, but as the goods train climbed a slight incline between Wigan and Preston, sparks from the engine set the sheet alight. Pixton and another mechanic were on the following train when it was stopped and, with other passengers, got out to see what was happening. They were shocked to see their aeroplanes blazing fiercely in the siding where the wagons had been shunted to burn themselves out. One of the passengers remarked, 'Well it will save somebody from being killed flying them'. It was a good example of the public's conception of aviation in those early days.

A.V. who was already in Blackpool was devastated by the news of the fire and it seemed he was on the point of giving up completely, as this was hard to bear after all the other disappointments along the way. It seemed as though things were just becoming right when this disaster struck. However, after the initial shock and a period of deliberation, A.V. decided on a plan of action and he and his team headed towards Manchester and Brownsfield Mill.

Leading the way, A.V., Humphrey, John Lord and Reg Parrott formed little groups from the workers and voluntary helpers working day and night to produce another triplane from spare parts. The new machine powered by a 35 hp Green engine arrived in Blackpool just after the start of the meeting and the team erected the triplane in record time. The crowd knew of the disaster and of the hard work to get an aeroplane to the event and the team were filled with pride as the spectators cheered loudly when A.V. climbed aboard. Alliott made a circuit of the field in the untested triplane, but on one of the turns the wing tip caught one of the pylons which had been placed as part of the race course and the machine flipped into the ground. Luckily A.V. was uninjured and the machine was repaired and flying again the following day and he went on to make a number of flights during the meeting. When the event ended he was awarded £75 as a 'Special Merit' prize.

In the meantime Humphrey had approached the railway company regarding the very serious loss of the two triplanes. Avro hoped that the Blackpool event would bring in orders as well as cash prizes, but LNWR would not consider compensation as all goods were sent at the owner's risk.

The flying school at Brooklands was becoming popular, but so too was the aerodrome itself almost to the point of overcrowding and by mutual consent with the management of the facility, Avro moved the school to Shoreham in Sussex.

The fourth production Roe III triplane had been ordered by the Harvard Aeronautical Society of the USA, and by coincidence great interest had been shown in the design by an American, Mr J.B. Martin, who attended the Blackpool meeting. Martin invited A.V. to take part in the flying meeting to be held in Boston, Massachusetts, from 3–13 September 1910. Alliott found time to marry his fiancée Mildred Kirk at the Holy Trinity Church in Blackpool on 20 August, 1910, and three days later he and Pixton left Liverpool on the vessel *Cymric*. Also on board was another pioneer aviator, Claude Grahame-White with his Blériot and Farman aircraft plus three mechanics. One of these mechanics was Benny Hucks, who like Pixton, was paying for flying lessons by helping to maintain Grahame-Whites's machines. Hucks was later to become famous as the first Englishman to loop an aeroplane and later as the designer of a starter for aircraft engines. At the meeting A.V. crashed his own triplane, which was Roe III number five, but after a short spell in hospital he returned to the meeting to take Harvard's machine into the air. The flying ground was at Squantum, a few miles from Boston, but it was nothing more than a swamp with just a short landing strip and no hangars for the aeroplanes. Temporary canvas hangars were eventually erected, but as no accommodation was nearby, both aviators and mechanics had to sleep under the wings of their

machines. Mosquitoes were a constant menace and the occasional skunk did not endear the area to the Britons. A.V. was to crash again, this time in the Harvard-owned triplane, but the Society did eventually receive a machine assembled from the wrecks of the two crashes. Pixton was joined by another Avro mechanic by the name of Halstead and together with A.V. the triplane was built and test flown before being handed over. Halstead was offered a job in Boston and decided to resign from the company and stay in the United States. A distinguished visitor to the meeting was President Taft who had long talks with both A.V. and Grahame-White with the latter winning prize money totalling $25,000. Instructions arrived from H.V. to sell spares and everything possible to pay for the return passage for Pixton!

After he returned to England Alliott was most gratified to receive a letter from Professor Huntington of Yale University who thanked A.V. for his contribution to the flying meeting and also praised him for the design of the triplane and his courage in taking to the air again after his first crash.

The first Avro 504 had a square engine cowling and inversely-tapered warping ailerons.

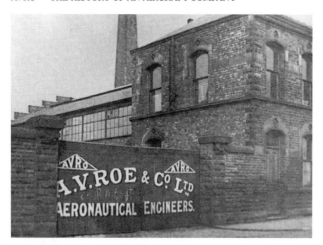

LEFT:
The Clifton Street works in 1914. The original building was demolished and its replacement occupied by a scrap dealer.

BELOW:
The *Daily Mail* sponsored Avro 504 to tour coastal resorts in 1914. The aircraft's engine was test run in the yard at Clifton Street.

BOTTOM:
In enemy hands. Squadron Commander Briggs' Avro 504 captured during the raid on the Friedrichshafen Zeppelin sheds. Briggs escaped from his captors and returned to England.

Back at Brownsfield Mill, Humphrey was continuing to search for suitable partners. He had a sympathetic hearing from the Lord Mayor of Manchester, Sir Charles Behrens, but nothing ever materialised. Two enthusiasts nearly became partners, but it was not to be. The first of these was C.R.L. Kenworthy who arranged for a banker's draft for £2,000 to be sent to the company after an agreement was signed. He then went to London to instruct his solicitor to draw up such an agreement. However, Kenworthy was under twenty-one years of age and his solicitor advised him against investing in the firm. Kenworthy had the courtesy to return to see H.V. to give him the disappointing news that his solicitor would not allow him to join Avro.

The second gentleman was F.S. Barnwell who, like Kenworthy, was extremely enthusiastic about joining Avro. The arrangements were progressing favourably, when suddenly he withdrew his offer. It emerged that he had a very good offer from a well established firm and even Humphrey had to agree that it would have been unwise of him not to accept; after all, the opposition's offer had excellent prospects while the Avro one was a financial risk. Although Barnwell was under no legal obligation he insisted on giving Avro full compensation for the time and effort which had arisen out of the proposed agreement. Together with the loss of finance, H.V. was sorry to lose Barnwell as he felt that the gentleman would have been a great asset to Avro.

Humphrey approached a catalogue of companies and individuals seeking investment, but all refused. A running advertisement in the *Manchester Guardian* every day for a week brought not one single enquiry. However, as he had great faith in the ultimate success of the company, H.V. dug deep into his pocket once more.

In September 1910, the sixth and final Roe III triplane was sold to Cecil Grace. Grace was an early aviator and had flown a number of types, but liked the Avro machine enough to buy it. He acted as a test pilot for Short Brothers and, indeed, assisted with the design of the Short S.27, but sadly he was lost in this machine when it disappeared while flying the English Channel on 22 December 1910.

The last triplane in the early series was the Roe IV which was powered by a 35 hp Green engine, but

was changed from the earlier versions by having a 'floating tail instead of a lifting tail' as Alliott described it. The top two wings had their span increased to forty-two feet while the lower wing remained at thirty feet.

Howard Pixton had been with the company for five months before he had his first flying lesson on 3 November 1910 and after a few flights he was allowed to practise taxying, but was under strict orders not to leave the ground. However, he soon got tired of this and, disobeying A.V.'s instructions, he took the triplane into the air. He was reasonably confident and felt at ease, that is until one wing dropped and he over compensated causing the other wing to follow! He pushed the control column forward, but too far, he then pulled it back and opened up the engine, but again too much! This kangaroo effect continued until he reached the boundary of the aerodrome and he had to make a turn, something he had never done before, but this was quite successful and he just scraped over the hangars and some telegraph wires before putting the machine down for a perfect landing! Now, full of confidence once more, he walked back to the Avro hangar, but there was nobody in sight. Pixton thought this to be a little strange as there were many about when he took off. He was soon to find that everyone had quickly disappeared when Pixton started his aerial antics! There were certainly no congratulations from A.V. as he was too indignant about the risks taken with his aeroplane, but the storm passed and after more

Some of the Avro employees at Clifton Street in August 1915. The young Roy Dobson is centre rear.

The first Avro Pike before its roll-out at Hamble in 1916.

flying lessons Pixton qualified as a pilot and was presented with Aviator's Certificate No.50 on 31 December 1910.

An amusing tailpiece on Pixton's first solo came from *Flight*'s Brooklands correspondent who reported 'While Pixton was a very daring and pretty flyer, his sudden movements must have put a severe strain on the bodywork'. He commented that, 'one dive and the sudden righting appeared to actually bend the body'. He also doubted that Mr Pixton would ever get through life unmaimed! Never one to miss a great public relations opportunity, A.V. commented that Avro had now produced a biplane-type machine with which Messrs Howard Pixton and Gordon Bell were conducting experiments!

Avro had indeed produced a biplane as Alliott had decided to concentrate on such a design. This conclusion came not only by the success of the competitor's machines, but also with the influence of Reg Parrott whose knowledge of aeroplane engineering and design were becoming widely recognised. The first biplane would be known as the Avro Type D.

The flying school produced a number of pilots who would go on to greater things. Howard Pixton was a natural flyer who, in years to come, would win the coveted Schneider Trophy for Great Britain; Hubert Oxley would become a test pilot for the Blackburn Aeroplane Company, but unfortunately would be killed after a structural failure in the aircraft he was flying; Freddy Raynham received his 'ticket' on 9 May 1911 and stayed with Avro for many years as a test pilot before becoming co-director of Kemps Air (later Aerial) Survey Company Limited and living in India he did a considerable amount of flying there; Ronald Kemp received his aviator's certificate on the same day as Raynham and they were to become close friends. Kemp also tested new aeroplanes and transferred from Farnborough to the Royal Flying Corps at the start of World War One. During his RFC service he continued to test fly military aeroplanes. He later joined Raynham in the air survey business and after the partition of of Pakistan and India he became consulting engineer to the Indian Government. All of these, plus many other Avro pupils, always held A.V. in great esteem and never forgot the debt they owed to him.

It was Pixton who first flew the Type D at Brooklands on 1 April 1911 and declared, 'The first flight was a complete success with the machine being viceless and easy to handle'. It was a statement to be used many times over the years after the maiden flight of a prototype aircraft! The Type D was flown later by a succession of pilots who agreed with Pixton's report. On 12 May he flew the biplane from Brooklands to Hendon in forty-eight minutes where he then gave an excellent flying demonstration to the Parliamentary Aerial Defence Committee. One week earlier, on 6 May, Pixton and the biplane were entered for the Brooklands to Brighton Air Race, but after an unusual lapse by the normally precise pilot, the aeroplane got lost and, after a series of occurrences which included landing on Plumpton Race Course to ask directions, Pixton decided to call it a day. He returned to Brooklands, but not until after joining a flying display which was being held at Haywards Heath.

On 15 June 1911, Commander Oliver Schwann, RN, flew the Type D at Brooklands and immediately bought it for £700. Stationed at Barrow-in-Furness, Commander Schwann was serving on the vessel *Hermione* which was an airship tender and arrangements were immediately made to despatch the biplane by rail up to the Lancashire port. The company insisted that a covered wagon be used as they did not want a repeat of the triplane railway disaster. After receiving the aeroplane Schwann made a number of modifications to the machine including replacing the undercarriage with floats. Tests were carried out in Cavendish Dock and, on 8 November 1911, Commander Schwann became the first British pilot to fly a British aeroplane off the water. The flight reached an altitude of approximately twenty feet before the machine fell back into the water and capsized. Schwann was only slightly injured and, after transferring to the Royal Air Force, he later became Air Vice-Marshal Sir Oliver Schwann.

During 1911 Avro received a seven-cylinder rotary engine from the Empress Motor Company of Stockport Road, Manchester for trials on any of the aeroplanes. A rather pleasant young mechanic by the name of Jack Alcock arrived at Brooklands as the Empress technical representative. The engine was not very successful, but Jack stayed on at Brooklands as he had been bitten by the flying bug. Unfortunately, it was not possible at that time, to learn to fly with Avro. However, Maurice Ducrocq, who had the next hangar took him on as a mechanic and taught him to fly. The young man later became Sir John Alcock, half of the Alcock and Brown team, first to conquer the Atlantic in a non-stop flight. A US Navy Curtiss NC-4 flying-boat had flown the Atlantic in May 1919, but via the Azores and Lisbon.

New Avro 504Ks awaiting collection at Hamble.

Instructors and mechanics of the Royal Flying Corps élite training unit at Gosport, Hampshire.

In July 1911 the *Daily Mail* once again showed its great enthusiasm for aviation by offering a massive £10,000 prize for a circuit of Britain race. This national newspaper made sure that the air race was well publicised with crowds at every stopping point and a massive 30,000 people gathered at Brooklands for the start. All of the British aeroplane builders made great efforts to take part and A.V. was no exception. He entered a Type D which was powered by a 60 hp E.N.V. engine and modified with strut-braced extensions to the top wings and shorter extensions to the lower mainplane. The Avro machine, flown by Ronald Kemp, was second off and climbed steadily to 700ft while being buffeted by a gusting wind. Suddenly, it began to lose height with the engine well throttled back, then at about 100 feet the extension of the lower left wing broke off and became tangled in the interplane wires. The aircraft spiralled down to the left and hit the ground with a shattering crash. Amazingly, Kemp crawled out of the wreckage with nothing more than a few cuts and bruises.

A.V. was most distressed, blaming himself for nearly causing the death of one of his pilots. The rushed modifications installed to make the machine go faster were to blame and the examination of the wrecked biplane showed that the workmanship was poor and not up to the standard demanded by Alliott. The result was that a stressman would be employed to work on future projects and, at all times, the aeroplane should be thoroughly inspected before it would be allowed to fly.

The British teams all had poor performances or bad luck and it was the French who swept the board. On 22 July 1911, the £10,000 Circuit of Britain prize was collected by Lt. de Vaisseau Conneau. The only British aeroplane to finish was flown by Samuel Franklin Cody, an American. Cody was known as 'Colonel' after King Edward VII had confused him with the famous 'Buffalo Bill'!

The Avro Flying School had its first military pupil in Capt. W.D. Beatty, Royal Engineers, who received his aviator's certificate on 30 May 1911 and continued to fly from Brooklands as much as possible: he ended World War One as a Lieutenant-Colonel and transferred to the newly-formed Royal Air Force. Besides the pupils, passenger flying was becoming popular and A.V.'s mother rode with her son to show confidence in his business. She later confided, 'I was very glad when the flight came to an end and I was safely out of the aeroplane.'

The fourth Avro Type D was to be used by Fred Raynham for an attempt to win the British Empire Michelin Cup No 2 which was over a circuit which

OPPOSITE TOP:
The Avro Spider fighter came too late to see service in World War One.

OPPOSITE BOTTOM:
Alexandra Park aerodrome provided an excellent facility for both the company and the military during World War One and its closure presented a problem for Avro.

started and ended at Hendon. Although not happy about the condition of the aeroplane, he took off from Brooklands and set off for Hendon, but he had not flown far when he ran into a fog bank. Climbing to 1,500 feet to clear any possible obstructions, he set course by compass, but the instrument seemed unreliable and he bent forward to adjust it. Suddenly, he found himself standing upright with the aeroplane spinning, but after two complete turns and some rapid action on his part, Raynham was able to pull the biplane level at 500 feet. He was badly shaken and after finding a clear patch and a suitable field underneath he landed safely to find himself at New Barnet. Seeking directions from a friendly local, he took off once more and headed for Hendon, but after landing there he decided to abandon the contest when it was found that the wing fabric had not been adequately doped as it was hanging loose and in a dangerous condition.

Raynham was, no doubt, the first pilot to enter a spin and live to tell about it even though he was not sure how he was able to effect a recovery. The prize was eventually won by Samuel Cody and he collected the £400 on 11 September 1911.

Prize money for any time contest was still the best source of finance for early aviators and Howard Pixton succeeded in winning the Manville duration prize of £500 on 4 October 1911. The award was for a British pilot who could put in the longest aggregate time in the air while carrying a passenger and this was to be completed on nine specified days. Pixton had flown both an Avro Type D and a Bristol Boxkite to build up the flying time and on the last day he was in the lead with three hours and seven minutes, but Cody put up an excellent three hours, sixteen minutes. Not to be outdone Pixton took to the air again and finished the day with a time of five hours and sixteen minutes, beating Cody by a comfortable two hours. Pixton was surprised to receive an extra £150 for the largest aggregate of hours flown by anyone throughout the season at Brooklands.

The Avro share of the prize money for 1911 was £112. 8s. 0d. and if it had not been for the disaster of the railway fire near Wigan, the company would have made a slight profit.

While Avro designs were still popular the firm was also in the market to build aeroplanes of other companies as specified by the prospective buyer.

In the summer of 1911 they had built a Curtiss-type two-seat pusher biplane and this was test flown at Brooklands in May of that year. Later, this machine was fitted with a main centre float and two wing tip floats for the Lakes Flying Company of Windermere. The director of the company and an aviation enthusiast was a local landowner, Captain E.W. Wakefield. Given the name *Waterbird*, this aeroplane first flew off the Lake on 25 November 1911 piloted by Mr H. Stanley-Adams. Although it flew some seventeen days after Commander Schwann, the *Waterbird* was generally regarded as the first successful British seaplane. In 1912 it was followed by the Avro Type E with a 50 hp Gnome rotary engine and this aeroplane became known as the Lakes *Seabird* after being fitted with floats. This machine, which was the first Type E, had been ordered by John R. Duigan, an Australian, who had built and attempted to fly his own aeroplane and had come to England specifically to obtain a Royal Aero Club licence. He joined the Avro Flying School and was awarded Certificate No. 211 on 30 April 1912, after taking his test in the Type E which he had ordered previously! Business commitments forced Duigan to return to Australia and the little biplane was sold to the Lakes Flying Company. Avro had also built the wings for another Curtiss-type for the Windermere-based company and this became known as the *Waterhen*. The *Seabird* was destroyed in a crash on 6 June 1915, when pupil pilot Ronald Buck stalled into the lake. Both the *Waterhen* and the *Waterbird* gave excellent service, with the former training a number of pilots for the Royal Naval Air Service in the First World War.

Howard Pixton reluctantly left the company after he had received an offer he could not refuse. He was happy to work for Avro, but as the firm's finances were always tight he was only receiving £2 per week from A.V. In an amicable agreement he left to join the British and Colonial Aeroplane Company (later Bristol Aeroplane Company) for a salary of £250 per annum plus one-third of any prize money.

The Sippé brothers, Sydney and Albert together with a friend named James Jenson, designed and built a small monoplane at Beckenham, in Kent in 1910. The machine was unsuccessful, but Sydney continued with his ambition of wanting to fly. He gained his Aviator's Certificate on 9 January 1912 and joined Avro soon after. His first major task was to fly Schwann's rebuilt Type D off the water at Barrow and this he did on 9 April 1912. This flight was recognised as being the first for a British seaplane to fly from British coastal waters as opposed to the *Waterbird* which flew from a lake.

In September 1911 a young man walked down Great Ancoats Street in Manchester, took a deep breath, and walked into Brownsfield Mill looking for a job building aeroplanes. He did get the job, but no-one at that time could imagine the impact this young chap would have on Avro and aviation in general. His name was Roy Chadwick.

The second Type E biplane made its first flight from Brooklands on 14 March 1912 in the capable hands of Lt Wilfred Parke, RN, who had begged a year on half pay from the Royal Navy to devote himself to aviation. This machine was much improved over the Duigan aeroplane by having a 60 hp water-cooled E.N.V. engine and an increase in wing area. The aeroplane was plagued by engine trouble through the design of the fuel system, but even after the change the aircraft crashed on take-off after engine failure on 20 April 1912. Parke was only slightly injured, but the Type E was badly damaged and it did not fly again until two months later when it went to Farnborough for

Avro Transport Company 504L seaplanes on Lake Windermere in 1919 still carried their military serial numbers.

trials. This aeroplane was later fitted with a 60 hp A.B.C. engine, but this proved unsatisfactory and the E.N.V. engine was fitted once more. The machine eventually went to Shoreham for use by the flying school, but on 29 June 1913 the aeroplane crashed killing its pupil pilot Robert Wright. This was the first ever fatal accident of an Avro machine.

Alliott complained bitterly that the War Office gave no help at all to British aeroplane constructors other than the Royal Aircraft Factory at Farnborough and Humphrey recorded that he was 'both surprised and delighted' when Avro received an order for three biplanes on 7 March 1912. Brownsfield Mill went onto overtime and the first of these aeroplanes was sent down to Brooklands on 27 April 1912. This type would be known as the Avro 500 and when asked about the change in the designating system and the high number for the first machine, Alliott put it down to 'drawing office swank'!

The Avro 500 was a modified Type E, but the fuselage was wider and a Gnome 50 hp engine was fitted. Parke flew the aeroplane for the first time on 8 May 1912, and later that day climbed the machine to 2,000 feet in under just five minutes. The following morning he took the Avro 500 from Brooklands to Laffans Plain, Wiltshire in twenty minutes, where the aeroplane was to be inspected by officials from the War Office. In the afternoon Parke put the Avro 500 through its paces with a

ABOVE:
The Sports and Social Club during a weekend break at the company's facility near Macclesfield. These activities still play an important part for the employees of today, but their facilities have improved somewhat!

OPPOSITE TOP:
Bathing beauties pose with the prototype Avro 536 at Ventnor, Isle of Wight in the summer of 1919.

OPPOSITE BOTTOM:
A joy riding 504 comes in to land on the sands at Southport. The small booking office was still in use in 1946 when the author made his first flight, unfortunately not in an Avro 504, but a D. H. Fox Moth of Giro Aviation!

faultless demonstration for the assembled representatives. The second Avro 500 was test flown for the first time at Brooklands on 5 June, 1912, and delivered to Farnborough later that day! On arrival the machine was immediately taken into one of the hangars where it was inverted in a rig for loading tests to be carried out. It passed all of the stringent ground tests with flying colours.

With orders building up the work force was expanding and a number of specialists were being employed. One such man was a timber buyer who started with Avro in April 1912. He was an experienced man who had purchased timber for the furniture trade for many years. There was obviously nothing that Avro could teach him although it soon became apparent that they would have to, because he insisted on buying curly grained wood — beautiful for furniture, but useless for aeroplanes where straight grained wood was essential. After years of buying with one ideal, he could not change his thinking and he finally left the company, but not before a large amount of wood was returned whence it came!

Early in 1912 A.V. had given up much of his flying in order to concentrate on his design work. With Roy Chadwick as his personal assistant and Reginald Parrott, Alliott established a drawing office at Brownsfield Mill. The office consisted of three drawing boards and three chairs as the sum total of the furnishings!

The three gentlemen put A.V.'s ideas into

practice when they designed the Avro Type F, which was a monoplane with a totally enclosed cabin and fitted with a 35 hp Viale engine. The deep fuselage completely enclosed the pilot keeping him protected from the elements, and clear window panels in the sides, roof and floor gave reasonably good vision. While the aircraft was under construction the works had a visit from the YMCA Junior Jaunters on 16 March 1912 and the normally placid Alliott was enraged to hear that one of the young visitors had tested the Type F's windscreen to destruction!

Parke took the cabin monoplane for its maiden flight on 1 May 1912, and the trials continued until 25 May 1912 when the aeroplane forced-landed after an engine failure on take-off en route for a demonstration at Hendon. The Type F did not live up to its expectations and only flew occasionally after its repairs. Richard Barnwell flew the aeroplane on 13 September 1912, but it was unlucky thirteen for him as the machine overturned on landing. Richard was the brother of Frank Barnwell who tried to invest in Avro in 1910, but who changed his mind after receiving a more financially sound offer. The Barnwell brothers had designed their own biplane in 1909 and a monoplane in 1911, but neither machine was a success.

Avro received a surprise boost on 17 May 1912, when the *Manchester Guardian* published a full-column article in which they apologised to the company for not realising earlier that they had a genius in their midst!

About that time Alliott also received some sad news when he heard that his friend E.V.B. Fisher

Japanese visitors view the Avro 547 at Hamble in 1920. Reg Parrott and Captain Hamersley are on the extreme left of the photograph. The aircraft in the background is a Renault-powered Avro 548.

RIGHT:
The Fuselage frame of the prototype Avro Baby.

and his passenger, an American financier Victor Mason, had been killed on 13 May 1912, at Brooklands in the crash of a Flanders F.3 monoplane. Fisher gave A.V. great help and encouragement during his early experiments at Lea Marshes and Wembley Park and had been awarded his own certificate on 2 May 1911. Fisher, who was secretary of the Shed-Holders Committee at Brooklands, had also founded the Brooklands Aero Club and was a well-known Egyptologist.

In July 1912 the *Daily Mail* sponsored a series of demonstration flights by an Avro 500 flown by Wilfred Parke. Humphrey arranged for every one of the work force to visit the Trafford Park area where the aircraft would be operated. The machine was the third of the War Office order and was delivered to Farnborough on 22 July.

Another enclosed cabin aeroplane from the Avro stable was the Type G biplane which was designed specifically to take part in the Military Trials due to be held on Salisbury Plain commencing 1 August 1912. Two aircraft were completed for the competition with one being flown by Wilfred Parke powered by a 60 hp Green engine while the second, piloted by R.L. Charteris of the All-British Engine Company, had a 60 hp A.B.C. engine. However, by the start of the event the second aircraft's engine was not ready so Parke's entry was the only one from Avro and even this machine had not been test flown before being taken by road and erected at Larkhill, where the trials were to take place. After its test flights the Type G was dismantled once again because the first trial was for speed of assembly and the Avro won this in a time of fourteen minutes and thirty seconds against eighteen other competitors. It also won the dismantling test in twelve minutes and again being reassembled in just eleven minutes! Until 7 August 1912 the Type G had received encouraging results with some officials liking the enclosed cockpit arrangement with the pilot and observer being sheltered from the wind and able to communicate easily, while others did not like the view from the cabin and this attracted much adverse comment. However, on the day in question, Parke took off for an endurance flight which was scheduled for three hours duration, but soon after, the skies darkened and visibility decreased rapidly. He decided to land as soon as possible, but came in downwind and too fast,

bouncing on touchdown and the aeroplane turned over breaking its back. The Type G was sent back to Manchester in two halves, But as Avro were experts at repairing aeroplanes the machine was back at Larkhill a week later.

While the trials were underway it was announced that the Central Flying School of the RFC had opened at Upavon on 17 August 1912. Seventeen pupils were on the first course with the aircraft fleet comprising of two Avros, two Shorts, one Maurice Farman, one Henry Farman and a Bristol.

As the trials continued an incident nearly ended in disaster for Parke and the Avro Type G, but the outcome provided data which was to help save the lives of future aviators.

On 25 August 1912, Wilfred Parke and his observer Lieut Le Breton, RFC, has just completed the three hours qualifying flight and the aircraft was approaching the aerodrome at a height of between 600 and 700 feet in preparation for landing. He put the machine in a spiral glide in order to lose height, but he soon found that the nose had dropped too much and the aircraft was slipping outwards. He pulled the stick back and to the left and the machine instantly started to spin, but he then opened up the engine, pulled the stick back hard and applied full rudder in the direction of the spin. This of course, only served to tighten the spin, but he quickly assessed that the rudder was the key and applied full opposite rudder. With the elevator still hard up the aeroplane came out of the spin just fifty feet above the ground and Parke made a circuit of the field before landing safely.

Parke and his observer owed their lives to the pilot's quick thinking and he was able to relate to others just how he pulled out of the spin and this, no doubt, served as the standard spin recovery technique. Fred Raynham had spun earlier, but was not clear on just what he did to survive, but 'Parke's Dive' as it became known, helped to provide the answer.

The trials ended in apparent failure for the Type G, but Avro were awarded £100 for completing the tests.

The Type G returned to Brooklands for further test flights and some modifications. On 22 October 1912 a broken water pipe cancelled out Fred Raynham's attempt to win the Michelin Endurance Prize.

The first Air Mail service in New South Wales, Australia was flown by an Avro 504 in June 1920. The photograph was taken at Lismore at the start of the service.

On 16 October 1912, Harry Hawker in a Sopwith-Wright biplane had made an attempt for the endurance prize, but was forced to land after three hours and thirty-one minutes. He tried again on two occasions and on the last of these he stayed in the air for three and a half hours on 23 October, 1912. At the same time Raynham was making his first successful attempt in the Type G and stayed airborne for three hours and forty-eight minutes, before he too was forced to land. As the competition was due to close on the last day of October, both pilots resumed their attempts on the 24th. Raynham took off just after dawn and Hawker joined him a few hours later. The Avro machine stayed in the air for seven hours, thirty one minutes and thirty seconds, thus establishing a new British endurance record by a very wide margin. Raynham could have stayed longer, but the oil in the Green engine was exhausted and he had to land. However, the record was not to stand for long as Harry Hawker was still circling over Brooklands and it was not until just after darkness fell that he landed the Sopwith machine. Not only had he set a new endurance record of eight hours and twenty-three minutes, but he captured the Michelin Trophy and walked off with £500 prize money. Needless to say, Alliott and the Avro team were extremely disappointed, but, at least, Raynham had written himself into the aviation record books, albeit for only a few hours.

One export order received in 1912 was from Portugal for a biplane to take part in the second anniversary of that country becoming a republic. Unfortunately, the ship carrying the aircraft encountered severe weather and its arrival in Lisbon was delayed. The Avro 500 made its first flight there on 10 October 1912 piloted by Copland Perry, a Sopwith instructor who was assisting Avro while Parke was on loan to Handley Page. The Avro machine was given the name *Republica* with this being painted on each side of the fuselage and flags of the Republic were attached to the outer wing struts. Many flights were made during the celebrations and the aeroplane successfully carried many officers and government officials. Unfortunately, engine failure forced it down in the River Tagus, but it was soon recovered.

On 30 August, Avro had received an order from

the Admiralty for a 100 hp Gnome-powered Avro Hydro-biplane and the aircraft was delivered to Eastchurch on 2 December 1912. The machine was an Avro 500 fitted with a centre float to which wheels were attached to make it an amphibian. Early in December 1912 the future brightened considerably when the War Office placed an order for four machines.

The year was to end on a sad note for Avro when it was learned that Wilfred Parke had been killed in a crash on 15 December 1912. Parke had taken off from Hendon for a flight to Oxford flying a Handley Page F.H.P.6, a two-seat side-by-side monoplane powered by an 80 hp Gnome. The engine was running rough, but was known to clear itself in flight. Ten minutes into the flight, with the engine pouring out blue smoke, the aeroplane began to turn back losing height all the time. At about forty feet, downwind, the machine stalled and dived vertically into the ground crashing on a golf course at Wembley, killing both Parke and his passenger Arkell Hardwick, Handley Page's manager. Parke was a pilot of great experience and a sad loss to the aviation scene.

One other order which deserves a mention was for Avro to build a Gnome-powered monoplane designed by Lieut R. Burga, a Peruvian naval officer. The monoplane, which had a number of unusual features including additional rudders, one mounted above and one below the forward fuselage, made its first flight from Shoreham on 11 November 1912.

In December 1912 the company was encouraged by a visit by Mr James Grimble Groves, JP, who was chairman of Groves & Whitnall Limited, a large brewery in Manchester. Mr Groves' son Peer had been one of a party to visit Brownsfield Mill and was so impressed by what he saw he told his father that somebody should help Avro. The cavalry had arrived at last!

After the initial and most encouraging talks, Mr Groves took a personal and almost fatherly interest in the firm and particularly in Alliott and Humphrey. He was keen to invest in the company and on 1 January 1913 it was agreed to make A.V. Roe and Company a Limited concern.

On 11 January 1913, the company was duly registered as A.V. Roe and Company Limited, with a capital of £30,000. The new company was gratified to receive a further order from the War Office for a further five Gnome-powered Avro 500 biplanes. With the increase in orders and the financial backing from the Groves family, new premises were sought and these were soon found in Clifton Street, Miles Platting, Manchester and the transfer of the seventy-five personnel and material from Brownsfield Mill was soon underway with the new works being opened on 17 March, 1913. Parrott and Chadwick had now been joined in the drawing office by Harry Broadsmith,

A two-seat Avro Baby at Hamble in July 1920. The peacefully grazing cows seem unaware that they are in the middle of a flying field!

who was later to make his name in Australia by helping to establish that country's first air routes.

Although aviation was becoming established throughout the world it still had its doubters, even on Avro's own doorstep. On 15 March 1913, Alliott had his lecture *Flying Machines* read to the Manchester Association of Engineers. In the discussion which followed, one member, quoting from an engineering journal read, 'it made an engineer ill to look at the way aeroplanes were constructed'. A second member said that two considerations would limit aeroplanes for military purposes. One was the great expense of the petrol used in the aeroplanes while the other was that it was too dangerous for warfare. Another member corrected him on both these points, but it served to remind Mr Groves, who attended the lecture, that he was still running a financial risk.

Luckily, Mr Groves' help was really much more than the cash he had invested, as he showed great interest in just about everything and was well liked by the employees. His influence was great and one of his early inputs was to inform the War Office and the Admiralty that he was now the Chairman of Avro and the Company could be relied upon totally.

The company could not have got a better man as the Groves family were well-known and highly respected. By a strange chance, they had already been connected with the Roes as Alliott's mother had started an orphanage in Patricroft and was pioneer of the day nursery concept. In her report for the year 1889 she had noted that Peer, Robbie, Douglas and Eric of the Groves family had all showed great self-denial by preferring to give ten shillings and sixpence each to the Home instead of having sweets and dessert during Lent.

At the end of 1912 A.V. had been sketching out a new design based on the Avro 500 and this aeroplane, to be known as the Type 504 was taking shape on the drawing boards at the new Clifton Street works. Alliott had his own way of designing with his scheme being to work out the size that the machine was going to be, the weight it would have to carry and from that he would determine the size of the wing spars and the distance apart they would have to be. He would then draw the spars in section in their relative positions and then, in freehand, he would sketch in the best wing section to suit! However, now with the help of Roy

Chadwick the design work had progressed a little more scientifically and their joint thinking started to go into the Avro 504. At a much later date, aeronautical experts acknowledged that A.V.'s wing sections could not have been designed better even today!

With the move Humphrey was finding it difficult to take care of both Everard and also of Avro as the two businesses were now separate geographically. Obviously, he did not want to run the risk of losing Everard and Company in case Avro failed, so he took in John Lord as a partner. John Lord was already showing great interest in the aircraft venture even though he was with Everard, but he would gradually spend more of his time with Avro and eventually he would be taken into the firm.

On 14 February 1913, the Fourth Aero Exhibition opened at Olympia and it was reported that for the first time the British machines held their own against the French. However, it was noted that some of the British aeroplanes had yet to prove their flying ability, but that comment could not be levelled at Avro because the centre piece of the company's display was an Avro 500. This aeroplane was proving to be quite acceptable in service and the machine exhibited was an improved version with the Gnome engine fully enclosed. His Majesty King George V visited the exhibition and was conducted around by senior officials from the motor car industry with the notable absence of anyone in aviation. Subsequently, the King passed by some of the more interesting exhibits, although on the displays he did visit he showed great interest in and knowledge of aviation and its achievements. Fortunately, one of the stands he visited belonged to Avro and A.V. spent some time with the King explaining the virtues of the Avro 500 and informing him of future projects. During the exhibition much interest was shown in the Avro 500 especially as it had been ordered by the War Office for the Royal Flying Corps. Besides the modified engine mounting, the aeroplane on display also had a steel shod rudder which slid up and down its spindle against a coiled spring and this acted as a tail-skid and the main undercarriage skid had a sprung metal tip to absorb the shock of bounced landings.

Back in Manchester more interest was being

When Avro 504s returned to the company for overhaul and modifications in the 1920s the new factory at Newton Heath provided much better accommodation than the cramped area of the earlier premises.

shown by prospective investors and Humphrey devised a scheme to encourage them. He arranged that any investor would receive 10% for Cumulative Participating Preference Shares and that Alliott and Humphrey would take all the Ordinary Shares for Goodwill. The profits to be divided one-third to Preference and two-thirds to Ordinary.

When their father, Dr Roe, heard of the proposed terms he condemned them strongly saying that it was not fair to the brothers themselves as very few companies pay 10% and it meant that their Ordinary Shares would never receive anything. In fact Humphrey was proved right because in the first years as a Limited Company, Avro paid the Preference Shareholders their 10% plus a Bonus of 2½%!

The construction of the new Avro 504 began in April 1913 with the Clifton Street premises already beginning to be short on space with Avro 500s, 501s and a 503 under manufacture. The Avro 501 was the number given to the Hydro-biplane which was delivered to the Admiralty in the previous December and an order for three more was underway. The Avro 503 was also being built and was already an improvement of the Type 501 by having a larger wing area through an increase in wing span. The Avro 503 was completed on 25 April 1913, with the machine being dismantled almost immediately before being despatched to 'Shoreham-by-the-Sea' as Avro brochures of the day described it. However, poor facilities and some personnel illness at Shoreham meant that the aeroplane took longer to assemble than expected and did not fly until 28 May 1913. The twin-float Avro 503 was eased into the river in the early morning mist and with Fred Raynham at the controls and Jack Alcock as passenger, the aircraft took to the air in fine style. Jack Alcock had gained

This excellent close-up of the Wolseley Viper engine installation of the Avro 552A also shows the new oleo undercarriage. This undercarriage was designed by Avro's George (later Sir George) Dowty who went on to form the famous company which still bears his name.

his pilot's certificate and was now an instructor at Shoreham for what became known as The Avro Flying School (Brighton) Limited. A mere six years later he would be world famous!

The Avro 503 proved to be an excellent machine and was soon being evaluated by the German Naval Air Service with Raynham being accompanied on early test flights by *Leutnant* Ernst Shultz who was, it was later established, empowered to purchase the machine on behalf of the German Government. He was so impressed that he insisted that he purchase that very machine and, never one to refuse money, Humphrey authorised the sale! The Avro 503 was dismantled and shipped to Germany during June 1913 and on 6 September 1913 a record was established when *Leutnant* Emil Langfeld made the first flight from Wilhelmshaven to Heligoland which was a distance of just over forty miles. The German Navy was so impressed by the Avro 503 that they acquired the licence to manufacture the aircraft themselves and the Gotha Company was selected to produce the machine. It was produced in Germany as the Gotha WD.1 and did sterling service for that country during the early part of World War One. A later design, the Gotha WD.2, which owed much to the Avro 503, was very successful and was exported by the Germans to Turkey.

The motorcycle journey between Brooklands and Manchester, as well as visits to Shoreham and other aviation centres, were becoming increasingly unpleasant for A.V. so he designed a completely enclosed version with retractable stabilising small wheels each side of the rear wheel.

The Avro 504 was almost complete by the end of June 1913 and with A.V. overseeing the design work, the fuselage was the responsibility of Roy Chadwick and his new assistant C.R.Taylor. With Chadwick's input Harry Broadsmith had designed the wings.

The aeroplane was delivered to Brooklands and the machine made its historic maiden flight on 28 July 1913 and, once again, Freddy Raynham was at the controls. Raynham, still only twenty-one years old was regarded as one of Britain's most experienced test pilots.

The first Avro 504 had its 80 hp Gnome engine encased in a flat rectangular nose cowling which spoilt the otherwise streamlined effect of the

An Avro Aldershot bomber being demonstrated at the Hendon R.A.F. Display in June 1922.

The Ventral gun position of the Avro Ava torpedo bomber was fully retractable, but provided little protection for its occupant from a would-be attacker.

aeroplane and this, together with the warping ailerons brought the only criticism from outsiders. One gentleman commented to A.V. that the aeroplane looked too light, to which Alliott quickly replied, ' It should rather be said that the machine is astonishingly strong for its weight. The War Office demands that certain stresses per square inch will not be exceeded. The Admiralty are more stringent, but the Avro people to be on the safe side keep within Admiralty requirements. The stresses of every part of the machine are most carefully considered by our Design Department and duplicate parts are then put to actual mechanical tests to see whether they stand up to the design stress'. The onlooker obviously made his comment to the wrong person as Alliott would have continued if one of his staff had not required his presence elsewhere!

The Circuit of Britain Race sponsored, once again, by the *Daily Mail* commenced on 25 August 1913 and Avro had hoped to enter the second Type 503 seaplane, but because of the outstanding number of orders the machine could not be prepared in time. A.V. was later informed that a seaplane entered by Harry Hawker was faster than the Avro 503. On the third day Hawker came down in the Irish Sea due to engine trouble, but he and his mechanic, who was flying as passenger, were

rescued by a passing ship which had witnessed the crash. As Hawker was the sole entrant in the race and had already completed 1,043 miles, which was the longest distance ever achieved in consecutive flights, he was awarded £1,000 of the proposed £5,000 prize money. The newspaper reported that a similar award would be offered for a similar competition in the following year.

The notoriety achieved by the Sopwith and Harry Hawker for their fine effort in the Circuit of Britain Race made A.V. more determined that come the next aerial event an Avro would be entered come what may. The following month the second Aerial Derby took place and the company entered the new Avro 504. Practically all of the aeroplane's test flying had been carried out by Fred Raynham and Alliott felt that he was the ideal candidate to race the machine. The race circuit of nearly one hundred miles started and finished at Hendon and the 504 put up a very creditable performance by finishing in fourth place at an average speed of 66.5 mph.

The race was won by a monoplane and this fuelled the ongoing controversy of biplane versus monoplane as the most efficient type of aeroplane at the time. With this very much in mind, Avro received a challenge from Dr M.G. Christie of Leeds for an aerial 'War of the Roses' for the *Yorkshire Evening News* Challenge Cup. Dr Christie

---

BELOW:
The second Avro 558 light biplane on its first appearance in September 1923 shows the chain drive from the 500 c.c. Douglas flat-twin engine.

---

BELOW RIGHT:
An Avro 504N fitted with a streamlined cowling for its Lynx engine.

ABOVE:
Final discussions before the first flight of the Cierva C.6 (Avro 574) Autogiro at Hamble in June 1926. On the left is A.V. Roe himself with Juan de la Cierva and Captain Frank Courtney.

ABOVE RIGHT:
Bert Hinkler poses with the Avro Avenger in a photograph which confirms that the aircraft had the cleanest lines of any of that period.

would represent Yorkshire by flying a passenger in a Blackburn Type 1 monoplane flown by Harold Blackburn himself while Humphrey would be in the Avro flying for Lancashire. The event took place on 2 October 1913 and started at Leeds with twenty minute stops at York, Doncaster, Sheffield and Barnsley with the finish at Leeds. The contest created great interest in the towns visited, but Fred Raynham flying the Avro 504 became lost in poor visibility and as he was not familiar with the area he decided to abandon the race. It was planned to repeat the event in the following year, this time in Lancashire. The course agreed was Manchester,

Blackburn, Blackpool, Liverpool and then return to Manchester. However, the First World War came and the 'air war' of the Roses of Lancashire and Yorkshire was completely forgotten.

The flying around Yorkshire proved to Raynham that the warping ailerons were very heavy and made long flights very hard work. The ailerons were replaced by more conventional types and after Raynham had re-tested the machine at Brooklands he declared the control was now excellent.

Raynham took the Avro 504 to Farnborough on 24 November 1913 for a series of tests and, much to everyone's delight, the aeroplane passed every one. With three hours fuel and one passenger on board Raynham took the 504 to 1,000 feet altitude in one minute forty-five seconds and during the speed trials the aeroplane achieved a speed of 80.9 mph over a measured distance. It was found that the machine stalled at 43 mph and with the speed range being an excellent 37 mph the 504 was a worthy challenger to the B.E.2. Other pilots who flew the 504 were impressed with all of its characteristics, it was nicer to handle than the B.E.2, which was finding favour with the Royal Flying Corps. The Avro 504 was showing itself to be well in advance of that aircraft.

At the end of 1913, Fred Raynham spared time from his test flying to grant H.V. one of his cherished wishes — he taught him to fly. Humphrey learned in an Avro 500, but he flew some of the other types, although his duties back in Manchester were obviously more important.

It was back to home ground for an exhibition at Belle Vue which opened on New Year's Day 1914 and it was to be the first showing of the Avro 508, a two-seat pusher biplane designed for military use. This machine was incomplete, but caused a stir in the aviation world as it was a complete departure from earlier Avro designs. As the local aeroplane builder, Avro had a large display stand even though the Show was to cover only three days. On the stand was the original Roe 1 triplane which made its last appearance before going into storage. This storage was to last for eleven years before the aeroplane emerged to be presented to the Science Museum in London in 1925. It can be seen there to this day. Fred Raynham gave flying displays in the Avro 504 over Belle Vue, although low cloud hampered this on the last day.

On 4 February 1914, Raynham flew an Avro 504 from Brooklands to Hendon and took the aeroplane to 15,000 feet which was almost 2,000 feet higher than the British altitude record. However, the flight was not officially observed and could not be submitted as an attempt. Not one to be denied, Raynham arranged for an official attempt on 10 February. Carrying Mr R.J. MacGeah Hurst as passenger, the 504 climbed to 14,420 feet over Brooklands to establish a new British height record.

At the 1914 Olympia Air Show, which opened on 16 March, A.V. Roe and Company Limited had a magnificent stand on which they displayed an Avro 504 seaplane, the Avro 508 and the brand new little Avro 511 Arrowscout. Although it had been seen in public before, at the Belle Vue exhibition two months earlier, the surprise of the show was the Avro 508 military pusher aeroplane. It was very similar to the F.E. (Fighting Experimental) and the Vickers E.F.B. 3, one of the famous Gunbus series, which was also on exhibition. The 508 had been a complete departure from the types the industry had come to expect

from Avro. In his search for speed A.V. had instigated the design of the Type 511 Arrowscout and it was certainly radical for the period. The single-bay biplane had a large sweep-back of the wings with the lower surface being flat. The interplane struts were faired between with fabric covering to form a single 'I' type strut. The 511 fuselage was scaled-down from the Avro 504, but one unusual innovation was the introduction of the flap-type airbrake fitted at the lower wing root trailing-edge. One feature insisted upon by A.V. was the fitting of safety belts to all Avro aircraft even though they were not considered necessary by some manufacturers and some aviators were thrown out of their aeroplane after a crash or even falling out while the machine was still in the air, with the latter happening to the great pioneer Samuel F. Cody on 7 August 1913. The foresight of A.V. was later accepted as a standard safety feature in aviation.

A number of aircraft were ordered during the Show and by the following month the *Daily Mail* had purchased the first Avro 504 to do exhibition flying at coastal resorts around Britain. They required the aircraft to be able to take-off from land or water, so Avro provided the machine with floats which could be interchangeable with the normal wheel undercarriage. The engine was also changed as it was felt that the powerplant originally installed, an 80 hp Gnome, would not be powerful enough for operations off the sea. It was fitted with a Gnome Monosoupape rotary engine which, although it had the same horse-power as the original, was much more efficient with greater power output.

The *Daily Mail* tour was an attempt to make the public air-minded and many resorts were visited with the aircraft making its debut as a seaplane from Paignton, Devon at the end of April 1914. The machine was being flown by Fred Raynham and George Lusted, but it was continually plagued by engine problems and it was this trouble that brought the prototype 504's career to an end. When war was declared in August the machine was at Shoreham fitted in the floatplane configuration, but it was immediately commandeered by the Admiralty. Two days later, on the 6th, Raynham took-off to deliver the aeroplane to the military, but the engine failed completely and the pilot was lucky to escape with

The company demonstrator Avian II, photographed in May 1927, displays its baggage compartment and hinged front cockpit for ease of entry.

his life when the aircraft was wrecked in a crash-landing.

The largest and last of the Avro 501— 503 type seaplanes was the Avro 510, an impressive machine with a top wing spanning sixty-three feet and the lower at thirty-eight feet. It was powered by a reliable 150 hp Sunbeam water-cooled engine and Alliott was convinced that this would be the aeroplane to win the 1914 Circuit of Britain race. The Admiralty ordered five Avro 510s and these were originally to be fitted with the Gnome 160 hp engine, but were adapted to take the Sunbeam as in A.V.'s 'Circuit' aeroplane. The latter was completed at Clifton Street on 15 July 1914 and

despatched to Calshot for flight trials before the actual race which was due to start there. Unfortunately it was never to be, as war was declared on 4 August 1914 and the Race was cancelled. The aeroplane was impressed into service alongside the other Avro 510s making a useful contribution in coastal patrol during the war.

The little Avro 511 Arrowscout made just two flights before appearing at Hendon on 23 May 1914. It was also entered in the Third Aerial Derby but A.V. was extremely disappointed with the aeroplane's performance and, after a few modifications had brought no improvements, he had the aircraft dismantled. It was later fitted with straight wings and a different undercarriage to be designated the Avro 514. On 5 June 1914, the day before the Aerial Derby was due, Fred Raynham was to test fly the 'new' Avro 514, but as he taxied out for take-off, the untried light-weight and streamlined undercarriage collapsed. Inevitably, the resulting damage made it impossible for the machine to take part in the Race and it was withdrawn from the competition.

On 1 July 1914, the Royal Naval Air Service was officially formed from the Naval Wing of the Royal Flying Corps. The Navy had given its pilots a free hand to conduct experiments best suited to naval flying. Captain (later Rear-Admiral Sir) Murray Sueter was their excellent mentor who had guided a certain Mr Winston Churchill of the Admiralty and the latter was well known for his interest in flying and the aviators. One incident which could have changed the course of history happened soon after, when Churchill, who was always being admonished about his flying as a passenger because of his Ministerial status, missed death by a whisker. Churchill had completed forty-five minutes dual instruction with Captain G.V. Wildman-Lushington of the Royal Military Academy when, on the next flight of the Short biplane which took place the following morning, that officer was killed when the machine stalled

and crashed.

In July 1914, a bright young Yorkshireman named Roy Hardy Dobson returned home after a holiday in Manchester. He had heard of Avro and his keen interest took him to Clifton Street where he applied at the door for a job. Alliott himself interviewed Dobson and asked him if he had any experience of mechanical drawing. He had not, but being a practical youngster he failed to reveal this to A.V and was sent along to Reg Parrott. Dobson commenced work with Avro at the beginning of August and two days later Britain was at War. Dobson always swore that it had nothing to do with him! He went to work in the drawing office under Roy Chadwick, but after six months he transferred to the materials testing department where he felt more at home. Dobson and Chadwick, Chadwick and Dobson, whichever way one looked at it they would go on to be synonymous with the name of A.V. Roe and Company Limited.

An Avian III seaplane on Southampton Water at Hamble in June 1928 just before delivery to Western Canada Airways.

# CHAPTER 3

# The First World War

On 4 August 1914, Germany rejected Britain's request for assurances that the neutrality of Belgium would be respected and war was declared.

In the summer of 1914 the War Office had ordered twelve Avro 504s and the Admiralty also ordered one as the build-up to a possible war had made it obvious that greater numbers of aeroplanes of all types would be needed. It was obvious to Avro that if war did come the current floor space would be inadequate for any increase in production. It was fortunate that Mather & Platt, a local engineering company had just completed an extension to their premises at Newton Heath just a mile away from Clifton Street.

When war was declared Humphrey immediately went to Mather & Platt's offices and met with Mr John Taylor, the Managing Director, to ask if Avro could take over the new building. The extension covered an area of 5,000 square yards and was not yet in use. A Director's meeting was already underway and the whole matter was settled in a few minutes with nothing more than a gentlemen's agreement between Mr Taylor and H.V. Immediate possession was granted and Avro also acquired new premises in Failsworth.

The small premises in Failsworth became known as the Empire Works which manufactured small metal components, but in 1936 the factory became the sheet metal facility for Avro with specialised 'tin bashers' having their own site, turning out some wonderful examples of precision metal work. The 'Empire' remained within the company right up to the British Aerospace days before it was closed on 31 October 1981, with the seventy-five workers being transferred to the Chadderton factory just over a mile away.

H.V.'s search for premises continued and he was able to rent a small building in Heath Street, Newton Heath which became known as the Heath Works. This too was a specialised site mainly for woodworkers and trimmers with a paint and dope section attached. It was in the latter that a fire started during the night of 1 May 1918 and the whole works was completely destroyed with very little equipment being salvageable. The Heath workers were spread around the local Avro sites, with the woodworkers moving into a timber yard owned by Evans & Company of Newton Heath, staying there until the end of the war. The timber yard later expanded and became Evans Bellhouse, which retained close links with Avro through specialised woodworking including, in later years, fairings for the bomb-doors of the various 'special' Lancasters.

Humphrey returned to Clifton Street to find that twenty or so army volunteers had been sent to guard the factory and after meeting the officer-in-charge, H.V., being an ex-army officer himself, suggested that they should have a rifle inspection to keep the men interested. The officer agreed with the theory, but only had two rifles between all of them and the two men on sentry duty would need those!

The Avro 504 had an inauspicious start to its wartime service, as it entered the record books by having the dubious honour of being the first British aeroplane to be shot down by the Germans. It was on 22 August 1914, that an Avro 504 of No. 5 Squadron, Royal Flying Corps, flown by Lieut Victor Waterfall, with Lieut C.G.C. Bayly as his observer, was brought down by infantry fire in Belgium.

In the early days of the war with air fighting in its infancy, Avro 504s as well as other RFC aircraft were regularly fired upon by British and French ground troops. The aircraft insignia consisted of Union Jacks painted on the aeroplanes in rectangular and in shield-shape on aircraft of the Royal Flying Corps and it was felt that markings of

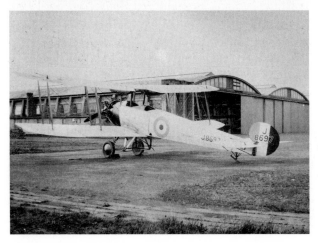

ABOVE LEFT:
The neatly cowled Napier Lion engine in the Avro Buffalo II. This aeroplane was purchased by the Air Ministry and converted to a seaplane, but after some experimental flying at Felixstowe any further development was abandoned.

ABOVE:
Confirmation that the famous Amelia Earhart did buy an Avro Avian as the crated aircraft is shown here being loaded onto the White Star steamer *Baltic* at Liverpool in July 1928.

LEFT:
The Avro Avenger II at Renfrew, Glasgow during the 1928 King's Cup Air Race. Piloted by a young 'Mutt' Summers, who later achieved fame as Vickers' chief test pilot, the Avenger won a prize for the fastest machine in the race.

BELOW LEFT:
Although the basic design was sixteen years old this Avro 504N was a newly delivered aeroplane when photographed at Renfrew in 1929.

a more conspicuous type should be carried. The famous roundel was adopted by the RFC on 26 October 1914, but the Royal Naval Air Service did not use a roundel officially until 11 December 1914. However, the RNAS roundel was used on the wings only and this consisted a red outer circle with a white centre in the initial stages.

On 16 September 1914, Humphrey was called to a meeting of aircraft manufacturers in the office of Winston Churchill. Churchill told the gathering that the Government must reduce the variety of designs and all manufacturers must build the B.E. type of aeroplane designed by the Royal Aircraft Factory at Farnborough, as it had been selected as the best for the purpose. H.V. raised the matter of the Avro 504s on order for the War Office. Were they to be completed? Churchill agreed, but added that the B.E. question could be settled at some later date. The B.E. situation died a natural death and orders for the 504 began to stream in steadily.

As the air war over France was gaining momentum, the Avro 504s were being flown from the rear seat with the observer sitting ahead of the pilot under the centre section of the upper wing with the operation of a machine-gun or other offensive weapon almost impossible. However, in October 1914, Second Lieut Louis A. Strange of No. 5 Squadron fitted his aeroplane with a Lewis machine-gun which was slotted into a metal tube taken from the tail boom of a crashed Farman biplane. The tube was suspended by a rope fixed to a cross member which enabled the observer to swing the gun in practically any direction. On 22 October Strange and his observer, Captain L.da C. Penn-Gaskell made the first strafing attack of the war when they fired on an enemy train in a siding at Perenchies and a month later Strange in his Avro 504 forced down a German Albatros two-seater near Neuve-Eglise.

The most famous action carried out by the Avro

An unusual venue to display an Avro Avian was this car showroom of Malayan Motors, Singapore in September 1929.

504 was the highly dangerous raid carried out against the Zeppelin sheds at Friedrichshafen on Lake Constance. On the outbreak of war squadrons of the RNAS carried out duties of escort and patrol along the coast and over the Channel. Once the routine work was established, the General Staff suggested that they go on the offensive with attacks on enemy airfields and airship sheds.

Under Wing Commander Charles Rumney Samson, a swashbuckling type who was one of the first naval officers to learn to fly, the Naval Air Unit was based at Ostend to assist in the defence of Antwerp. Samson personally led aeroplane raids, but also designed an armoured car and amused himself by raiding in enemy occupied areas, creating as much havoc as possible! A number of raids were carried out successfully against enemy targets and besides the damage caused, the new Zeppelin Z-1X (LZ-25) was destroyed on 8 October 1914.

The real prize wanted by Samson was the Zeppelin sheds at Friedrichshafen, but these were almost in Switzerland and careful planning had to be taken for such an attack.

An order had been received by Avro to supply four 504s each fitted with underwing bomb racks capable of carrying 20lb bombs. A secret unit was formed by Commander P. Shepherd with two pilots and eleven mechanics of the group arriving in Manchester for instruction on the type. The Park

Works at Newton Heath was visited by Squadron Commander E. Featherstone Briggs, RN, on 29 October 1914 when it was made clear to him that the only way the aircraft could be ready in the time-scale specified with the order was for him to accept parts which had already been condemned by the Aeronautical Inspection Department (later Directorate) for the War Office order. They were quite good, but did not comply with AID specifications and Lieut Briggs examined the parts, agreeing they were safe. The AID, then as now, insisted on perfection and it was felt that although the parts were slightly below standard, the aviators were not at risk.

The completed aircraft were crated and despatched to Southampton immediately where they were loaded aboard the vessel *Manchester Importer* (H.V. thought it a pity that it wasn't the *Exporter*!) with the ship sailing to Le Havre that evening. The crates were then transported to the French airfield at Belfort where they were hidden in barns away from prying eyes until the attack could be undertaken. The aircraft were erected, but the late arrival of the additional pilots delayed the raid and then poor weather stopped flying for three days.

It was a tribute to the builders that the raid itself would be the first time that the aircraft had ever flown, as there had been no time for test flights. Each fitted with four bombs, the Avro 504s taxied out for take-off on 21 November 1914, but the machine being piloted by Flight Sub-Lieut R.P. Cannon (No. 179) broke its tail skid on a rough patch and this prevented it taking part in the attack. The other machines took off successfully for their 125 mile flight to the target with Briggs (No. 873) leading then, at five minute intervals, followed Flight Commander J.T. Babington (No. 875) and then Flight Lieut Sydney Sippé (No. 874) — the latter, of course, was an old friend of Avro. The aircraft, to avoid Swiss neutrality, had to fly a course to Mülhausen and then over the Black Forest to Schaffhausen, then they had to turn southwards to reach Lake Constance. They made the trip at an altitude of 5,000 feet, before flying low over the Lake to avoid detection and then climbed to 1,500 feet to drop their bombs. One of Sippé's bombs failed to release, but all the others dropped successfully, damaging a Zeppelin in its shed and also a number of the surrounding

buildings, but one bomb hit a gas-making plant causing it to explode violently with heavy damage to the surrounding area. Briggs was shot down and badly beaten by German civilians before being rescued from them by the military. He later escaped and returned to England where he commanded the experimental station at Eastchurch.

The daring raid was carried out with fine skill which earned praise from the chivalrous members of the German Air Service. Back in Manchester the news of the raid was greeted with great delight, especially when it was found that the attack was carried out just twenty-three days after the official order had been placed with Avro!

Wing Commander Samson's unit, known as the Eastchurch Squadron, named after their home base in Kent, had been at Ostend since 27 August. They made another contribution to Avro 504 history when one of their machines, flown by Flight Sub-Lieut R.H. Collet, dropped four 16lb bombs on the Ostend — Bruges railway line, disrupting German supply trains for almost a week.

An important raid carried out by Avro 504s did not receive as much publicity as the attack at Friedrichshafen, but in terms of effectiveness it was no less worthy. On 24 March 1915, five aeroplanes of No. 1 Squadron, RNAS under Squadron Commander A.M. Longmore set out to bomb the dockyard at Hoboken near Antwerp, but only two aircraft were able to reach their objective. Squadron Commander Ivor T. Courtney and Flight Lieut Harold L. Rosher, with the latter flying No. 874, Sippé's aeroplane in the Zeppelin sheds raid, dropped their bombs from 1,000 feet causing damage in the dockyard and more importantly, destroying two coastal-type U-boats (U-B class) which had just arrived from Scheldt.

Interestingly enough, the RNAS often referred to the 504 as the Avro 179, which was the serial number of the first Avro 504 to be accepted and, later, was the aeroplane which suffered the broken tail skid in the Friedrichshafen raid and had to retire from the attack. An aircraft which did take part, No. 875, was shot down by ground fire on 16 February 1915, while being flown by Flight Lieut E.G. Rigall.

The 504 continued in front-line service, but with the rapid development of new fighter aircraft, the machine was employed on anti-Zeppelin patrols.

ABOVE:
A well detailed shot of the wing construction of the Avro 627 Mailplane.

ABOVE RIGHT:
Norman Giroux was famous for his pleasure flying from Southport sands both before and after World War Two. This Avro 548 of Giro Aviation flew thousands of passengers from April 1932 until the outbreak of war.

RIGHT:
Indian State Airways ordered four Avro Tens, but financial problems led to the delivery of only one of them. The aircraft was later taken over by the Viceroy of India.

On the night of 16-17 May 1915* the Avros were out on patrol and two machines, piloted by Flight Sub-Lieut R.H. Mulock and Flight Commander A.W. Bigsworth, both made interceptions. The Zeppelin LZ-38 under the command of *Hauptmann* Karl Linnerz was on a raid to bomb Southend and Ramsgate when Mulock attacked, but the airship was able to climb into cloud and escape. Bigsworth located the LZ-39 near Ostend, climbed above it and dropped four 20lb bombs onto the envelope. The bombs went right through the airship without exploding, but did damage to the Zeppelin's structure forcing it down safely behind the German lines. Both of these airships were to meet their end shortly afterwards with the LZ-38 being destroyed in its shed at Evère after a raid by the RNAS on 7 June 1915. The LZ-39 was repaired and

In the early 1930s orders were received from many parts of the world for Avro training machines and their variants. This aeroplane is the company's Type 626 demonstrator showing the availability of a rear gunner's position.

became operational again, but on 18 October 1915 it was hit by ground fire and came down near Leuze, Belgium and was burned by the crew to avoid capture.

The Avro 504C was specially developed by Avro and the RNAS for anti-Zeppelin duties. The aircraft had an extra fuel tank in the front cockpit area and a number of them had a Lewis gun fitted into the centre section to fire upwards at an enemy

*Exactly twenty-eight years later Guy Gibson was to lead another force of Avro aeroplanes — Lancasters on the famous Dams raid.

airship. About eighty of this type were supplied and other versions, the Avro 504B, E and G were all developed for the RNAS. An Avro 504B was used in early trials for deck arresting on ships while a 504C, given the designation 504H became one of the first aircraft to be launched by catapult.

The modifications to the 504C included the strengthening of various parts of the aircraft: catapult pick-up points were fitted and a new padded seat and neck support were provided for the pilot. These modifications were supervised by Squadron Commander E.H. Dunning who made history on 2 August 1917, when he was the first in the world to land an aeroplane on a ship that was underway. HMS *Furious* was steaming at twenty-six knots into a headwind of twenty-one knots

His Excellency Hakki-Bey, the Egyptian Charge d'Affaires in London inspects Egyptian Army Air Force pilots with their Avro 626s at Lympne, Kent in September 1932. These aircraft were about to depart for Cairo in a massed delivery flight. Egypt eventually ordered twenty-seven 626s

which gave Dunning a combination of forty-seven knots against which to land his Sopwith Pup on the ship's deck. Unfortunately, before the catapult trials could commence, Dunning was killed on 7 August in his third attempt to land on the ship. The *Furious* had a great headwind coming over the deck and in an attempted overshoot the Pup was blown over the side into the water with Dunning losing his life. The catapult tests with the Avro 504 were now without a pilot, but Flight Commander R.E. Penny, who had been an associate of Dunning, volunteered for the job. The launch was completed successfully with Penny landing safely.

In Manchester Avro was having difficulties in coping with success as both the War Office and the Admiralty were in competition for the Avro 504, with each of their technical departments making a detailed study of the aeroplane and both wanting different specifications. Neither would give way as the company sought to avoid production difficulties, but as the War Office order was received first their machines were completed and

The fuselage construction of the only Avro Tutor II. Changes in the wing struts and the addition of a tail wheel were the modifications from the earlier model, but as they were of no advantage, production continued on the Tutor 1.

The Avro 624 airliner under construction at Newton Heath showing its original semi-circular nose design.

delivered before the Admiralty aircraft. As more orders flooded in, the troubles started once more.

Female labour was introduced into suitable departments and as the early arrivals proved to be most satisfactory, the facility at Failsworth was operated mostly by women. H.V. felt that the labour matters were too important to delegate to

The pilot's cockpit of the Avro 642. Slightly different from the airliners of today!

Accommocation in the Avro 642's cabin was for sixteen passengers, but in this photograph taken from the cockpit door, the camera's lense could only show twelve.

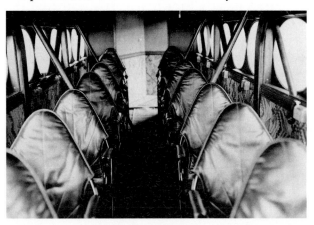

others, so he dealt with employee matters himself along with his other duties. One situation of which he became proud was when Roy Dobson had been sacked! Humphrey had Dobson in line for promotion, so he was not happy when he heard from Dobson's manager that he had been dismissed. H.V. listened to both sides and decided that the trouble had been caused by Dobson's surplus energy and eagerness, spoilt by the inexperience of youth. His manager would not take Dobson back into his department, so H.V. placed him in the Progress Department managed by Harry Broadsmith. It was the making of Dobson as he was ideal for the job, a live wire who would get things done. Broadsmith was a steadying

influence and the perfect man to train him and it was fortunate for the future of the firm that Humphrey stepped in when he did!

It was at this time that Humphrey heard from the War Office that his application to rejoin the army had been overturned. In fact, he had been granted a commission again as a Lieutenant in the Manchester Regiment's 12th Service Battalion, but this was cancelled because of his position as Managing Director of A.V. Roe and Company Limited.

The build-up in orders continued apace and H.V. received a visit from a Captain Wheatley of the Military Aeronautics Directorate — an independent department of the War Office — who asked for more Avro 504s, but he was reminded that the company was well underway with the orders received. 'Can you deliver more?' Wheatley enquired. Humphrey replied that they could guarantee delivery on any order. 'Good', said the officer and he ordered another hundred aeroplanes on the spot!

Aircraft were completed at Park Works where they had their engines tested, before being dismantled for delivery to the services. They were then towed through the streets to London Road (now Piccadilly) Railway Station where they would be transported by train to one of the many Aircraft Acceptance Parks. It would have been ideal to fly them out from a field in Newton Heath, but nothing was entirely suitable. However, a field at Trafford Park once owned by Manchester Aerodrome Limited, which has ceased operating in 1913, was being used for occasional visits by the Royal Flying Corps. To help with the delivery problem Avro erected a portable hangar which proved to be most useful and even some of the newer Avro types were flight tested from there.

In 1916 the Society of British Aircraft Constructors was formed for the Government to have a representative body with whom they could deal directly on questions connected with aircraft manufacture. Humphrey was to be the representative for A.V. Roe & Company Limited and was present at the first ever meeting of the SBAC committee.

Meanwhile, A.V. himself had decided that the expansion at Manchester was unsatisfactory and his dream was to build a new plant in pleasanter surroundings. After touring a number of areas in search of a 'green field' site he discovered the ideal place at Hamble in Hampshire. The 100 acre site was on firm grassland which stretched down to Southampton Water. Alliott and his wife Mildred had motored around the Southampton area, but as soon as he saw the large field at Hamble he turned to her and said, 'This is our spot'. He immediately telegraphed his co-directors and arrangements were made to purchase the site and, within two weeks, Avro had purchased the 100 acres plus a mile of the foreshore. They were later to buy another 200 acres.

A.V. wanted a Garden City similar to the one devised by Bournville and he employed the services of Harry Fairhurst, a well-known Manchester architect and artist, to design the whole facility. The ambitious project would consist of a factory and a garden-town consisting of 350 artistic houses. The aircraft assembly area would be a large rectangular building with full span doors and a floor space unimpeded by roof supports. Only twenty-four houses had been completed when the Government took control of all building materials and, although the factory was able to undertake production, the remaining staff houses were put on hold, but were destined never to be built.

The Avro 642 in its final form when delivered to Midland and Scottish Air Ferries in 1934. It was later sold to an operator in the Far East and provided excellent service before it was destroyed by the Japanese in New Guinea during 1942.

Reginald Parrott became General Manager and was later succeeded in that position by the Reverend Everard V. Roe who eventually became the Vicar of Hamble's Parish Church. The Manchester factories were now under Harry Broadsmith, but the design team which under the twenty-three year old Roy Chadwick, consisted of C.R. Taylor and Frank Vernon, remained at Manchester.

Despite his age Chadwick was responsible for all the aircraft design work and, of course, remained so for the rest of his life. Everything connected with aeroplanes came easy to him and his aviation knowledge was unsurpassed. He was, arguably, the finest aircraft designer in the world.

One of Chadwick's designs that was not a success was the Avro 521, a 110 hp Clerget-powered reconnaissance aircraft which was first flown late in 1915. The aeroplane had its maiden flight from Trafford Park in the hands of Fred Raynham with Harry Broadsmith in the rear cockpit standing with a dummy machine-gun to check the wind resistance and any extra drag. Raynham found the machine to have disagreeable flying characteristics, but the Avro 521 was sent to Farnborough on 20 January 1916 for official trials. There it became known as the 'Avro Scout 1811' for some unknown reason and it then went on to the Central Flying School (CFS) at Upavon with the warning: 'This machine plunges its nose viciously towards the ground in a right hand turn!' It did in fact crash on 21 September, 1916, killing its pilot Lieut W.H.S. Garnett. The aeroplane's reputation

prompted the War Office to cancel an order for twenty-five of the type, but as they were already under construction, it is possible that they were converted to Avro 504s.

With pressure of war and the constant search for aircraft types for various roles, the design team were busier than ever with machines like the Avro 519, 522 and 528 emerging from the drawing boards and all of these variations on the Avro 515, a large tractor biplane. However, none of them seemed to pass the experimental stage.

One type which did make the headlines was the Avro 523 which was known as the Pike. This machine was a large twin-engined pusher biplane fighter which was delivered from Manchester to Farnborough for testing on 29 January 1916. Trials showed that performance was reasonable, but not up to standard to justify large-scale production. The Pike was involved in an extraordinary incident soon after take-off from the RNAS experimental establishment on the Isle of Grain for a demonstration to officials of the Admiralty. The pilot, Fred Raynham, had great difficulty in controlling the aeroplane as it was extremely tail heavy. Roy Dobson, who was by that time a qualified pilot, was in the rear acting as observer, but this position was a long way from Raynham as the pilot's cockpit was forward of the wing. There was no communication system for the crew, but Dobson realised that there was something wrong and Raynham signalled to him that he could not get the tail up. The pilot feared that if he throttled back or switched off the engines the Pike might stall and Dobson assessed the situation quickly — he must act like ballast! He climbed out of the rear gunner's position and, straddling the fuselage with nothing to hold on to, he inched his way forward just missing the whirring propellers with his toes! He grabbed the bracing wires under the centre section and squeezed through them, climbed over Raynham and then fell headlong into the front gunner's position. The balance of the aeroplane was restored and Raynham landed safely. It was a brave deed which saved the aeroplane and possibly their lives. Afterwards, 'Dobbie', as he was known said, 'I like flying, but I would not care to do that again!'

The Manchester facilities were still expanding with Avro building its own large factory at Newton Heath, but the restrictions on building

materials in the south saw Hamble emerge as an experimental site only, although some 504s were built there during 1918. Hamble did have the advantage of having a slipway into Southampton Water and Avro was able to offer the use of this facility to Westland of Yeovil who were building Short 184 seaplanes under licence. In February 1917 an Avro design team under Roy Chadwick arrived at Hamble to work on new projects and to modify and improve current aircraft. There were now forty people working in the design office and they were delighted to find that their new offices were light and airy and well lit during the darker hours. Despite the trauma of the complete move from Manchester, Chadwick had to secure accommodation for his men and himself, carry on with the design of the Avro 504J dual-control training aeroplane, but also push ahead with the Avro 530 two-seat fighter which was in direct competition with the Bristol F.2B. The 530 flew for the first time on 4 July 1917, but failed to secure a large production order because of the shortage of available engines. The Avro 530 was originally designed with a 300 hp water-cooled engine, but the manufacturer, Hispano-Suiza, could not supply one to Avro by the time the aircraft was completed so the aeroplane made its early flights with the 200 hp version. The performance was quite acceptable and the 530 was pleasant to fly, but the engine supply problem hit the design once more as the 200 hp Hispano-Suiza was needed for the highly successful S.E.5A fighter. The Bristol F.2B Fighter powered by a 275 hp Rolls-Royce Falcon engine, went into service and became the RFC's best two-seat fighter of the war. This aeroplane, known affectionately as the 'Brisfit', gave excellent service to the RFC and, later the Royal Air Force, for many years after the war ended. The Avro 530 design was later fitted with a 200 hp Sunbeam Arab

OPPOSITE TOP:
The woodworker's apron was still the main attire in the 1930s and here an Avro Five wing is under construction at Newton Heath.

OPPOSITE BOTTOM:
The Avro Ten *Faith in Australia* was attempting a world record flight when it crashed in Ireland. The aircraft was rebuilt at Newton Heath and Woodford before flying back to Australia. Relaxing during the work are (L to R) Bill MacGregor, Alex McKenzie and Jack Caulfield.

The four engined version of the Avro 642 named *Star of India* was the Viceroy of India's personal aircraft. Delivered in December 1934 the machine performed well and was transferred to R.A.F. service at the start of the war.

The Avro 671 autogiro was the Cierva C.30A built by the company under a licence agreement. This particular example photographed at Woodford was delivered to the French Army in July 1934.

engine, but this version was flight tested as the war was drawing to a close, so production was not required. A civil high-speed touring version was proposed by Chadwick in 1920, but this was not pursued.

Roy Dobson, who had become famous throughout the company with his exploits in the Pike, was again on the mat. This time it was Reg Parrott at Hamble who was 'after a piece of

THE FIRST WORLD WAR

Dobson's tail'. Apparently 'Dobbie' had been caught spending much time with an old Ford car in one of the huts vacated by the builders at Hamble. Dismissal would have been harsh so he was allowed to return to Manchester where John Lord took him under his wing. Despite the odd spot of trouble, Dobson had great potential, combining great ability with untiring energy and under Lord he went on to become assistant manager and eventually Works Manager. The rest is history.

By the middle of 1917 the firm had increased considerably in size and was on a much firmer financial base. It was at that time that Humphrey applied for, and received, a commission in the RFC and he resigned his position in the company from 31 July 1917. On the day before he left, H.V. hosted a visit by Sir George Toulmin, MP and both gave a speech to the work force assembled outside the Park Works. Sir George expressed his thanks to the workers and told them how important their work was. The speeches were received enthusiastically and it was satisfying to H.V. before going off to war.

Humphrey, who was a bachelor, had the feeling that he would not return so he sold his shares to members of the Roe family at a low price. After the transaction A.V. had over half the company shares with the whole family owning nearly three-quarters of them. A.V. Roe & Company Limited was still very much a family concern.

Although H.V. was a qualified pilot he was over forty years old and the RFC would not allow him to fly as such, but after several applications he reported to the School of Military Aeronautics at Reading on 8 December 1917. He qualified for flying as an observer and was posted to the Independent Force of the newly-formed Royal Air Force. This Unit was being organised by Major-General Hugh M. (later Lord) Trenchard in eastern France. Trenchard known as 'Father of the Royal Air Force' was aware of H.V.'s former senior position in the aviation industry and his organising ability, but he did not press Humphrey to join his staff. Humphrey made no secret of the fact that he wanted to fly operationally and later had the satisfaction of taking part in bombing raids against German military targets. However, there was no fairy tale ending as H.V.'s operations were not made in Avro aeroplanes, but in the rather draughty front cockpit of an F.E.2B which, though outmoded for daytime operations, proved to be excellent for night raids on the Western Front. H.V.'s war service ended when his aeroplane crashed on landing in darkness and a couple of fractures took him to hospital in Hampstead. Shortly after the war he married Doctor Marie Stopes, an authority on sociology who, in later years, was a pioneer of birth control.

In 1916 the Commanding Officer of No. 60 Squadron, RFC, Major Robert R. Smith-Barry, insisted on staying in active service with his unit which, at that time, flew Nieuport Scouts. His insistence came from the fact the too many of his young pilots were being killed by a lack of flying training and general ability in the air. A crippled leg had restricted Smith-Barry's activities, but he was determined to do something about the poor training. He took the unprecedented step of writing direct to Major-General Trenchard, General Officer Commanding the RFC in France. The letter read,

'No attention whatever has been paid to the fundamental importance of instruction in the mere manual part of flying. The writer has been surprised to find how little interest in flying is taken by many young pilots who come out to the Front. They have to be ordered to go up from the very first; they never ask permission to fly even for a practise flight. Before the war young pilots were begging to be allowed up. This is largely due to the mental supineness of instructors in England whose attitude towards flying is reflected in all the pilots they turn out.

' It is submitted that a good way to remedy this would be a School of Training for instructors, where they could (a) have their flying taught to the very high standards necessary before they can teach with confidence and ease; (b) be combed out if they do not speedily reach this standard; (c) be given definite lines upon which to instruct. The institution of such a school would produce an *esprit de corps* among instructors and improve the atmosphere surrounding the whole business of instruction.'

This letter produced startling and immediate results with Major-General John Salmond (later Sir

The busy production lines at Newton Heath in the 1930s showing Tutors for the R.A.F., Avians for private owners and Avro Ten trimotors for airline and military service.

The Newton Heath scene today used for storage by the Co-operative Society.

John) being detached from Trenchard's staff to return to England to re-organise pilot training.

A qualified instructor at the Central Flying School himself, the now Lieut-Colonel Smith-Barry was given command of No. 1 Reserve Flying School, RFC stationed at Gosport, Hampshire. He soon evolved a technique for a new method of flying instruction which covered the system of explanation and then demonstration. Many aspects of aviation were still a mystery and many trainee pilots found it difficult to understand control movements. These new methods met with the full approval of the General Staff and orders were drafted that all instructors should use the Smith-Barry system. The Unit was to be expanded and developed to become the School of Special Flying with the sole objective being the advanced training of instructors. The school was formed in August 1917 and expanded with the addition of No. 27 and No. 55 Training Squadrons. Now a Colonel, Smith-Barry selected the Avro 504J as standard aeroplane for the school and this unit was the first recipient of that type. The Avro 504 could be loved or hated, as some regarded earlier versions as over-sensitive aeroplanes which needed careful handling, but others enjoyed flying them. Smith-Barry had chosen wisely as the Avro 504J was a superb training aeroplane with light and powerful controls which had a positive response. The aircraft's controls were ideal for his training techniques as the pupil's fault could be detected early in the programme. The instructor could speak to his pupil through a speaking tube and this means of communication became universally known as the 'Gosport Tube'. Many famous aviators learned to fly on the Avro 504J including Prince Albert, who later became King George VI, and pilots who were to distinguish themselves in a later war. The 504 was used for training until well into the 1930s with Battle of Britain aces like Douglas Bader and Robert Stanford-Tuck being just two of its thousands of pupils.

The Avro 639 Cabin Cadet was flown at Woodford during 1933-34, but the aircraft was overtaken by the development of the more advanced Avro Commodore.

At Avro's, when the decision was taken to standardise on the 504J, their troubles commenced in earnest for a massive demand for the machines was immediately created and such fantastic figures as a production rate of 1,200 aircraft per month were seriously discussed. It was obvious that this output was far beyond the company's resources and large contracts were placed for other companies to build the aircraft. Eventually, there were eighteen firms building complete machines and countless others making parts. Two very great difficulties were encountered immediately; the first was that, although the drawings were perfectly intelligible to the Avro staff, many of whom had grown up with the aeroplane, they were far from being readable to outside manufacturers. The other difficulty was in the supply of engines. It appeared that owing to the obsolescence of the 100 hp Gnome Monosoupape, which was the design power plant for the Avro 504J, contracts for the engine had been allowed to run down and there were not sufficient stocks of the engine nor was it

Pleasing on the eye, the Avro Commodore was well ahead of its time. The prototype's all-silver colour scheme was changed to an attractive light blue fuselage with a dark blue cheat line as in this photograph.

LEFT:
The Commodore's cabin layout was unusual as the two pilot seats had only one control column which could be swung to either side. Two passengers could be accommodated or three if less luggage was carried.

possible to increase production rapidly to meet the great demand for the Avro 504J. The situation was met by drawing in from every aerodrome, both in England and in France, all available rotary engines including 130 hp Clergets and both 80 hp and110 hp Le Rhônes. The larger engines would not easily fit into the 504J and, in consequence, the detail of the machine, including the fuselage and engine mounting, had to be redesigned. This resulted in a new type, The Avro 504K.

These changes naturally retarded production and the new aeroplanes did not begin to appear until the end of 1917. The production then went ahead at a great rate with the Avro plants turning out over 200 per month and the eighteen contractors who were building the aeroplane augmented production to such an extent that more than 5,000 were produced in the twelve months preceding the end of the war. The total wartime production of the Avro 504-type was 8,340, of which A.V. Roe and Company built 3,696, while other contractors turned out 4,644. Had the war continued, the rate of production would have been tremendous with plans already drawn up for Avro to produce 500 machines per month. After the war, Lord Weir, in an address in Manchester, stated that no other aeroplane had been ordered in

such large quantities and that one third of Britain's supply of silver spruce had gone into the construction of the Avro 504s.

However, apart from the initial problems of drawing deciphering, there were no serious production problems with any of the sub-contractors.

Expert inspection was, of course, necessary on every piece of timber to ensure that the quality and the grain were correct. The moisture content had to be controlled plank by plank and frequent bend and impact tests were made to check the strength of the various specifications.

Some of the spruce had to come from the west coast of the United States and delivery was unreliable due to the U-boat menace in the Atlantic. Alternatives had to be used and waste cut down to a minimum with this being achieved by laminating spars, the splicing of spars and also the use of box spars. An alternative timber was Oregon pine.

The Smith-Barry School was élite; his own standards were high and his people had to be as near perfect as possible or they were posted away. It is on record that some pupils soloed in forty minutes and had absolute mastery of the aeroplane in all circumstances of flight in just a few hours. Those who witnessed the flying of Gosport's Avro 504s were amazed at the skill of the pilots and a special feature of the School was spot landings where the pilots were taught to put their aeroplanes down on a predetermined spot. This necessitated the development in training of cross-wind landings and in side-slip approaches. Pilots would come in over the hangars, turn quickly, side-slip steeply with the aeroplane's nose well up and then drop their wheels gently onto the grass in front of the tarmac. The result of this training was a mastery of the forced landing, which was fairly frequent in those days, but this now held no terror for the pilot who, if he was trained at Gosport, was equal to any situation. The local people became used to seeing aircraft landing in the smallest of fields and also touch their wheels down on roadways, many times having to hop over cars presumably to the distress of the unsuspecting motorist.

Maintenance of the machines was paramount in the mind of Smith-Barry. Legend has it that when an aeroplane came out of the workshop after an overhaul, the Colonel himself would take the machine up for a test flight and when he landed, if their was a speck of oil on his immaculate field-boots, heaven help the NCO in charge!

Smith-Barry's senior team were as expert at flying as he was and they needed to be or they would not have been tolerated. Deputy to the Colonel was Major F.P. Scott, who taught the Chilian Air Force to fly after the war; Captain H.G. Smart became a Group Captain and commanded RAF Martlesham in the late 1930s. Captain Rex Stocken was an exceptional pilot and a born instructor, but the exploits of the Avro 504s in the hands of other pilots such as Captain Williams, Captain Foote, Captain Duncan Davis and Major Brearley have become almost legendary. Captain Williams' speciality was to land between two hangars and then turn completely round after touchdown and finishing the landing run in 'C' Flight's hangar. The others could not complain as he was 'C' Flight commander!

The instructors were certainly special and some 'unusual' behaviour was overlooked, but Smith-Barry had the best and it showed with the quality of the pilots that graduated from the School. The combination of the Avro 504 and the best instructors proved to be a winner. Colonel Smith-Barry left the service after the war ended to become a landed gentleman and later, a noted art specialist and connoisseur. During World War Two he was seriously injured in a crash while delivering an Avro-built Blenheim from Woodford to the RAF.

At the beginning of 1918 two gentlemen came to Avro who would both play important parts in the company's future, but in different ways. On 1 January 1918 a young man by the name of Charles Edward Fielding started in the materials test house. Teddy Fielding was to rise through the ranks to become Production Director and was involved in every type of aircraft manufactured by Avro up to the 748, the last aeroplane to bear the famous name. He saw the construction of the 748s underway before he retired in 1961.

The second gentleman to come to Avro actually was returning from the war. Harold Rogerson, a childhood friend of Roy Chadwick, had joined Avro in December 1913 as assistant mathematician and proved himself to be most useful under the watchful eye of Reg Parrott. Soon after war was declared, Rogerson enlisted in the army and the company was sorry to lose him. Early in 1918 Chadwick heard the Rogerson had been badly wounded resulting in the amputation of his right arm. Roy Chadwick then approached A.V. to apply for Rogerson to be invalided out of the service as his work could be of more value to the aviation industry. He was overjoyed to rejoin the company, this time at Hamble where the drawing office was now located.

A pleasant surprise came on 20 February 1918 when the company was notified that Alliott Verdon Roe had been awarded the OBE for his devoted service to aviation. It was richly deserved, but the unassuming Alliott played down the honour as much as possible.

Chadwick had designed an advanced single-seat fighter known as the Avro 531 Spider. Powered by a 110 hp Le Rhône, the Spider incorporated many features learned from nearly four years of war, but the performance was no improvement on the

This Avro Prefect for the Royal New Zealand Air Force is awaiting acceptance in July 1935. The R.N.Z.A.F. has restored a Prefect to flying condition and the machine takes part in air shows around that country.

fighters currently in service and even the change of engine to a 130 hp Clerget brought little improvement. In April 1918 the Spider had been flown to Gosport for some development flying by the instructors of the School of Special Flying, but it appeared that the pilots treated the flying of the aeroplane as nothing more than a pleasant interlude. After the war the Avro 531A — a modified version of the original — was made into a racing aircraft fitted with a Bentley BR1 engine which had a power output of 242 hp at sea level. This became known as the Avro 538 and as a structural defect restricted the aircraft to flying straight and level the machine was used as a hack by J.C.C. Taylor — the chief engineer of the Avro Transport Company — to fly around the joyriding sites to check on the condition and maintenance of the Avro 504s used by the company. Joe Taylor had joined Avro as an apprentice in 1915, but he had enlisted in the RFC in 1916 as an observer. He later became a pilot in the RAF, but rejoined Avro in 1919. Taylor was one of the founder members of the exclusive Avro 504 Club which exists today.

There was some flying from the field next to the Park Works in Newton Heath even though the highly industrialised and populated area made the operation a risky business. The proposal of the Americans to build Handley Page 0/400 heavy bombers under licence in Oldham, brought with it the prospects of a new airfield to be built by the Americans. On 20 October 1917, the Manchester City Council received confirmation that an Air Acceptance Park was to be built at Didsbury in south-east Manchester and the airfield would be known as Alexandra Park after the nearest railway station. Sometimes known as Didsbury the aerodrome became No. 15 (Manchester) Air Acceptance Park and the airfield became operational in May 1918, when the first aeroplane to use it was ferried from there. Avro rented a hangar there and both delivery and test flying were carried out, but when the war ended further construction work on the airfield was cancelled.

After the twin-engined Pike, another large twin

OPPOSITE TOP:
Avro Tutors in service with the R.A.F. at Abu Sueir, Egypt in 1935. These aircraft belonged to No. 4 Flying Training School, a unit which is still active and currently flies the British Aerospace Hawk from Valley in Anglesey.

OPPOSITE BOTTOM:
The first of many! The prototype Anson nears completion at the Newton Heath works.

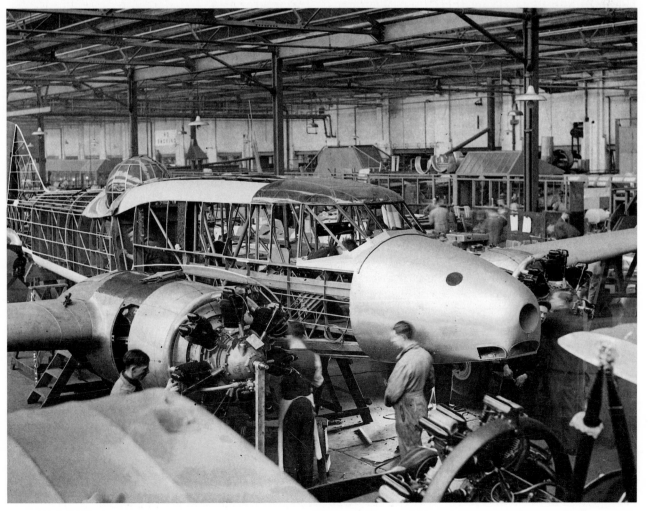

was being developed from that aeroplane with changes in the wings and tractor-type engines instead of the pushers: this machine was the Avro 529. The first aircraft was completed at the Park Works and sent to Hamble for test flying, but the second aircraft was unfinished when it was despatched to Hamble because the floor space at Newton Heath was urgently needed for the great increase in production of the Avro 504. On 4 March 1917 a test flight of the 529 nearly ended in disaster when the rudder collapsed during a turn, but the aeroplane landed safely. Roy Chadwick and his stress people made a close inspection of the damaged rudder and redesigned the structure. An improved version was the Avro 529A with higher powered engines which resulted in excellent performance. Both aircraft were flown to the Aeroplane Experimental Station at Martlesham Heath in Suffolk, arriving there on 31 October 1917. This was only eight days after the 529A had its maiden flight, but during the trials at Martlesham this aeroplane also had a rudder failure in a test flight on 11 November 1917. Unfortunately, this incident caused the aircraft to crash injuring both crewmen.

The last in the series of twin-engined aeroplanes to appear before the war's end was the Avro 533 Manchester. Once again, this was an improved version of the previous aeroplanes, but this time the machine was manufactured entirely at Hamble. Confusion over the type and delivery of the

engines added to the lateness of assembly, and constant changes in specification did not help the situation. The Avro 533 Manchester Mk.1 and the 'later' 533A Manchester II both made their first flights within days of each other in December 1918. The performance of these aeroplanes was excellent as the military trials at No. 186 Development Squadron at Gosport and the AES at Martlesham had shown. Further trials were completed by both Avro and the military, but the need for a bomber or photo reconnaissance aircraft had disappeared with the signing of the armistice. The Manchester III was under construction, but the work was terminated and the machine was scrapped. In March 1919, Chadwick unveiled plans for a passenger-carrying version to be designated Avro 537, but the proposal was dropped and eventually the Type 533 jigs were dismantled and taken away by the scrapman.

Though a number of excellent designs came from Avro during World War One, none really made the grade through one reason or another. It was an aeroplane designed before the war and developed successfully that helped the company to survive and also pushed the firm's name to the fore in the aviation industry — the Avro 504.

An Avro 626 fuselage under construction with a telescopic gunsight and Vickers machine-gun already in place. The .303-in gun was synchronised to fire through the propeller arc.

## CHAPTER 4
# Peace Once More

**P**eace came at 11 am, on 11 November 1918, when the armistice was signed and hostilities on the Western Front ceased. At the end of the war the Royal Air Force was the largest air force in the world with 27,333 officers, 263,410 other ranks, 22,647 aeroplanes and nearly 700 aerodromes. The price of an Avro 504 to the War Office was nearly £900, but the engines took the largest slice of the cost with the Gnome Monosoupape being £696 while the Le Rhône was £770, so the profit on each aeroplane was not great.

Victory brought numerous problems for the wartime factories and Avro was no exception. The new plant at Newton Heath was specifically designed for large scale production and was now almost complete, but the end of hostilities meant the virtual end to large orders of aeroplanes. Production of the 504K continued, but at a greatly reduced rate and the orders placed with sub-contractors of the type were cancelled completely.

Finance was becoming a problem once more and much to Alliott and his fellow director's sadness, jobs had to be shed; but Humphrey returned from the war and immediately began to search for orders.

With the future uncertain, Chadwick was working on the Avro 504L, a seaplane version of the 504K. He also felt that a light aeroplane was badly needed and A.V. encouraged him to proceed

The first Avro 636 for the Irish Air Corps shortly before delivery to Baldonnel in August 1935.

with the design providing the cost was kept to a minimum. The design had to be drawn around a 35 hp Green engine as it was the only 'free' powerplant available. Amazingly, this engine had been preserved by Fred May of the Green Engine Company Ltd and was the very engine which was fitted to the Avro Type D in which Howard Pixton attempted to fly to Brighton on 6 May 1911!

The new little aeroplane became known as the Avro 534 with the name Popular, but this was soon changed to Baby and construction began in February 1919.

Fred Raynham had tested a number of aeroplanes during the war and in the latter stages flew the Martinsyde Buzzard fighter, an excellent fighter which went into the record books as being

the fastest type produced in Britain after reaching a top speed of 144.5 mph at ground level. This aeroplane suffered the same fate as some of the Avro types as the war ended — production was not necessary. However, Raynham decided to stay with that company and Avro needed to find a top test pilot. They found him in Squadron Leader Harold A. Hamersley, an ex-Avro 504 instructor. On 4 February 1919, Hamersley flew the Avro 504L off Southampton Water at Hamble. The handling was excellent, but the general performance was poor with the 130 hp Clerget driving a four-bladed propeller giving insufficient power for the type. The RAF had already dropped the idea of any new type of seaplane trainer and news of the 504L's poor showing did not help to revise their thinking.

During this period the *Daily Mail* was offering a £10,000 prize for the first non-stop flight across the Atlantic and as always, Alliott was excited by the prospect of the award, but also the fame which could go with it. Roy Chadwick proposed a large biplane powered by a Rolls-Royce Falcon engine of

LEFT:
The tandem cockpit arrangement of the Type 636 is well illustrated here.

BELOW:
The fourth production Anson 1 on its transport dolly at the Newton Heath works before transportation to Woodford for assembly in March 1936.

275 hp with the Avro team working out that the range and fuel efficiency of the aeroplane would be ideal for an attempt at the crossing. The aircraft was given the Type number 535, but after much discussion between A.V. and Chadwick both expressed concern on the reliability of a single engine to cross such an expanse of ocean. If the engine should have failed there would be little chance of rescue for the pilot. Presumably, Alliott gave some thought to the days he spent at sea and the long voyages without ever seeing another vessel. After some consultation it was decided to cancel the project.

The Air Navigation Bill, which would later dictate the rules of civil flying, was still awaited, but Avro was able to get clearance to fly the public over the Easter period in war surplus Avro 504s. The weekend was a great success and a number of ex-wartime pilots were engaged by the company to fly the 504K aircraft which had been converted to three seaters and the age of the 'Five Bob Flip' began. This activity became known as a 'joy-ride' and the obvious locations for such an operation were the holiday resorts where people were just starting to have holidays again in the first year after the war. Beaches at Southport, Blackpool and Weston-Super-Mare were selected and fields around Manchester, Harrogate and Scarborough were also used. The Avro Transport Company was established and a scheduled service from Alexandra Park, Manchester to Blackpool and Southport and return began in May 1919 after the Navigation Regulations were issued on 30 April 1919. Blackpool Corporation invited John Lord to a meeting of the Council on 6 May 1919 and after presenting a fine case for a scheduled air service, Avro obtained their full authority to operate the 'airline' from the town and he also received permission to use the site opposite the Star Inn as a terminus for the Manchester to Blackpool via Southport service.

On 14 May, a party of Blackpool officials visited the Avro Transport headquarters at Alexandra Park and then, highly satisfied, they were flown home. Britain's first scheduled domestic air service commenced operations on 26 May 1919 when two aircraft took-off from Alexandra Park. The service was flown for eighteen weeks and four days without mishap, but weather conditions caused the cancellation of a few flights. The operation was flown without the promised government subsidy and the *Blackpool Times* for 7 June 1919 ran the following advertisement:

The Avro Air Service which has been running daily between Blackpool, Southport and Manchester for the past fortnight, leaves Blackpool at 12.00 noon and Southport at 12.15 pm and arrives at Alexandra Park, Manchester at 12.45 pm. The machine, on its return journey, leaves Alexandra Park at 2.00 o'clock and arrives at Southport at 2.30 pm and Blackpool at 2.45 pm.

The fare between Manchester and Southport or Manchester and Blackpool is:-
£5 5s 0d  Single      £9 9s 0d  Return

Tickets can be booked by letter or by telephone from the Officer in Charge of Civil Aviation, Alexandra Park Aerodrome, Manchester. The telephone number is Central 3332, 3334 or 3335.

Passengers desirous of travelling from Blackpool or Southport can obtain tickets by telephoning or writing to :-
A.V. Roe & Co
Brighton Hydro
Blackpool      Telephone 697

The Avro Air Service pleasure flights were quoted as:

| | |
|---|---|
| Short Circuit (round Blackpool) | £1.1s.0d |
| Blackpool and St. Annes | £2.2s.0d |
| Looping the Loop | £2.2s.0d |

These joy-riding trips were flown daily in the summer months from the end of May from 10 am to 8 pm.

The *Gazette News* was a great supporter of aviation in that region and on 29 July 1919 published the following:

*Blackpool's Flying Record*
Blackpool has broken every record in the matter of pleasure flying since the A.V. Roe Company established their aerodrome on the sands at South Shore on May 10th. They have just recorded their 10,000th flight there without any mishap that caused personal injury and although the flying ground has been moved

**ABOVE:**
The wings for the fourth Anson were shipped to Woodford at the same time as the fuselage and the completed aircraft was delivered to No. 48 Squadron at Manston, Kent in the following month.

**LEFT:**
Down in the drink! The first Anson casualty was in June 1936 when this 48 Squadron aircraft forced landed in the sea off the Kent coast.

**BELOW:**
Three Ansons of No. 215 Squadron based at Driffield in Yorkshire head back to their airfield after a familiarisation flight in February 1937.

further south, to a point just beyond Star Inn, making it necessary to plod through a great deal of very loose sand to get there, the place is still a great attraction for holiday-makers. There is always a huge crowd when flying is in progress. The booking office is a special attraction, the people swarming round to watch the passengers book for their guinea 'flips' or two-guinea 'aerobatic' flights. Sometimes they are rewarded with some very good humour. On Saturday for instance, two Blackburn mill-hands thought they would have a flight to complete their round of Blackpool's joys. One demurred at the idea of 'doing in' a guinea for five minutes 'Coom on. A'v a coople o'guineas' returned the other leading the way. They were each handed the usual souvenir card. 'Wot's them?' they asked.

'Why' replied the clerk. 'they are for the pilot to write his name on.' 'Wot for?' inquired the materialistic operatives! And the battery of questions was set going again when they were rigged out in their flying gear, to the vast amusement of the crowd and themselves, for they were bent on having as much fun as they could for their guineas. The story which has been going round is of a miner who broke the record for pleasure flying by having 70 'flips' at a guinea a time is not verified by the Avro Co. The record is still held by a wealthy Lancashire man 'in cotton' who had 120 flights during his Blackpool holiday sampling every known 'stunt'. The record for a single pleasure flight belongs to a titled Colonel of the King's Own Scottish Borderers, who astonished the booking clerk by saying, 'I don't want a ten minute flip. I want an hour or two.' 'But it costs £20 an hour,' explained the clerk. 'I don't care about the price,'

The 'office' of an Anson Mk.1 showing the pilot's gun sight for his fixed forward-firing machine-gun.

returned the Colonel. 'Give me a machine and I'll tell the pilot when I want to come back.' His flight cost £40. How flying appeals to the workers on holiday is shown by the fact the Avro machines are never so busy as when there are a large number of charabanc trips in for the day. Many of these visitors seem to come for the express purpose of having a fly. Men, who prefer a muffler to a collar, readily pay an extra guinea for something more than a straightforward 'flip'. They want thrills.

The company operated on a nationwide scale carrying 30,000 passengers in nearly two years without a single accident, but not paying its way the Avro Transport Company was wound up. The only real benefit to come from the operation was that it helped to foster air-mindedness in the nation.

One successful firm was the Berkshire Aviation Company Limited which was owned by the brothers F.J.V., a former Avro apprentice and G.D.V. Holmes, who later divided the company in two! Other pilots involved and who later became famous in their own right were Alan Cobham, later

A rare photograph of the 20mm Hispano cannon installation fitted below the cabin floor of an Anson for anti-shipping attacks. Squadron Leader W. E. LeMay of No. 206 Squadron used this weapon to great effect against German E-boats in the Channel during 1940.

An Avro 637 of the Kwangsi Air Force of South China before its delivery to Luichow via Hong Kong. It is reported that 637s went into action against the Japanese, but no details are available on how they fared!

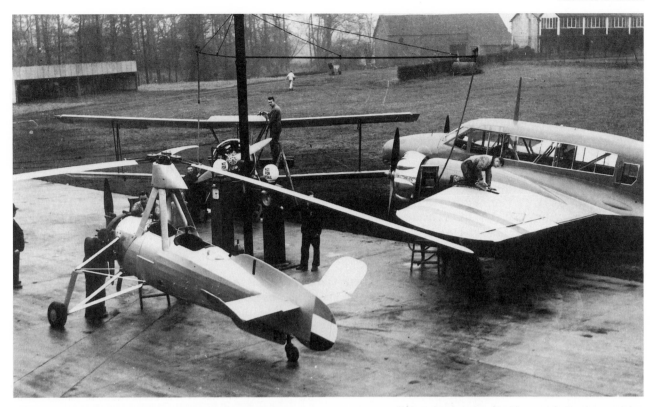

A variety of Avro aircraft refuelling at Woodford in December 1937. The three types were all for export with the Anson for the Irish Air Corps, the C.30A autogiro was for Yugoslavia while the Avro 626 was destined for Portugal. In the background is the famous Club House which continues to be used today.

Sir Alan, famous for his aerial circus and the pioneering of air-to-air refuelling; O.P. Jones, who became Captain and chief pilot for Imperial Airways and BOAC's senior pilot, who did not retire from flying until 1955 after more than 300 Atlantic crossings and 'Jimmy' Yuill, who was one of the founders of Lancashire Aero Club.

The Avro 534 Baby was ready to be test flown on 30 April 1919 which was Roy Chadwick's twenty-sixth birthday and as this aeroplane was all his own work he had hoped to fly it on its maiden flight. However, the job was given to Hamersley and the Baby was in the air for less than two minutes when it suddenly went out of control at 300 feet and crashed into the river bank. It was a bad crash, but Hamersley was not badly injured and in his report he felt that he accidentally switched off the ignition. However, the investigation into the crash showed that it could

have been an airlock in the fuel system. A few days earlier, on 25 April, Hamersley had ignition trouble with the new Avro 536, a modified 504 built to accommodate four passengers, but on this flight the trouble was rectified before any incident occurred. This was indeed fortunate because one of the passengers was Lord Birkenhead, the Lord Chancellor, who visited Hamble and had been offered a flight in the aeroplane by A.V. Another version of the 504 was flying at that time and this was the Avro 504M, sometimes referred to as the 'Limousine'. This type had a totally enclosed cockpit for two passengers who sat in a staggered seat arrangement behind the pilot and achieved some fame by landing outside a church in Chorley Wood, Buckinghamshire to pick up the newly weds, Mr Robert Hamilton and his wife Nora, to take them on their honeymoon. After refuelling at Bournemouth the aeroplane flew on to Fowey in Cornwall, landing there just four hours after collection.

The Japanese had paid Avro for rights to build the 504 in that country, but finance was still a problem for the company. Alliott and his senior managers recognised that they would have to diversify and plans were drawn up to build and market a 12 hp saloon car. The firm bought the patent rights for an epicyclic gearbox which would give the car a real edge over any competitors. The work would be undertaken in Manchester with the production line taking up most of the floor space although an area would still be available for the repair of aircraft. The Hamble factory would be able to cope with aircraft production as orders were slow in coming and design of the vehicle's body would be in the drawing office. The engine and other parts of the car were designed at Newton Heath and the vehicle was tested successfully with a number of cars being built. The car, costing £425, included some innovations such as adjustable seats and a sliding roof, but on 6 May 1920 production was ended by mutual agreement when Crossley Motors Limited of Manchester bought three-fifths of Avro shares, acquiring a controlling interest in A.V. Roe & Company Limited. Crossley appointed Henry Fieldes, MP as the Chairman with the Crossley chief William (later Sir William) Letts asking Alliott and John Lord to remain on the Board of Directors, but not before reminding them that Crossley had the voting majority! The Crossley 25/30 saloon was achieving excellent sales and the Avro factory manufactured bodies for this model, but also supplementing the finance was the production of a variety of toys, tin baths, bassinets and a particularly good billiard table.

Good news came to the Avro people on 15 June 1919 when they heard that a Vickers Vimy aircraft flown by their old friend Jack Alcock had made the first non-stop air crossing of the Atlantic. The aircraft, piloted by Alcock and Lieut Arthur Whitten Brown had made the crossing from St Johns, Newfoundland to Clifden, County Galway, in sixteen hours, twelve minutes. Both were knighted for this feat, although Sir John Alcock did not live long enough to enjoy the honour as he was killed whilst trying to land his Vickers Viking aircraft in thick fog near Rouen, France on 18 December 1919.

Just ten days after Hamersley's crash in the Avro Baby a second aircraft of this type flew successfully. However, Avro classed this as the 'first' Baby as it was built up from the engine and other parts salvaged from the wreck which was too badly damaged to be repaired. Hamersley was

enthusiastic about the aeroplane and on 21 June 1919 he won the handicap section of the Aerial Derby at Hendon with an average speed of 70.3 mph.

Alliott had always been interested in the Schneider Trophy competition and Hamersley's win in the Aerial Derby encouraged him to start thinking about the contest once more. As the race was to be held on 10 September 1919 at Bournemouth, it gave Avro a little over two months to prepare for it, but A.V. and Chadwick were soon thinking along the same lines with a Baby-type aeroplane fitted with one of the higher-powered engines which were becoming available. The Schneider aeroplane was the Avro 539, a single-seat seaplane designed around the 240 hp Siddeley Puma engine and after being built at a rather expedited pace, the 539 made its first flight from Hamble's waterfront on 29 August 1919 with Hamersley as pilot. The elimination trials were to be held at Cowes, Isle of Wight on 3 September, but the aeroplane damaged a float after hitting a floating log and returned to Hamble for repairs. After some negotiation A.V. persuaded the Schneider Committee to postpone the trial until 8 September and this was of great benefit to Avro as, besides the repair, it gave the company a chance to make some improvements to the machine. With these modifications the aeroplane was designated the Avro 539A and was due at Bournemouth on the 10th, but only as reserve to the Sopwith Schneider and the Supermarine Sea Lion, which had been designed by R.J. Mitchell of Spitfire fame. However, fog turned the competition into chaos and it was eventually abandoned with the Italians being asked to organise the next Schneider event because of their fine showing.

The Government sales of ex-service aeroplanes at extremely low prices meant that the manufacturing companies would find it difficult to build and market new machines and it was a great relief and encouragement to Avro when the Department of Civil Aviation announced a proposal to offer prizes totalling £64,000 for three categories of commercial aircraft. The proposal, dated 14 August 1919, covered single-engined aircraft, twin-engined passenger 'airliners' and amphibious seaplanes or flying-boats. With available finance still a problem for any new project, Roy Chadwick was instructed to use as many Avro 504 parts as possible. A.V. liked the idea of using three sets of wings, but Chadwick thought that a triplane would be a retrograde step. A.V. won the day and the Type 547 was commenced with the aeroplane being powered by a 160 hp Beardmore water-cooled engine. Hamersley was again the pilot for a maiden flight when he took the 547 into the air for the first time on 6 February 1920 and although his report 'for public consumption' was that the machine handled like the 504, in truth the 547 was very sensitive on the controls and was difficult to land even in a moderate wind. A second 547 with a 240 hp Siddeley Puma was constructed and was exhibited at the Olympia Aero Show in London on 9–20 July 1920. This aircraft, the Avro 547A, went to Martlesham Heath from Hamble on 2 August, 1920 to take part in the trials which, it was hoped, would eventually bring some prize money to Avro. Competing against five other types, the 547A failed to qualify for an award because it was unstable and did not reach the minimum speed of 100 mph. On the landing test the aircraft damaged an undercarriage strut, but it got down safely,

RIGHT:
The first Avro-built Hawker Audax is being prepared for flight at Woodford soon after its arrival from Newton Heath.

BELOW:
Another licence-built aircraft was the Bristol Blenheim and, with test pilot Sam Brown aboard, the first Avro-produced machine prepares for its maiden flight at Woodford in September 1938.

taxyied in and parked in front of the hangar being used by the trials aircraft. As Hamersley and his mechanics were discussing the bent undercarriage, the machine collapsed onto the tarmac! The aircraft was patched up and flown back to the Hamble for permanent repairs and returned to Martlesham Heath on 12 October to continue the trials. This time it was flown by a young Australian by the name of Herbert John Louis Hinkler, DSM who joined Avro earlier that year. Bert Hinkler was an excellent pilot but even his talents could not improve matters and the aeroplane was rejected. It was later dismantled at Hamble.

On 1 June 1920, Hinkler had taken the first machine to Croydon for demonstrating to S. Instone & Company Limited and while his flying made the aeroplane look satisfactory, Frank Barnard of Instone was not impressed and felt that

King George VI tours the Anson production line at the Newton Heath works in March 1939. His Majesty is accompanied by Roy Dobson and Sir Frank Spriggs.

he could not recommend the purchase of this aircraft. A further demonstration later in the month just served to confirm the decision.

In the previous November Avro had opened an office in Australia as many aviators there had flown with the RFC in the war and the Avro 504 was well-known to them. Harry Broadsmith had been sent from Manchester and a number of crated 504s with enough component parts to start an assembly line had followed. Broadsmith and some Australian colleagues had formed the Australian Aircraft & Engineering Company at Mascot, Sydney. The Queensland and Northern Territory Aerial Services (QANTAS), Australia's first airline,

was officially formed on 16 November 1920 with a Sunbeam Dyak-engined Avro 504 being their first aircraft. Broadsmith, wearing his salesman's hat, had persuaded QANTAS to look at the Avro 547 for its passenger services which had been proposed between Charleville and Katherine, a sector in its Melbourne to Darwin route. Surprisingly, QANTAS purchased the Avro 547 for £2,798 on 30 November 1920 and the crated aircraft left Southampton for Sydney where it was assembled at Mascot. The 547 made its first flight in Australia on 2 March 1921 piloted by Paul McGinness, who had founded the airline with Fergus (later Sir Fergus) McMaster and Hudson (later Sir Hudson) Fysh, but as he landed the aeroplane the undercarriage gave way and deposited the 547 unceremoniously on its belly. Ginty McGinness, an experienced pilot with several aerial victories to his credit during the war, walked away from the aircraft uttering unprintable comments! The aircraft was repaired and fitted with a stronger undercarriage, flying again on 8 April 1922. On 6 May the 547 came second in the Australian Aerial Derby which took place at the Victoria Park Race Course, Sydney when, piloted by Hudson Fysh, it averaged 69.5 mph. However, it was then restricted to joy-riding flights over Sydney Harbour and never flew on the intended routes because it was allowed to fly only in good conditions and operate from airfields with smooth surfaces. The 547's certificate of airworthiness was withdrawn and the machine was scrapped with its fuselage serving as a chicken-coop on the outskirts of Sydney for many years. QANTAS sought compensation from Avro, promising never to do business with them again if an agreement was not reached. There is no record of compensation and QANTAS did buy from Avro again, but not until

1946 when they purchased three Lancastrians!

The 547 had been a great disappointment and the fuselage of a third machine, which was never assembled, hung from the hangar roof at Hamble for many years before it was taken down and burnt in 1925.

Roy Chadwick had longed to fly the aeroplanes he had designed and, with A.V.'s blessing, had taken flying lessons with Hamersley in the company's Avro 504K. As a fully qualified flying instructor, Hamersley was excellent and Chadwick was soon awarded his private pilot's licence.

Chadwick had built up his flying experience with a number of cross-country trips and one was planned for the afternoon of 13 January 1920 with a flight in the Avro Baby. He took-off normally and was flying low over Hamble when a down-draft smashed the aeroplane into some trees before it crashed into the garden of A.V.'s brother Everard's vicarage. The aircraft was a total wreck and Chadwick was very seriously injured and rushed to the Royal South Hants Hospital where surgeons worked untiringly on his fractured arms, pelvis

An aerial view of Woodford flight sheds in 1939 with Ansons and Blenheims awaiting delivery.

and kneecap. Two months later he was not progressing as he should and his first attempt at walking with the aid of crutches was an extremely painful experience. Even going to Bournemouth for complete rest and recuperation did not help, but the father of Chadwick's fiancée Mary Gomersall suggested they contact Sir Arbuthnot Lane, a pioneer in the technique of bone grafting. He was transferred to Lane's nursing home in London and underwent a long operation when the specialist had to break all the mended bones and reset them using his own techniques. Chadwick was still very ill, but his determination and a lot of care and devotion put him on the road to recovery.

Chadwick was going to be laid up for a long period, but he insisted on being informed of important events at Avro and his friend Harold Rogerson kept him up-to-date. A succession of visitors, including A.V., kept him happy and eager to return.

In Manchester the Crossley 'saving' or 'intrusion into' — depending on which side of the fence one was sitting — the affairs of A.V. Roe & Company Limited were becoming public and it was revealed that of the 50,000 shares, Crossley had bought 34,283! Of the remaining shares, A.V. held 6,118, John Lord 1,604, with the remainder being smaller investors. The main thing for the employees was that the company was allowed to continue under its own name.

The Avro Baby involved in Roy Chadwick's crash was described as a total wreck, but amazingly the aeroplane was rebuilt using the engine and some of the basic airframe. From his sick bed Chadwick had suggested a number of modifications and these were incorporated into the rebuild programme. The machine was completed and immediately purchased by Bert Hinkler late in April 1920 after an agreement had been reached with A.V. and John Lord. The aircraft was sold for a nominal price as Hinkler had proposed a record-breaking long-distance flight and Alliott loved the idea and the prospect of the publicity which would surround such an attempt.

Publicity there certainly was as Hinkler took off from Croydon in the morning of 31 May 1921 and made a tremendous 650 miles non-stop flight to Turin, Italy in just nine hours, thirty minutes using only twenty gallons of fuel. He then flew on to Rome, but returned to the Hamble in short stages due to engine problems. It was not widely known, but his original plan was to fly all the way home to Australia! Anyway, the media of the day wasn't to know that and his epic flight to Turin made the front pages of newspapers all over the world. Hinkler was later to receive the Britannia Trophy for the most outstanding flight of the year.

Roy Chadwick, still using sticks, had hobbled back into Hamble's drawing office during May 1920 and the success of Hinkler's flight did more than anything to help him on the way to a full recovery. One of his first jobs was to commence the redesign of the Baby into a two seat aeroplane with dual controls for training purposes.

This new Avro Baby was designated Type 543, but it was completed too late to take part in the Olympia Aero Show which opened in London on 9 July 1920. An admirable substitute was found with Hinkler's little record breaker which drew large crowds for the duration of the show. As mentioned previously, the Avro 547A was the centre-piece of the Avro stand.

After the show closed the Baby was transported to Hendon, where it was erected and flown by Hinkler into second place in the Aerial Derby Handicap Race on 24 July. Also taking part was a landplane version of the Schneider aircraft, the Avro 539, but this was forced to withdraw from the race through a bad fuel leak which saturated the pilot D.G. Westgarth-Heslam and an emergency landing was made at Abridge, Essex during the first lap. The winner of the race was a Martinsyde Semiquaver flown by Frank Courtney, who was later to become part of the team at Hamble. He was lucky on this particular day for, after winning, the aeroplane somersaulted upon landing and, fortunately, Courtney was uninjured.

The third Avro Baby had a plywood-covered fuselage and slightly shortened lower wing and this version, the Avro 534B, brought more cheer to Roy Chadwick as, piloted by Hamersley, it won the

---

OPPOSITE TOP:
Patrolling over the Forth Bridge in March 1939 this Anson from No. 233 Squadron was based at Leuchars near St. Andrews.

---

OPPOSITE:
A peaceful scene at Ringway on 25 July 1939 as the prototype Avro Manchester awaits the crew for its first flight.

When this photograph was taken of the Rolls-Royce Vulture engine installation in the prototype Manchester, no-one could have envisaged the problems ahead or that those problems would lead to the development of the war's greatest bomber, the Avro Lancaster.

Royal Aero Club Trophy with Hinkler and his Baby coming a close second. Unfortunately, the Avro 543B was destroyed in a crash on 4 August, 1920 which badly injured Westgarth-Heslam when he was en route to Martlesham Heath to take part in the Avro 547 trials. Investigation showed that a choked carburettor had forced the aeroplane down, but as the machine was landing, the universal joint in the control column failed and the aircraft crashed.

The Director-General of Supply and Research, Air Vice-Marshal Sir Edward Ellington and his technical staff issued the Specification 2/20 (D of R

Type 4B) which was for a long-range heavy bomber. This would be Avro's first entirely new military aeroplane since the end of the war and Chadwick was given the task of designing the machine. The power plant would be a 650 hp Rolls-Royce Condor III and the new aeroplane would be known as the Avro 549 Aldershot. Two prototypes were completed and Hamersley and Hinkler flew early test flights commencing in September 1921. A lack of lateral stability brought a number of modifications to the tail assembly, but the problem was not cured until the fuselage was lengthened. Competitive trials were held against the De Havilland D.H.27 Derby with the 549 being flown by Hinkler. The lengthened version appeared in the new types park at the RAF Display at Hendon on 24 June 1922.

The Aldershot Mk.II, fitted with a 1,000 hp Napier Cub water-cooled engine made its first flight at the Hamble on 15 December 1922 in the presence of Air Vice-Marshal Sir Geoffrey Salmond and other senior RAF officers with A.V. acting as host. The aircraft took-off after a short run and after an excellent handling demonstration Bert Hinkler made a fast downwind run at something like 140 mph before bringing the Aldershot in for a short landing. The display was indeed impressive and the aircraft gave excellent service to the RAF, with the Aldershot Mk. III being operated by No.99 Squadron until it was replaced by the Handley Page Hyderabad after the Air Ministry abandoned single-engined heavy bombers.

Back in Manchester the new factory at Newton Heath had commenced operation with the employees from the Park Works and the old Clifton Street works moving in. On 23 August, 1920 the Newton Heath factory became the Head Office of the company to the great delight of the personnel, but the date 23 August would mean great sadness just twenty-seven years later as it would be on that date that the great Roy Chadwick would meet his death.

At Newton Heath, Crossley had installed John Hubble as General Manager and this tall, rumbustious chap kept the work-force on their toes. Teddy Fielding noted that all of the employees knew the saying; 'Never trouble Hubble, lest Hubble trouble you'. Roy Dobson, as

works manager, had therefore to prove his worth on the job and was more than a match for Hubble, especially when the aircraft work began to return.

About that time Teddy Fielding recalled a test flight in the Avro Aldershot which could have ended in disaster;

'We took off from Alexandra Park airfield in Manchester to carry out speed trials at different altitudes, avoiding the clouds to get the best results. After the tests were completed we descended, but there was no aerodrome in sight. Bert Hinkler, who was the pilot, asked me if I could recognise anything and looking through the bomb-aimer's window I saw "Ferodo Friction Linings" on the roof of a factory. This was in Chapel-en-le-Frith and I told Hinkler that we were south of Stockport so he set course by compass. This, however, had not been "swung" so there was compass error of forty degrees! As a result we flew south-west instead of north-west. Luckily, as we cruised along Hinkler recognised Crewe and then followed the railway line almost exactly to Alexandra Park.'

A different error setting in the compass could have taken them over the Peak District — a graveyard for many aircraft with navigational problems.

The Air Ministry issued Specification 3/21 (D of R Type 7a) for a sea reconnaissance and fleet gunnery spotting biplane capable of deck-landing and in May 1921 A.V. Roe & Company Limited was invited to tender.

Chadwick's answer to the tender was the Avro 555 Bison which was the result of his extensive

The prototype Lancaster in its original triple-finned form at Boscombe Down in January 1941. Just over one month later the aircraft was flying with the twin fins which became standard after early handling trials showed the need for larger rudders. The aircraft in the background is a Blackburn Roc.

study of naval aircraft. Both he and A.V. had visited the naval air station at Lee-on-Solent and the seaplane base at Calshot and even went to sea on the aircraft carrier HMS *Argus* to study deck take-off and landing techniques and hangar stowage below decks.

The Bison first flew in November 1921, but a number of difficulties were encountered in both performance and stability with Chadwick making a number of modifications over the months before the problems were solved. Finally, the Bison was sent to Martlesham Heath on 4 August 1922 for trials with its contemporary which, rather strangely, was known as the Blackburn Blackburn! On 19 August both aircraft flew down to Gosport where they were to be stationed for deck-landing trials. On the 22nd the Bison made three deck landings on the *Argus* as did the Blackburn aeroplane.

In later years a naval aviator was to write; 'In both types a 450 hp Napier Lion engine towed an unwieldy contraption about the sky.' In both cases that quote summed it up nicely as they were uncommonly ugly, but the reason for the cumbersome appearance was the need for the Fleet Spotter-type aircraft to provide accommodation for a pilot, observer, wireless operator and gunner. A deep fuselage was necessary to carry a plotting table and radio equipment. Communication between the observer and pilot was effected by means of an internal ladder from the main cabin to the pilot's cockpit perched high in the forward fuselage. Avro publicity of the day noted;

'The Avro "Bison" was specially designed for the British Air Ministry as a Deck Landing Fleet Spotting aeroplane. The Mark II version of this machine is used by the Fleet Air Arm in considerable quantities and has proved a conspicuous success. It is undoubtedly one of the best aeroplanes yet produced for the purpose of alighting on and taking off from an aircraft carrier.'

The publicity was quite correct as forty Bisons were supplied to the Fleet Air Arm and served with a number of squadrons including operations from both HMS *Eagle* and HMS *Furious* until the type was retired from service late in 1929 with the arrival into the Fleet Air Arm of the excellent Fairy IIIF. An amphibian version of the Bison was also built.

The two-seat Avro 543 Baby had flown at the end of July 1920 but although the aeroplane was most successful and impressed many in the aviation world, no orders were forthcoming. It showed itself as a fine aeroplane when Hinkler and Chadwick flew the little machine to an altitude of 11,000 feet and in the 1921 Aerial Derby an ex-RFC pilot, Captain Thomas Tulley, averaged 73.67 mph before engine trouble forced him to land at Brooklands and he was not able to get back into the race.

A development which interested Chadwick was the use of a Baby's fuselage and tail surface by a Mr H.G. Leigh with a smaller wing and six narrow-cord aerofoils in a Venetian-blind configuration replacing the normal wings. This experiment was carried out at Hamble in December 1920, but the results, if any, are not known.

With the 1920 Aerial Derby in the past, Hinkler decided to have his own Avro Baby shipped to Australia and during the journey he undertook a number of his own modifications to make single-handed overhauls possible and also to be able to remove cylinders, pistons and other engine accessaries without having to remove the engine completely. He exhibited the aircraft at the Royal Sydney Show during the Easter Holiday commencing 11 April 1921 and made a number of display flights afterwards. He then made the historic flight from Sydney to Bundaberg non-stop in less than nine hours with a fuel consumption of thirty-five miles to the gallon. Hinkler landed in his home town of Bundaberg's main street and taxyied up to the garden gate of his mother's home! On 27 April he departed from Bundaberg for the return flight to Mascot, Sydney, but en route he encountered a tropical rain storm and set the aeroplane down on a remote beach only to have it overturn in soft sand. After being dismantled and taken the sixteen miles to Newcastle by horse and cart it was shipped to Sydney by rail and soon repaired. However, Hinkler decided to return to England, so he sold the Avro Baby to Harry Broadsmith and the aircraft had an extensive career before it was finally grounded in 1937. This aeroplane can still be seen in the Queensland Museum, Brisbane, along with a later aeroplane of Hinkler's, the Avro 581 Avian prototype.

One interesting customer for the Avro Baby was

The effectiveness of camouflage can be seen in this photograph of the second prototype Lancaster taken in June 1941.

the Russian Government and, with the usual type of privacy, the aircraft was collected by a Russian pilot for delivery to Moscow in May 1922. It is known to have been the first delivery to Moscow from England.

The last version of the Baby was the Avro 554 Antarctic Baby which had been designed specifically for the Shackleton-Rowett South Polar Expedition. The two-seat floatplane was capable of being dismantled quickly, but being assembled again using gloved hands without any rigging problems. With full consultation and guidance of the famous explorer Sir Ernest Shackleton, Chadwick provided the ideal design. The 80 hp Le Rhône rotary engine changed the nose of the aircraft and, of course, folding wings were essential. Trials took place on Southampton Water

with the 554 being flown by the Expedition's pilot Major C.R.Carr. The aeroplane was loaded aboard the auxiliary-sail steamship *Quest* at Tower Bridge, but well into the voyage the vessel suffered engine trouble and went direct to Rio de Janeiro without the scheduled call at Cape Town. This was indeed unfortunate as Avro had shipped essential spares for the Baby to the South African port and during the exploration the aircraft was never flown! The vessel did call into Cape Town on the return journey and the spares were collected and, with the complete but unused aeroplane, the *Quest* arrived back in England on 16 September 1922.

The interesting Antarctic Baby was purchased by Captain R.S. Grandy on behalf of Bowring Brothers Limited of St Johns, Newfoundland in June 1923. Before it left Hamble the aircraft was fitted with a wheeled undercarriage and test flown as such, but on arrival at its new home, it was fitted with skis. It was to be based on one of Bowring's vessels, the *Neptune* for seal spotting from the air, but a superstitious crew would not allow it to fly. However, in May 1924 Captain Grandy took off from an icefloe alongside another of Bowring's vessels, the *Eagle* and delighted the company by spotting a herd of 125,000 seals. The machine was flown for three more seasons also piloted by 'Jack' Caldwell and proved to be very successful by locating nearly 400,000 seals, but was finally retired in 1927 when it was replaced by another Avro machine, this time, one of the new Avians.

The design of the Antarctic Baby did more than produce a fine aeroplane; it made Sir Ernest Shackleton into a good friend of the Chadwick family and, just before his death, Roy Chadwick named one of his last designs as a tribute to the famous explorer. The Avro Shackleton bore the name well as it served in front line service with the Royal Air Force for over forty years.

On 15 February 1923, Sir William Letts of Crossley invited the national press to tour their Manchester factories which, of course, included Avro at Newton Heath where the production of car bodies was well underway. A.V. got wind of this and quickly despatched Chadwick with a number of fine models and large photographs of Avro aircraft to remind the assembled pressmen that aeroplanes were still being designed and produced at Hamble.

One of the models taken to Newton Heath was of the twin-engined Avro 557 Ava which was designed for long-range coastal patrol work. It had evolved from the Avro 556 which had been Chadwick's study for the Specification 16/22 (D of R Type 9) which was to be a torpedo-bomber. Two Avas were built and tested during 1924-27 and when things began to look promising the Admiralty adopted the Mark VIII torpedo as standard equipment. The smaller size of this weapon made an aeroplane like the Ava unnecessary, so no further machines of this type were built.

Alliott, always the brilliant inventor, studied many things and with the Avro Car long gone he started to look at the idea of a substitute for a motorcycle. In 1923 he produced the single-seat Monocar, which had two main wheels with two small outrigger wheels to provide support when the vehicle was stopped. The engine was a 2.75 hp Barr & Stroud with kick start, three speed gearbox and chain drive. The driver sat in an adjustable

car-type seat in an enclosed body which had a collapsible hood for inclement weather and a small space for luggage behind the driver. Its fuel consumption was 100 mpg at a cruising speed of 25 mph and the price was only £75. To prove that the driver was free from road dirt or engine oil, A.V. would demonstrate the Monocar wearing a light grey suit, but it did not catch on and only one machine was made, registration HO 9530. Three years later A.V. designed an improved Monocar which was powered by a 350 cc Villiers engine and was used extensively by him on trips between Hamble and Manchester with the vehicle clocking up over 30,000 miles. Again, only one was built and this Monocar's registration was OT 3664; this famous machine can still be seen in Southampton's excellent Hall of Aviation.

A third Monocar was built by A.V. in his home workshop and used constantly until just before he died.

In August 1923, the newly-appointed Under

Test pilot Bill Thorn smiles for Sandy Jack's camera during an inter factory flight in an Anson.

Sam Brown ready to taxi the first production Lancaster for its maiden flight from Woodford in October 1941. This aircraft served with the R.A.F. until March 1944 when it was lost on a raid to Essen.

A production Manchester at Woodford early in 1942. The aeroplane served with No. 49 Squadron until June of that year when it was reported missing during an attack on Emden. Avro-built Blenheim IVs awaiting collection are on the airfield.

Secretary of State for Air, the Duke of Sutherland, offered a prize of £500 for the winner of a competition for single-seat light aeroplanes with engines not exceeding 750cc. The *Daily Mail* also showed interest in the light aeroplane competition and offered an additional £1,000. On hearing of the newspaper's prize money, the Duke put up a further £500 to equal the *Daily Mail*'s amount.

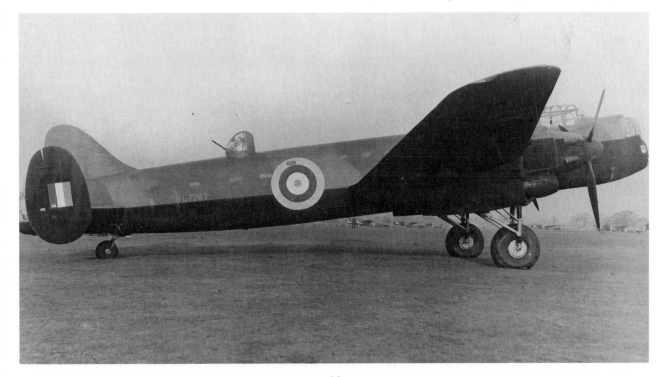

Both A.V. and Chadwick showed great interest as their ideas on ultra-light aircraft were similar and the prize money was always an added attraction, especially as the Duke's extra contribution was only for British competitors flying all-British aeroplanes.

The competition was to take place at Lympne in Kent 8–13 October 1923 and Chadwick's machine was a biplane design, the Avro 558, of which two aircraft were built at Hamble specifically to fly in the trials. In an unusual step A.V. personally designed a monoplane which was known as the Avro 560 and this too was entered in the contest.

Chadwick's aircraft was of small overall dimensions, low structural weight and the first Avro 558 powered by a B & H twin-cylinder, air-cooled motorcycle engine and flown by Hinkler. The second 558 had a 500 cc Douglas motorcycle engine which was also twin cylinder, horizontally opposed. This machine was flown by Hamersley who, with G.S. Bush, had paid for this aeroplane's construction. The latter aircraft performed much better as on the first day Hamersley completed four laps of the twelve and a half mile Lympne circuit, reaching an altitude 6,750 feet, to win £100

in prize money. Engine trouble plagued Hinkler and on 13 October with him flying A.V.'s Avro 560, the 558 was flown by Lieut Barrett, but this machine was damaged when it was forced to land by high winds. The high aspect ratio cantilever monoplane 560 won high praise when, being flown by Hinkler, it completed 80 laps of the circuit covering 1,000 miles with a fuel consumption of 63.3 mpg. Both came out of the event with some satisfaction for A.V. and Chadwick, but with little prize money. Hamersley flew his Avro 558 at Hendon in the Royal Aero Club Light Plane Race on 27 October 1923 and finished a very creditable third.

Early in 1924 the Air Ministry were seeking an aeroplane which could replace the De Havilland D.H.10 on the Cairo to Baghdad air route and which could be used as both passenger and ambulance aircraft. The Avro Aldershot seemed to be the ideal size for the specification and the Hamble drawing office began to look at this aeroplane to suit the requirement. However, it soon became clear that a newly-designed fuselage would be required for the new aircraft. The Avro 561 Andover had six feet added to the Aldershot dimensions in order to accommodate twelve passengers or six stretcher cases. The RAF were most impressed by the machine and its performance almost matched that required, but it was to be Avro's bad luck once more when the desert air route was handed over to Imperial Airways for them to operate instead of the services. The changeover resulted in an order for only three Andovers from the RAF, with the first of these being displayed at Hendon on 28 June 1924. The three eventually went into service and operated from Halton for a number of years. A civilian version of the Andover — designated Avro 563 — was built specifically for airline service for main routes. This was also a twelve-passenger aircraft, but had a toilet and baggage space at the rear of the cabin. After some trials at Hamble and airworthiness flights at Gosport, the 563 was loaned to Imperial Airways in the summer of 1925 and made a number of cross Channel flights from Croydon to Paris, but the aircraft was not retained by the airline. The Avro 563 did eventually find a home, with the RAF! After extensive testing the aeroplane was accepted and joined the military Andovers at Halton in January 1927.

After an all-night session a tired looking Roy Dobson uses a dictaphone in his office at Chadderton.

# CHAPTER 5

# Woodford Aerodrome

**E**arly in 1924 a serious problem arose when the airfield at Alexandra Park was scheduled to be closed and Avro received official notice of this in May of that year. The aerodrome was owned by Lord Egerton of Tatton and with the Air Ministry's lease about to expire he made it clear that if he sold or rented out land the new user would never allow flying to take place in the future. Anyone entering into a sale or lease agreement would have to comply

with his wishes. Manchester Corporation showed obvious interest in the land for the building of council houses and it was they who were successful in securing the land as Lord Egerton presented Alexandra Park to them free of charge.

Avro was allowed to test and deliver aircraft from the site until 30 August 1924, but as that date approached A.V. and a small team were frantically seeking a new flying field. They eventually found a suitable location at New Hall Farm near Bramhall in Cheshire which was approximately fifteen miles from the Newton Heath factory. An auction was held at Alexandra Park on 17

Roy Chadwick introduces the Avro York to Roy Dobson and the production team at Chadderton in 1942. The first York had a twin-finned configuration.

September to dispose of equipment and the occupiers were given notice that all buildings had to be removed by 30 November 1924.

The new site became known as Woodford, which was the name of the small village adjacent to the field. The area consisted of a large field with a few useful buildings, but there was the possibility of expansion and that was one of the requirements during the search for a flying field.

Avro bought a small double hangar from Alexandra Park and also a larger one which could be used for assembly of aircraft. An ex-World War One cloth hangar was also purchased. Affectionately known as 'the tent' it was erected while the permanent hangars were being rebuilt. The store was established from old Mills bomb boxes from war surplus and a large cupboard was bought locally to help with bits and pieces. The main problems were with the water supply and there was no electricity, but after initially using buckets to carry water from the nearby stream, running water was arranged. The electricity was another matter, as carbide lamps and car headlights were used for illumination and, in fact, great adaptability and ingenuity was required as electric power did not become available to the site until 1933!

It was January 1925 before any real work could commence and the airfield gradually came to life with expansion continuing in the following years. The flight sheds developed with the building of hangars No.1 and No.2 during 1933-34. In 1936 the No.3 hangar and canteen were built and in 1938 began the huge task of draining and levelling the site of the New Assembly building. Number 4 hangar was built in 1939 and in the following year the No.5 hangar was erected. The New Assembly building had an extension added in 1943 which later became known as 'finals'. In 1955 the area between No.2 and No.4 hangars was levelled off and roofed over to become hangar No.3A.

As Avro began to move into Woodford, the Lancashire Aero Club was looking for a new home as, under the presidency of Lord Leverhulme, they had applied to the Royal Aero Club for official recognition and affiliation, but with the closure of Alexandra Park their application for membership was suspended until a flying field could be found. The club went through a difficult period and negotiated the use of a field at West Timperley, but

Sam Brown and Bill Thorn ready to board a Lancaster for a production test flight in March 1942.

as this was uncertain Avro stepped in and offered the club the use of Woodford aerodrome and its facilities. The club's only aeroplane was the LPW glider which had been built by Manchester enthusiast John Leeming with a number of his friends, including Avro foreman Tom Prince and a colleague from Newton Heath, Arthur Ainsworth. The LPW Glider, as it was known, would certainly feel at home as it had been built from surplus wood and parts from Avro! The glider was later powered by a Douglas motorcycle engine, but was never termed successful.

In November 1924 the Air Ministry announced that it would subsidise the formation of a number of aero clubs and the Lancashire Aero Club was underway when two D.H.60 Moths were acquired under the Ministry scheme. The second Moth was delivered to Woodford by Alan (later Sir Alan) Cobham and this aeroplane G-EBLV still flies today nearly seventy years later. On delivery of this aircraft, on 29 August 1925 an air pageant was held at the aerodrome and on 26 September a large air display attracted more than 25,000 people with participation from the RAF, Lancashire Aero Club and a small number of private owners and, of course, A.V. Roe & Company Limited. The display was a spectacular success and even today air shows still attract large crowds to Woodford.

The Lancashire Aero Club benefited once more from Avro generosity when the Company presented them with an Avro 504R Gosport.

For the Air Ministry's Two-Seat Light Aeroplane Trials held at Lympne from 29 September to 4 October 1924, Avro produced the Type 562 Avis. Two of this type were entered with the first machine being powered by a 32 hp Bristol Cherub II engine while the second had a 35 hp Blackburn Thrush as a powerplant, but the latter aircraft did not compete. The first Avis arrived at Lympne by road as the geared Cherub was late in being delivered, but this aircraft had already been test flown at Hamble with the Thrush in place and Avro mechanics worked through the night to install the preferred engine. Unfortunately, the engine only developed half power and the aeroplane had difficulty in getting airborne, but late in the afternoon of 30 September Hinkler was

able to take off although he did not attempt the course circuit and landed soon afterwards. Working through the night once more, the Cherub was converted to direct-drive and on 2 October Hinkler beat thirteen other contestants to win the Grosvenor Challenge Trophy and £100 by flying around the twelve and a half mile course at an average speed of 65.87 mph. The exuberant Hinkler flew back to Hamble with his wife as passenger, but with a celebration night stop at Croydon en route!

In 1924 Oxford University planned an expedition to the Arctic and after George (later Sir George) Binney had approached Avro about a spotter aircraft, John Lord agreed to supply a machine suitable for the demanding task. A special three-seat 504 was assembled at Hamble and designated the Avro 504Q. Entry into the specially designed cabin was by a door on the starboard side of the fuselage and there was a sliding hatch in the top for the navigator to work in the open whilst checking bearings and mooring points. The aircraft was equipped to carry a sledge and an alternative

The prototype York nears completion in Chadderton's experimental department. The aircraft was soon to be transported to Ringway for assembly and test flying.

A day's production of Lancasters at Woodford in 1942.

engine cowling for sub-zero temperature operations was also carried. The twin floats were strengthened to act as skis if the aircraft was required to land on snow.

The Avro 504Q was launched from the slipway at Hamble and flown off Southampton Water by Bert Hinkler on 11 June 1924. This was cutting it fine as the expedition was due to depart from Newcastle-upon-Tyne on 14 July, but this delay had been caused by the late arrival of the 160 hp Armstrong Siddeley Lynx engine. The aircraft was also test flown by the Expedition's pilot A.G.B. Ellis and 'Joe' Taylor, who had also been employed as engineer. Soon after landing the aircraft was dismantled and loaded into three packing cases for despatch by rail to Newcastle. The 504Q sailed with the Expedition's team and the rest of its equipment on the SS *Polarbjorn* to Spitsbergen. It was subsequently erected in four days and nights at an abandoned whaling base at Green Harbour in the Arctic Circle by Ellis, Taylor and Fred (later Sir Frederick) Tymms, the aircraft's observer and navigator. Piloted by Ellis with George Binney on board the aeroplane was flying from Green Harbour to Liefde Bay on 15 July when engine trouble forced the machine down into the sea. It was eventually recovered, but not until after an eighteen hour battle with heavy seas and gale force winds. More engine trouble and a collapsed undercarriage plagued the flying operations, but

on one flight that took place on 8 August 1924 the aircraft reached a latitude of eighty degrees fifteen minutes, which was the farthest north ever reached by an aeroplane at that time. The engine was removed and returned to England with the team, but the airframe was left at Liefde Bay to assess the effect of Arctic weather on wood and fabric aeroplanes. The Oxford Expedition eight years later found the structure to be in fine condition apart from the areas eaten by polar bears!

Over the years the magnificent Avro 504 was developed into a number of types for many roles and with a variety of powerplants. The Avro 504N could be fitted with no less than six different engines and, once again, proved to be an excellent training aircraft. Besides being exported to many countries the 504N was used in large numbers by the RAF and after the usual service trials with two modernised 504Ks, which had been in storage at Newton Heath since the end of the war, the Air Ministry ordered a batch of 100 Avro 504Ns with production commencing in 1927. After an incredible 511 total order, production ended in March 1932. Many of the 504N version found their way into the civil market and at the start of World War Two seven were impressed into service with the RAF and these aeroplanes were powered by 215 hp Armstrong Siddeley Lynx engines. Two of the aircraft were destroyed in a fire on Hooton Park race-course in Cheshire before they could join the service and two more were reduced to spares after their first inspection! However, the three remaining aircraft joined up in 1940 and were used by the Special Duty Flight to tow gliders forty miles out to sea, sometimes operating only twenty miles from occupied France. The aircraft were used at Christchurch, Hampshire and each day they would tow the gliders and release them for the benefit of the Radar (then Radio Direction Finding) operators to establish if radar could detect wooden gliders should the Germans attempt such an invasion. The 504s then came home to Manchester as part of the Development Unit of the Central Landing Establishment at Ringway where they were used to develop glider towing techniques for the Airborne Forces. It is a wonderful tribute to this fine aeroplane that, besides training many famous pilots of the RAF, as previously mentioned, thousands of others learned to fly on the Avro 504. It is interesting to note that both Commander (later Admiral) Minoru Genda and Commander Mitsuo Fuchida who planned, with the latter leading, the raid on Pearl Harbor on 7 December 1941 which brought the United States into World War Two, learned to fly on licence-built 504Ks. Manufactured by the Yokosuka Naval Arsenal, the aircraft was known as the Yokosuka K1Y1 in the Imperial Japanese Navy and later versions were built in Japan until 1940.

It is also a great tribute to the aircraft that it was to play its part in two world wars with a fine contribution as a fighter, bomber and trainer in the First World War and then, albeit in a much smaller, but important role, in the Second.

Early in 1926 the 504 was revised once again in an updated low-powered version the Avro 504R, which was named the Gosport in honour of the system of flying instruction which made Avro training aeroplanes famous the world over. It was to be the final version of the 504.

The first two prototype Gosports were built at Hamble and after the early, but hardly required, test flights the second of these was presented to Lancashire Aero Club by Sir William Letts at Woodford on 16 April 1926. The third Gosport built at Newton Heath was put through its paces by Hinkler at Yorkshire Aero Club's air display held at Sherburn-in-Elmet during August and was immediately sold abroad. Interest in the Gosport was great with overseas visitors arriving almost daily at Woodford to see for themselves and sample the fine handling qualities of the aeroplane.

The 100 hp Monosoupape version was the favoured engine in the early Gosports, but later machines could use the 100 hp Bristol Lucifer and the 150 hp Armstrong Siddeley Mongoose. Ten Gosports were delivered to the Argentine Air Service in June 1927 and the type was also built under licence at the Military Aviation Factory at Cordoba which opened in October 1927. The factory eventually built 100 Avro 504 Gosports with the first locally-built example making its maiden flight on 2 October 1928. The Gosport was also sold to Estonia and Peru.

The Lucifer-powered Gosport was going to be known as the Avro 504S, but this type number was never used as the Avro Alpha, a 100 hp engine built by Crossley, was becoming available. The fourth Gosport was to be the first aircraft to be fitted with this new engine and a unique public relations opportunity presented itself in the prospect of a record flight.

The Director of Civil Aviation, Sir Sefton Brancker, was always seeking new avenues to further the cause of aviation. John Leeming of Lancashire Aero Club suggested a landing and take-off from the top of one of Britain's mountains and Sir Sefton was greatly taken by the idea. Leeming returned to Manchester and approached Avro with the proposed attempt at such a flight. Roy Dobson, who was Works Manager at that time, was extremely keen and supervised the preparation of the Alpha-powered Gosport. The mountain chosen for the landing was the 3,118 feet Helvellyn in the Lake District with the original plan being for Leeming to fly the machine while Hinkler accompanied him in another aircraft. Unfortunately, the poor visibility in the Lakes spoilt the first attempt, but on 22 December 1926 with Leeming and Hinkler together in the Gosport they took off from Woodford and headed north-west. An excellent landing was made on the summit of Helvellyn and Leeming was amazed to see that their touch-down had been witnessed by a solitary climber. He clambered out of the aeroplane armed with pencil and paper to get signed confirmation of the landing. The witness could not have been better as it was Professor John Dodds, a lecturer in Greek at Birmingham University, who readily signed before watching the Gosport take-off safely for its return flight to Woodford. The flight did receive a fair amount of publicity, but it

The Minister of Aircraft Production, Sir Stafford Cripps, addresses employees in Chadderton's canteen during a visit to Avro in January 1943.

also made aviation history and a commemorative plaque was later erected on the mountain at the place the aeroplane had landed.

At the RAF Air Display at Hendon on 3 July 1926 the company surprised everyone by showing a brand-new private venture single-seat fighter, the Avro 566 Avenger. It was an attractive aeroplane powered by a 525 hp Napier Lion engine, but as for other experimental fighter types at that time no orders were forthcoming. This aeroplane was fitted with a higher powered Napier Lion becoming the Avro 567 Avenger II and although it was raced a number of times putting in reasonable speeds no

OPPOSITE TOP:
In November 1942 King George VI and Queen Elizabeth visited Woodford. Her Majesty is seen chatting to Roy Chadwick with Teddy Fielding in attendance. Looking on are His Majesty the King with Roy Dobson, Sam Brown and Sir Hartley Shawcross.

OPPOSITE BOTTOM:
During the Royal visit the King, in the uniform of Marshal of the Royal Air Force, inspected Woodford's Home Guard. Accompanying His Majesty is Major Bill Thorn, test pilot by day and unit commander by night! The officer following is Group Captain E. C. Dearth, Avro's service liaison chief.

real interest was shown. The Avro 571 Buffalo, a two-seat torpedo-bomber suffered the same fate and even a more powerful version which was later fitted with floats was the only one sold to the Air Ministry. In the immediate post-war years and well into the 1920s there was a lack of demand for newly-designed military aircraft and it was left to the civil side of A.V. Roe & Company Limited to prove its place in aircraft manufacture.

The Cierva Autogiro Company was formed in Spain in 1924 after Don Juan de la Cierva had carried out a number of experiments with 'rotating wing' aircraft. The Spanish Aviation Ministry assisted Cierva to build the C.6A autogiro which was basically an Avro 504K fuselage and tail, but with a modified undercarriage and a four-bladed rotor mounted on a pylon to replace the wings. The modification to the 504K was carried out at the Military Aircraft Works in Madrid and the machine was first flown by Lieut A. Gomez Spencer, a pilot of the Spanish Flying Corps, on 1 May 1924.

In England the Air Ministry was showing interest in these trials and Harry Wimperis, Director of Scientific Research, invited Cierva to bring the C.6A to Farnborough for a series of demonstration flights. On 15 October 1925 the autogiro was very ably displayed by Frank Courtney, a pilot who was closely associated with the trials in Spain. Later demonstrations led to an order from the Air Ministry for two of this type of autogiro to be built by Avro. The Hamble-built machines were Cierva C.6C, known within the Avro company as the Type 574. Courtney flew the first Avro-built example on 19 June 1926 and just two weeks later he impressed King George V with an excellent performance during the RAF Display at Hendon. Avro were hailed as leaders of the Display by showing two aircraft to the public for the first time, the 566 Avenger and the Avro 574 autogiro. On 7 January 1927, Courtney was lucky to survive a crash from 120 feet when a rotor blade became detached and the machine came down at Hamble. A number of autogiros, using various Avro Type numbers, were built and tested using both 504 and, later, Avian parts, but the most exciting machine was the Cierva C.30. This custom-designed autogiro was a tremendous advance from earlier part aeroplane, part autogiro machines and Avro were so impressed that they acquired a licence to put the C.30 into full production at Newton Heath.

The new version known as the C.30A became more familiar as the Avro 671 Rota and the first order for the type came on 14 February 1934 when the Air Ministry ordered ten, later increased to twelve, to be used for investigation into the effectiveness of the autogiro in Army Co-operation work. The Avro Rota also went to sea on 9 September 1935 when it made a number of deck landings on the aircraft carrier HMS *Furious* and followed this, a few weeks later, with a similar exercise on HMS *Courageous*. One machine was

fitted with floats and successfully flew off the River Medway at Rochester, Kent on 15 April 1935. Besides the service aircraft another sixty-six Rotas were produced for both civilian and export markets, with orders from the latter coming from Australia, China, Hong Kong, India, Lithuania and Russia. The C.30A version also wore the German swastika as forty were built by Focke-Wulf while a further twenty-five were manufactured in France by the Loiré et Olivier company. The last Avro-built Rota left Newton Heath in June 1938.

It was during World War Two that the Avro Rota proved its potential. One of its tasks was to provide a target for radar calibration duties, but because of the area in which it had to operate, off Britain's east coast, the Rotas would have to have a fighter escort! Six of these machines were built up from a number of dismantled civilian airframes and a total of seventeen Rotas saw war service with the RAF. In February 1942 the little autogiros were formed into their own unit which was known as No. 1448 Flight stationed at Halton under the command of Squadron Leader A.H. Marsh. Marsh was an experienced autogiro pilot and had flown a number of early test flights and was the pilot involved in the trials of the float-equipped version which was tested on the River Medway. After being joined by a number of older fixed-wing aircraft such as the de Havilland Hornet Moth the Unit's strength was enough to warrant squadron status and in June 1943 it was renamed No. 529 Squadron. The Avro Rotas continued to give excellent service until the war's end when some went back into civilian service. A few examples of this unique machine can still be seen in various museums around the world including the Science Museum in London, the RAF Museum at Hendon and the Shuttleworth Trust at Old Warden, Bedfordshire.

This Dam Busting Lancaster was the second aircraft to be converted to carry the 'Upkeep' weapon and although it took part in the test drops at Reculver, Kent, it was not used on the actual raid, possibly through damage received in the trials. Another machine using the same code-letters AJ-C did attack the Dams.

# CHAPTER 6

## Hinkler and the Avian

The autogiros under design and construction by Avro brought a number of benefits to the company and it was the fuselage of an Avro 576 (Cierva C.9) which became the basis of a new light aeroplane. Hinkler had test flown the first C.9 in September 1927, but it was the fuselage of the second machine that was transformed into a biplane, the Avro 581 Avian, the prototype for an extremely successful series of light aeroplanes. Roe and Chadwick had their eyes firmly on the *Daily Mail*'s Light Aeroplane Trials, a competition for two-seat aircraft, to be held at Lympne, Kent, from 10–18 September 1926. The Avro Avian retained the 70 hp Armstrong Siddeley Genet engine as used by the C.9 as it was the most powerful available under the powerplant weight restriction of 170 lb. The low structural weight of the aeroplane and the Genet engine made the Avian a promising machine, but trouble with the Genet's magneto forced the aircraft to be eliminated from the trials. However, all was not lost as Hinkler won a six-lap race on the final day. Upon returning to Hamble the Avian was fitted with an 85 hp A.D.C. Cirrus engine to replace the original and with shorter span wings the aeroplane was redesignated the Avro 571A. Hinkler was pleasantly surprised to hear that he had won a £200 prize presented by the Society of Motor Manufacturers and Traders who sponsored the race. A number of other races were entered with reasonable success and this encouraged Avro to put the Avian into production in a modified and much advanced form which would be designated Type 594.

Hinkler had some ideas of his own and persuaded Avro to sell the 581 Avian prototype to him for £750 complete. He designed a new wide-track undercarriage and made a number of other changes making the engine more accessible for maintenance. On 27 August 1927 he took off from Croydon to fly the 1,200 miles to Riga in Latvia to complete the urgent signing of a contact on behalf of William Beardmore Limited. With the aid of an extra fuel tank situated in the front cockpit Hinkler completed the journey non-stop in ten hours fifty minutes, thereby breaking the world record for a long distance flight by a light aeroplane. While the 581 was at Riga it was inspected by officers of the

After the Dams raid Wing Commander Guy Gibson V.C. and some of the crew members visited the Avro factories at Chadderton and Woodford. Gibson was photographed relaxing in Chadderton's board room during a break in the proceedings.

Latvian Air Force and this eventually led to an order for Avians from Avro.

Hinkler's objective had always been to fly to Australia and he was convinced that his little Avro 581 was the aeroplane to take him there. He had assessed the aeroplane's performance over the months and with further modifications he would make an attempt. Wings designed by Chadwick for the Avro 594 Avian were fitted, as was a new Fairey all-metal propeller and the undercarriage was strengthened to combat the possibility of a rough-field landing. Then he was ready and early in January 1928 he resigned his position as Chief Test Pilot for Avro.

One woman and three men watched Hinkler in his tiny Avian take off from Croydon at dawn on 7 February 1928, heading south-east for Australia some 11,500 miles away. The woman was Bert's wife, Nance, who firmly believed that Hinkler

In August 1943 Woodford's production lines were turning out seven Lancasters every day.

would beat the record for the journey established nine years earlier by Ross and Keith Smith in a Vickers Vimy. Aviation experts doubted that the Avian would be able to endure the flight with the possibility of sand storms and tropical winds along the route. Hinkler's night stop in Rome was a little more than he bargained for because after landing in the evening moonlight he was promptly arrested and marched off to the lock-up as he had, mistakenly, landed on a military airfield instead of the civil aerodrome. His anxiety cost him most of the night's sleep and he was not in the best of moods when the British Consul rescued him from the military and he was able to continue the flight. Hinkler landed twice in the Middle East, inflating his rubber dinghy to sleep in, but he suffered from the oppressive heat and had bad bouts of cramp. On the leg to Karachi he had a few anxious hours with a leaking fuel tank, but upon his arrival he was suitably elated to learn that the world was beginning to take notice of his attempt on the record. A newspaper in Sydney gave some fantasy

A popular visitor was Mrs Eleanor Roosevelt, wife of the United States President, seen here sharing a joke with Roy Dobson and Laura Bailey at Chadderton.

to the story by reporting that Hinkler had taken out a policy with Lloyds of London and would, 'net a considerable sum' if he beat the record. He was well ahead of the Ross Smith record and the newspapers around the globe were lyrical over the feat with one American paper calling him 'Hustling Hinkler'. The Commonwealth Government reported that they could not subscribe to such a wild enterprise, but when Hinkler took off from Timor on 22 February for the 850 mile flight over water to reach Australia there just happened to be a number of warships along his route! Hinkler landed safely in Darwin to a hero's welcome just fifteen and a half days after leaving London, covering the 11,005 miles in just 128 flying hours with fourteen night stops along the way. The flight had cost him just fifty-five pounds, but it was after he reached Australia that his troubles started. On the flight to his native Bundaberg he was forced to land in the bush and once again slept in his inflated dinghy. After taking off he flew to Longreach where he was also received a great welcome, but things turned a little sour when a souvenir hunter tried to steal his goggles and others placed their children on the aeroplane's wings. All of this, of course, did not go down too well with Hinkler. In the towns and cities the welcome was much the same with an

estimated 80,000 people turning out to see him in Sydney. He led a triumphal parade perched on top of a lorry while the little Avian, wings now folded, was towed behind. The public relations machine worked overtime for Hinkler with the tiny Avro Avian catching much of the adoration and many Australian boys born in 1928 were named Herbert. He was offered film contracts, lecture tours and many public appearances which he just did not have the time to attend. The only 'official' upset came when he flew the Avian into Perth as certain religious leaders reproached him for arriving on the Sabbath and thereby decimating their congregations!

On a humorous note, many of his fans worked out just how much money he would receive from his Lloyd's policy, with newspapers speculating on some fantastic amounts. However, they were shocked to hear that Hinkler would not receive one penny because, although he had begun to negotiate such a policy, he pulled out thinking that his premium money could be used more effectively on his expenses for the journey!

His admirers in Australia came to his rescue because after donations from various parts of the country he amassed something in the region of £10,000 and the title, which later followed him, of 'Australia's Lone Eagle'. He left the Avian in Australia where it now resides in the Queensland Museum at Brisbane along with the Avro Baby from his earlier flight to Bundaberg. The town of Bundaberg is still extremely proud of its famous son and in recent years the townsfolk subscribed to have the house he used while he was flying at Hamble, to be dismantled brick by brick and reassembled in the town as the Hinkler Museum.

Bert Hinkler went on to greater glory and established more records, but his many friends at Avro were saddened to hear on 7 January 1933 that his aircraft had gone missing on another record breaking attempt. He was flying a de Havilland Puss Moth to beat C.W.A. Scott's time of eight days ten hours to Australia completed in April 1931. The Italian Apennines were on Hinkler's route and it was there in April 1933 that a small band of Italian charcoal burners came across the wreckage of an aeroplane 3,000 feet up in the mountains. The confirmation of his death cast a shadow over Avro both at Manchester and Hamble as he had died as he liked to fly, alone.

The South African Air Force fitted floats to one of its Ansons for handling trials for seaplane pilots.

Although the purchase of new military aircraft was not lucrative during that period the Air Ministry continued to issue specifications. The Specification 17/25 for a single-seat fleet fighter was received by the company in June 1926. Chadwick with Harry Broadsmith — back from Australia — as his assistant, Jock Ratcliffe as chief draughtsman and the rest of the team in Hamble's drawing office, who were already extremely busy on modifications to the Bison, Ava, Aldershot, Andover and the autogiros as well as new work on the Avian, now took on the design work for this new fleet fighter. Chadwick set his ideas down for a sleek looking biplane fighter with this coming to be known as the Avro 584 Avocet. It was to be an all-metal stressed skin aircraft powered by a 230 hp Armstrong Siddeley Lynx, but unfortunately the design did not allow for wing folding as required for carrier operations. A simple and efficient system was devised to unbolt the wings and attach them again without too many rigging problems. However, no matter how simple the system was it was not looked upon favourably by the services. Only two prototypes were built as the Avocet's performance was not impressive and these aircraft were flown with both land and float

undercarriages. The two aircraft were evaluated by the Fleet Air Arm at Martlesham Heath in February 1929 and the second aircraft which had been refitted with floats, after landplane trials, was passed on to the High Speed Flight in September 1929. The unit operated from Calshot in Hampshire, just across Southampton Water from Hamble and was formed solely to allow pilots to practise for the Schneider Trophy races.

It was another disappointment for Roy Chadwick that the only military aeroplanes being sold by Avro were the older designs such as the Avro 504N and the Gosport.

The Avro 594 Avian continued to arouse interest in the private flying market and was proving itself to be a most popular aeroplane. Avians, in common with other types, were ordered in a variety of marks with the choice of seven different engines! Once again, records were there to be

OPPOSITE TOP:
A familiar sight on Greengate outside the Chadderton factory was a complete Lancaster fuselage on its trailers. After assembly at Woodford the aircraft was delivered to No. 83 Squadron and survived the war, but went to the scrapman in November 1946.

OPPOSITE BOTTOM:
With hardly any space to spare Chadderton's floor area was completely covered with Lancaster components as this photograph taken in June 1944 will testify.

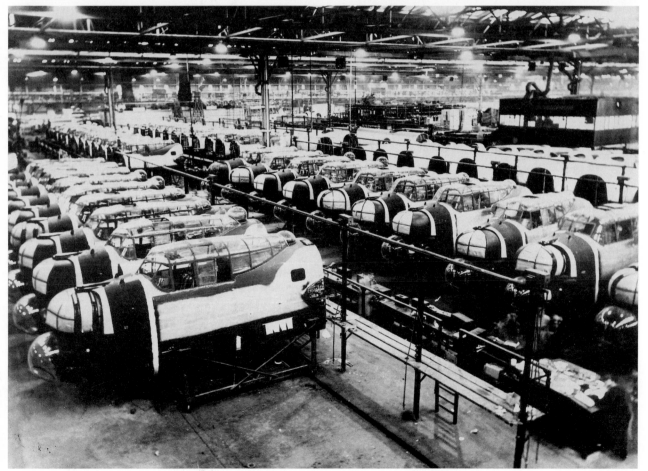

**ABOVE TOP:**
The prototype Lincoln made its first flight from Ringway on 9 June 1944 in the capable hands of Sam Brown. Originally known as the Lancaster IV, the Avro super bomber was too late to see action in World War Two.

**ABOVE:**
The first Lancastrian airliner leaves the snows of Woodford for delivery to B.O.A.C. at Croydon in February 1945.

**LEFT:**
A Lancastrian's cabin showing just thirteen seats which now would be the passenger load for a small commuter aircraft!

The beautiful lines of the Tudor 1 are shown in this photograph of the prototype before its maiden flight.

broken and there was no shortage of aviators who wanted to write their names into the record books. One of these was Captain W.N. Lancaster who, with his passenger Mrs Keith Miller, wife of an Australian journalist, took off from Croydon on 14 October 1927. Their Avro Avian III named *Red Rose* was heading for Australia, but it certainly did not go into the record books as it took over five months to get there! With numerous breakdowns and the odd forced landing, the flight was horrendous enough and more so after a delayed take-off from Rangoon when Mrs Miller found a live snake at her feet! She killed it with a spare joystick and quickly threw it overboard! The Avian eventually arrived in Darwin on 19 March 1928, but with little notice being taken by the locals — it was not the reception they would have got if they had landed there in the time Lancaster had originally estimated.

Famous Australian aviators had a penchant for Avro aeroplanes and their most famous pilot Sir Charles Kingsford Smith ordered a special single-seat long-range version of the Avian which he named *Southern Cross Junior* after his record breaking Fokker Tri-motor *Southern Cross*. Sir Charles's great ambition was to establish an England-Australia record by beating Hinkler's time. On 9 October 1930 he departed from Heston and after a trouble-free flight he arrived in Darwin just ten days later to capture the record. Sir Charles purchased another Avian which became the *Southern Cross Minor* and in pursuit of another record he took off from Melbourne for a 'wrong-way' flight to England on 21 September 1931. Unfortunately, he was struck down by illness in Turkey and had to abandon the attempt.

Bill Lancaster, who was still searching for any record at all, now planned an attempt on the England to Cape Town record. Sir Charles had sold *Southern Cross Minor* to Lancaster who departed from Lympne on 11 April 1933 and during the flight the aircraft disappeared without trace. He had taken-off at dawn in a blaze of publicity in attempting to beat Mrs Mollison's (Miss Amy Johnson) record for a solo flight to Cape Town which took place in the previous November. It was later found that Lancaster had refuelled in Barcelona and also at Oran, Algeria, before heading out over the Sahara. He had landed at

Reggane to refuel, but despite warnings not to take off as he appeared to be tired, Lancaster departed. Nothing was ever heard from him again, that is, until 1962 when a French Foreign Legion patrol found the wrecked Avian and Lancaster's mummified body. The crash site was approximately 200 miles south of Reggane and his log showed that he had stayed alive for eight days afterwards.

The crash had been caused by a fuel blockage, but on landing the aeroplane lost a wheel and flipped over. The Avian remained in surprisingly good condition after twenty-nine years in the desert and the wreckage was recovered in 1975 to be displayed in Australia.

In May 1926 the Air Ministry had purchased a Fokker F.VII three-engined transport aeroplane and this aeroplane amazed spectators by looping the loop on its arrival at Martlesham Heath. The aircraft was of advanced construction and in 1928 Roy Chadwick, Roy Dobson and Harry Broadsmith visited the Fokker factory in Amsterdam to study drawings and production techniques of the F.VII. The Avro team recommended that the licence should be obtained to produce the machine in England and their

Bill Thorn brings the Tudor over Woodford during its first flight in June 1945.

favourable report was accepted with the Avro-built aircraft becoming known as the Type 618 or Avro Ten, so called because it accommodated eight passengers and two crew. The aircraft had a fabric covered welded steel tube fuselage with wooden structured wing with plywood covering. The welded tube fuselage frame became a feature of Avro aeroplanes and in 1929 the Avian IVM adopted this type of structure.

Powered by three 240 hp Armstrong Siddeley Lynx engines the Avro Ten production totalled fourteen aircraft, all built at Newton Heath. It was the Australian connection once again when the first order for the aircraft was for five machines for Sir Charles Kingsford Smith who, with Charles Ulm, had founded Australian National Airways Limited. These aeroplanes were delivered in the winter of 1929-30 and immediately went into service establishing a wide route network, but the depression forced the closure of the services in July 1931. Two aircraft were lost, but the others were sold including one purchased privately by Ulm for a proposed round-the-world record attempt. Ulm in the Avro Ten, named *Faith in Australia* departed from Sydney on 21 June 1933 to fly the empire route around the globe, but problems with the fuel system and later one of the engines cost valuable time and it took seventeen days just to reach England. Intent on the world flight he took the aircraft to Ireland where

A striking view of the Tudor 1 over the Cheshire countryside.

he would refuel for the Atlantic crossing. His point of departure would be Portmarnock Sands, but the weight of the fuel caused the aircraft to sink in the sand collapsing the undercarriage. All looked lost when the tide came in and lapped around the aeroplane and it would have been the end, but the oil magnate Lord Wakefield telegraphed Ulm to have the machine salvaged and repaired as he would cover the costs. With temporary repairs completed the aircraft was flown 'home' to Woodford where it was rebuilt by Avro.

The story did not end there because in the middle of October 1933, Ulm took the Avro Ten back to Australia and in doing so set a new record of six days eighteen hours.

In 1928 Avro was joined by an experienced pilot who would serve the company well over the following seventeen years until he was forced to

retire in 1945 through high blood pressure. His name was H.A. Brown or 'Sam' as he was known to one and all. He had flown in the First World War and afterwards had a period of flying joy-riding Avro 504s from the sands at Blackpool. From 1921 to 1926 he spent an enjoyable time in Spain training pilots of the Naval Air Service, but then accepted a job as flying instructor at the Lancashire Aero Club. He became a popular figure at Woodford and quickly rose to become chief flying instructor of the club, often flying Roy Dobson in the Avro Avian which had been presented to the Club by John Lord.

The Avro Gosport which had been presented to the Lancashire Aero Club crashed on Bramhall Golf Course near Woodford on 21 October 1928 killing both occupants. The subsequent investigation into the accident concluded that the passenger had interfered with the aircraft's controls.

Chadwick was on the military trail once more

A July 1945 photograph of Avro's famous communications Anson lovingly known in the company as 'Aggie-Paggie' because of the aircraft's registration letters.

Sir Roy Dobson received his knighthood in the 1945 New Year's Honours.

when he designed the Avro 604 Antelope, a high performance day bomber powered by a 480 hp Rolls-Royce F.XIB engine. The Air Ministry had issued the Specification 12/26 for a bomber-type aeroplane with a top speed of 160 mph. The attractive Antelope made its first flight in August 1928 in the hands of a new recruit, Flight Lieut Frank Luxmore, DFC. He had joined Avro at Hamble after the departure of Hinkler and was proving to be an excellent test pilot. It was Sam Brown who flew the first Antelope to Martlesham on 13 September 1928 for comparative trials against the Hawker Hart and the Fairy Fox II. The Antelope was of advanced construction for its day, with the structure mainly of duralumin including the covering of the fuselage sides. This machine might have laid the foundation for a whole series of similarly built aeroplanes, but in the RAF's final assessment, although all three aircraft were comparable, it was felt that for maintenance the internal access to the structure offered by conventional fabric coverings was preferable. The winner of the competition was the Hawker Hart, with this machine going on to give the RAF many years of excellent service.

The Antelope was displayed at the Olympia Aero Show in London from 16–27 July 1929 and although the aircraft attracted a great deal of interest, no orders were forthcoming. The aeroplane eventually ended its days at Farnborough as a test-bed for newly-designed variable-pitch propellers.

# CHAPTER 7
## Avro Changes Hands

The shares in Crossley Motors Limited had plunged to their lowest ever price of 1s.6d and the *Financial News* dated 25 May 1928 carried the following statement:

'As recently foreshadowed, arrangements have now been completed whereby Sir William Letts has sold to the Armstrong Siddeley Development Company Limited, the whole share capital of A.V. Roe & Company Limited, the well-known aeroplane manufacturers of Manchester and Hamble.

'A sum of over £270,000 in cash has been paid by Sir William M. Letts to Crossley Motors Limited for the acquisition of their shares, which show them a profit of more than £200,000 on their original investment in A.V. Roe & Company Limited.

'For the last eight years Crossley Motors Limited have held the majority of shares in A.V. Roe & Company Limited and during that period Sir William Letts has acted as managing director of the latter company.

'The fact that Crossley Motors had sold their interest in A.V. Roe & Company Limited was announced in the "Financial News" of May 2 last, but at that time the name of the purchaser was not known.

'A.V. Roe & Company Limited is a private company, registered in 1913, and until the sale now announced has been controlled by Crossley Motors. The capital is £50,000 in £ shares, £20,000 being in 10 per cent Cumulative Second Preference shares and £10,000 Ordinary, all issued and paid up.

'For the year ending October 31 last Crossley Motors reported a loss of £65,518, but the report stated that, in considering the accounts, it should be known that if the accumulated profits and reserves of A.V. Roe & Company Limited, in which the company had a large interest, had been distributed, instead of retained as working capital, the adverse balance arising from the year's operation of the company would have been eliminated.'

This statement was, no doubt, the talking point at a banquet held at the Savoy, London on 8 June 1928, to honour Alliott Verdon Roe and his pioneering activities in the field of aviation. The attendance was marvellous for besides HRH The Duke of York, there were many pioneers of flying in Britain, government ministers, serving officers and others connected with aviation at that time. Senior managers of Avro attended, including H.V. and his wife Dr Marie Stopes.

The banquet, organised by the Royal Aeronautical Society, was on the twentieth anniversary of A.V.'s first flight and, although not officially recognised it was acknowledged to be the first time an Englishman had left the ground in a powered aeroplane of his own design.

Back in Manchester, Roy Dobson heard that a Mr John Sword in Scotland had been considering purchasing a number of Avro Avians, but had now switched his attention to the de Havilland Moth. Dobson, never one to stand about, caught the next train to Glasgow even though it was a Friday night and a meeting with Mr Sword turned the decision in favour of Avro. This meeting was the start of a lifelong friendship between the pair and when the Kelvin Construction Company, headed by John Sword, became part of the Hawker Siddeley Group they were responsible for building all of the new factories for that organisation, including the massive Chadderton facility for Avro.

After the take-over of the company, Avro employees feared for their jobs, but Armstrong Siddeley chief executive John Siddeley (later Lord Kenilworth) assured A.V. that there would be no changes as he planned to allow both Avro and Armstrong Whitworth to continue building aeroplanes. It was felt that the Hamble site was too detached from Newton Heath and Woodford, but it was allowed to carry on with design work and experimental flying. However, by the beginning of 1929, Roy Chadwick and his design team were back in Manchester and fears that Armstrong Whitworth's excellent chief designer, John Lloyd, might take over from Chadwick soon receded as John Siddeley kept his word.

When the Avro Ten was shown at Olympia in 1929 the company also exhibited a scaled-down version of that machine which had been completely designed by the Avro team. The smaller aircraft was powered by three Armstrong Siddeley Genet Major engines and had accommodation for four passengers and the pilot and so, carrying on the theme, it became the Avro Five, known in the company as the Type 619. Orders for this aeroplane came from Australia, Kenya, China and Hong Kong and the progressive design team then came up with the Avro 624 or Avro Six, but only two of this type were sold. Chadwick liked the high-wing airliner configuration and designed an even larger aircraft, the Avro 642, which could be ordered in either a two- or four-engined version. Marketed as the

Avro Eighteen, once again, only two of this type were ever delivered, but one of these was certainly a prestigious aeroplane as it was bought by the Viceroy of India, Lord Willingdon. The 642 gave excellent service for six years before being taken over by the RAF at the beginning of World War Two.

The Avro Avian continued to sell well both at home and abroad with fifty-one being assembled in Canada by the Ottawa Car Manufacturing Company. The Whittlesey Manufacturing Company of Bridgeport, Connecticut, USA also obtained a licence to build the Avian and plans for the production of the aeroplane in large numbers had to be shelved when the United States went into recession. Manufacture was getting into its stride under the supervision of Teddy Fielding and between 14 March and 15 May 1929 an amazing thirty-eight Avians were completed! Unfortunately, this good production run came too late to save Whittlesey as the company went into receivership soon afterwards.

The Sports Avian was introduced in 1930 and the Avro 625 Avian monoplane also appeared. Two of this type were entered in the 1930 King's Cup air race, but because both aircraft were handicapped they did not feature in the placings. However, for the record, the race was won by Miss Winifred Brown of the Lancashire Aero Club in an Avian III. It is also interesting to note that an Avian III was purchased by Fred Raynham, Avro's famous test

Lord Mountbatten's Avro York leaving Ringway to return to India after overhaul in August 1945.

The end of an era! The last Lancaster leaves Yeadon in October 1945.

pilot, in 1928. He was at that time involved in the air survey business with Ronald Kemp and the aeroplane was for his personal use.

The Avian's achievements in racing and long distance flights are many, but production ended in August 1933 when Avro began to receive orders for their later types. Very few Avians survived after World War Two, but besides the examples of the machine overseas, a beautifully restored Avian IIIA can be seen in Manchester's Museum of Science & Industry. This aircraft was first delivered to Liverpool and District Aero Club on 6 July 1928 and was rescued from the Ringway Airport fire dump by the Northern Aircraft Preservation Society (now The Aeroplane Collection) who have loaned it to the Museum where restoration was completed to exhibition standard by Basil Carlin.

A.V.'s interests were many and one of his passions was for water-borne aircraft. However, it still came as a great shock to all at Avro when he submitted his resignation from the company to John Siddeley at the end of October 1928. Alliott was to take a controlling interest in S.E. Saunders Limited of Cowes, Isle of Wight, well-known builder of high-speed motor-boats and which had aviation experience in building the hull for T.O.M.

Roy Chadwick studies a drawing in his office at Chadderton.

ABOVE:
The Tudor 2 roars down Woodford's main runway before landing from its first flight on 10 March 1946

OPPOSITE TOP:
A Lincoln of No. 57 Squadron in August 1945. The colour scheme of all white upper surfaces with black undersides was designed for operations against the Japanese.

OPPOSITE BOTTOM:
The Tudor 2 prototype roll-out at Woodford.

Sopwith's famous Bat Boat amphibian. During World War One they had produced hulls for the large Curtiss America flying-boats assembled in England and before the war's end Saunders had built two of these machines under licence.

Samuel Saunders had made it known that his company wanted to expand into the aviation business and after secret negotiations it was announced that A.V., John Lord and Harry Broadsmith were to invest £42,500 in that company. Further backing was secured from a number of finance houses.

It was a blow to A.V. Roe & Company Limited for besides losing A.V. himself and Harry Broadsmith, the departure of John Lord was felt deeply. Lord was the force that drove Avro for, although he had only entered aviation through H.V., he had become highly respected as, besides being a most amiable man, he was also a shrewd

business man whom few bettered. At a later stage he held high office in the Society of British Aircraft Constructors (SBAC) and was liked and respected by all other manufacturers.

The company became known as Saunders-Roe Limited and as makers of Saro flying-boats produced some fine aircraft from the Saro Cloud in 1931 up to the magnificent Princess flying-boat, also the SR-53 rocket fighter and Skeeter helicopter.

At the end of 1928 Chadwick had been studying a design to replace the Avro 504Ns in the RAF as the basic 504 type had been the standard trainer for twelve years and the Air Ministry had asked companies to investigate a possible replacement aircraft. Chadwick came up with the Avro 621 which, unknown at the time, would make a worthy replacement.

Alliott Verdon Roe was knighted in the New Year Honours of 1929 for his pioneer work and services to aviation. It was certainly not going to go to his head and he made it known that he was still the old A.V.; *The Aeroplane* for 6 March 1929 featured the following report:

The Honour to Mr Roe
'No honour yet given in connection with aeronautics has been better deserved than the knighthood conferred on Mr A.V. Roe. Though a thoroughly competent committee, after considering irrefutable evidence, decided that

the first flight by a British subject in England was made by Mr Moore-Brabazon on a foreign aeroplane and though there is good evidence to show that the first flight made in England was made by Mr S.F. Cody, a citizen of the United States on a British aeroplane, there is no doubt that Mr A.V. Roe did in fact make the first series of experiments in this country to be ultimately crowned with success.

'Moreover those little hops of his, which were not officially flights, were the basis on which was ultimately built a business which has probably done more than any one firm to establish the good name of British aircraft all over the world. From those hops at Brooklands in 1908 came the longer hops on Lea Marshes and at Wembley in 1909. And from them came real flights at Brooklands in 1910 with the old Green-engined tractor biplane.'

The report continued to list the achievements of A.V. and ended:

'In congratulating Mr A.V. Roe on this honour we must not forget to join with him when recognising the great work which the Avro Company has done, his brother Mr H.V. Roe who not only financed his experiments in 1909–10 and formed A.V. Roe & Company Limited with his own money, but managed all the business affairs of the firm so ably until the middle of the 1914–18 War, when he deliberately gave up a very profitable business to join the Royal Flying Corps, although over the age for a pilot, and in consequence suffered severe injuries in a crash on active service after a gallant night-bombing raid over German territory.

'Also we must couple with the brothers Mr R.J. Parrott and Mr Roy Chadwick, the former as engineer and the latter as designer, who have been responsible for the high quality of Avro workmanship and cleanliness of Avro design, which has contributed so largely to the world-wide reputation of the firm. They are also honoured by this long-delayed recognition of Mr Roe's services to the nation and they will be the first to rejoice in his elevation.'

---

After the Tudor 2's maiden flight those closely involved with the aeroplane gathered for a photo call. From the left are, Alf Sewart, Bill Thorn, Roy Chadwick, Teddy Fielding, Jimmy Orrell, Arthur Bowers and Jack Dobson.

# CHAPTER 8
# The Successful Tutor Series

Avro was determined that the replacement of the legendary Avro 504 should be by another Avro aircraft and with Chadwick's design of the Type 621 well underway, the factory at Newton Heath was busy comparing welded steel structures with their usual wooden ones. It was found that the tubes did not corrode internally as had been forecast and the advantages of such a rugged frame was being confirmed throughout the world from both Fokker and the metal Avro Avians which were going into service at that time.

The Type 621 was delivered to Martlesham for trials on 4 December 1929 and made its first public appearance at the 1930 Hendon RAF Display. Roy Chadwick himself entered the aeroplane for that year's King's Cup Race when, flown by J.L.N. Bennett Baggs it averaged 108.3 mph. The first powerplant was a 155 hp Armstrong Siddeley Mongoose, but Chadwick was already looking at alternatives.

The aircraft received excellent reports from its early trials with the handling qualities being superb. The Air Ministry ordered a batch of ten aircraft for service trials at a number of training stations including Gosport. Three 621s were purchased by the Irish Air Corps who named the machine the Triton.

The parent company was keen that Avro aircraft should be fitted with Armstrong Siddeley engines and Chadwick found no problems with that, selecting the A.S. Lynx of some 215 hp as the alternative powerplant for the Avro 621. Two prototypes were built with this engine and the aeroplane proved to be a winner with great interest already being shown in a number of overseas military and civilian operators. In June 1932 the Avro 621 was adopted as standard trainer for the RAF and given the name Tutor. Production techniques included jig-built components to ensure interchangeability and methods of mass

production were starting to be used. The first deliveries to the RAF went to the Central Flying School at Wittering and a team of instructors formed a display team which specialised in inverted formation flying, with this routine being a feature of many air displays in the years that followed. In all 394 Tutors were delivered to the RAF and a floatplane version was known as the Sea Tutor. When production of the Tutor ended in March 1936 a total of 795 aircraft had been built at Newton Heath and assembled at Woodford. A further fifty-seven Tutors were licence-built in South Africa and three assembled in Denmark. Apart from the RAF and British registered aeroplanes, the Avro 621 had been sold all over the world, spreading the company name across the globe as the 504 had done previously. Tutors in the RAF served as trainers into World War Two and it is known that at least one of the type was operated as a communications aircraft in the Western Desert until 1942. The Danish aeroplanes were stored in a hangar during the German occupation, but were destroyed when Danish saboteurs blew it up on 22 November 1943. The RAF also used the navigation trainer version of the later Avro 626 with the seven machines ordered being known as Avro Prefects.

Britain's sole surviving Tutor has been preserved and still flies regularly with the Shuttleworth Collection at Old Warden, Bedfordshire. One of the four Avro Prefects supplied to the Royal New Zealand Air Force has recently been restored and still flies regularly at Ohakea on New Zealand's North Island.

The excellent qualities of the Type 621 attracted many interested parties including some of the smaller air arms and Avro were quick to realise that there would be an excellent market for a multi-role version of the aeroplane. Out of the 621 development came the Avro 626 aircraft which would be sold with conversion kits capable of

The first Tudor 2 after the redesign of the tail surfaces, but these modifications plus other structural changes increased the aeroplane's weight and reduced the performance.

changing the operation of the machine from initial training to bomber, reconnaissance, navigation, night flying or even seaplane trainer. The aeroplane also had a third cockpit which could be used as a gunner's position should that requirement arise. The foresight of the company once again produced a winner with nearly 200 sold to fifteen countries with the last Avro 626 being delivered to Egypt on 4 April 1940! Yet another version of the basic 621 came when the third prototype Avro 626 was converted into an offensive aeroplane with the fitting of a forward-firing Vickers gun for the pilot and a Lewis gun in the rear cockpit. A varying bomb load could be carried and in this configuration, the Avro 637, was ideal for the Kwangsi Air Force of Southern China who ordered eight of the type.

After the take-over by Siddeley it was planned that the Avro operation at Hamble would be scaled down and eventually terminated, but it was not until 14 December 1932 that the move was completed. The Avro premises were taken over by Air Service Training Limited who occupied the site until 1960.

The *London Gazette* for 2 May 1933 carried an announcement that by deed poll in the Supreme Court on 28 April 1933, Sir Edwin Alliott Verdon-Roe, formerly Edwin Alliott Verdon Roe of Hamble House, Hamble, Southampton, Aeronautical Engineer abandoned the surname Roe and in lieu thereof adopted the surname of Verdon-Roe.

As the Avro 604 Antelope failed to secure any production contract, the second airframe was intended to be made into a two-seat fighter designated the Avro 608 to be named the Hawk. The change was commenced in 1928, but was slow and before any work could be completed the project was abandoned with modifications and a change of engine making it into the Type 622. This type too did not progress, as Avro heard of a requirement for a mail-carrying aeroplane in Canada. After consultation with Canadian Airways, Chadwick produced the design for the Avro 627 called, appropriately, the Mailplane, with the machine capable of ski or float operation and having inertia engine starting, blind flying equipment and a fire-and-waterproof mail compartment forward of the pilot. The engine was a 525 hp Armstrong Siddeley Panther, but after it arrived in Canada for trials it was fitted with a Pratt & Whitney Hornet of similar capacity. However, the Canadian Government greatly reduced its financial allotment to civil airlines with the mail contract being hit and in consequence Canadian Airways could not invest in new equipment and the aeroplane was shipped back to Woodford. With the Panther engine installed once more the Avro 627 was exhibited at the SBAC Show at Hendon in June 1932 and Sam Brown flew the aircraft in the 1932 King's Cup Air Race at Brooklands on 8–9 July. The aeroplane established the fastest speed yet recorded for the race when it averaged 175.5 mph flying to Woodford and then back to Brooklands on the 8th and then flew at 170 mph around a short circuit on the 9th, but because

the full course was not completed the 627 was unplaced.

Conversion of the Mailplane into a day bomber designated Avro 630 was not undertaken and the 627 was fitted with a 700 hp Armstrong Siddeley Tiger engine with the machine becoming the Avro 654 high performance test-bed when it appeared at Woodford in June 1933. This machine was not as successful as Chadwick and his team had hoped. A number of test flights were undertaken by Sam Brown and his assistant Sidney 'Bill' Thorn, but the aeroplane seemed overpowered and without further changes it was dismantled in June 1934.

Out of the success of the Tutor as a military training aeroplane came a smaller version designed specifically for club or private flying. The Avro 631 Cadet closely resembled its military predecessor, but was much lighter as wood had replaced metal in various parts of the structure. The 631 first flew on 15 March 1932, but did not appear in public until 14 May 1932 when Sam Brown took the aeroplane to the east coast for the official opening of Skegness Aerodrome. Brown

Tudor nose sections under construction at Chadderton in 1946.

In order to restore the lost performance, a Tudor 2 was fitted with Bristol Hercules radial engines and designated Tudor 7. This aircraft is shown nearing completion at Woodford in March 1947.

showed off the Cadet's fine handling qualities with a magnificent aerobatic display. Roy Dobson took part in a Cheshire air race and flew the Cadet into fourth place with an average speed of 114 mph.

The Irish Air Corps, who had purchased three Tutors in March 1930, liked the concept of a lighter and cheaper version and ordered six Avro Cadets from the company before the prototype had even flown! The aircraft was powered by a 135 hp Armstrong Siddeley Genet Major compared with the 215 hp of the Tutor's Lynx, but the lighter weight enabled the Cadet to produce a more than adequate performance for civilian operators. The largest user was Air Service Training who had taken over the A.V. Roe facilities at Hamble and were well established as experts in flying instruction from basic to advanced trainer. They operated seventeen Cadets at one time and found the aeroplane to be ideal for all phases of instruction.

The Avro 643 was an improved version of the Cadet which had a roomier fuselage and raised rear seat giving the instructor a much improved view. The Type 643 was issued with a Certificate of Airworthiness on 9 March 1934 and was sold to a number of private operators, but a higher powered

Avro 643 Mk II Cadet received a significant boost when the Australian Air Board ordered twelve of this type for the Royal Australian Air Force in September 1935 with deliveries from Manchester beginning two months later. Two further batches of ten aircraft each were ordered for the RAAF and were delivered between December 1937 and March 1939. The Mk II Cadets gave excellent service during World War Two and in 1946 sixteen of them were sold by the Australian Government to civilian users. At least one of these was still flying in the late 1980s.

In 1946 Chadderton proudly displayed the company name for the first time. Although built just as the war clouds were gathering, the factory never advertised the name for obvious reasons!

Other versions of the Cadet were studied and the Avro 633 Cadet Fighter and another trainer development, the Type 663, reached the drawing board stage, but were not continued.

One of the problems of the Type 631 Cadet for private and club owners was that the wings did not fold for hangar storage. It was a requirement for light aeroplanes in the 1930s and Avro remedied the problem by introducing the Avro 638 which was popularly known as the Club Cadet. The prototype first flew from Woodford in May 1933 and the first production aeroplane joined two Avro 631s when it was bought by Lancashire Aero Club. Unfortunately, the aeroplane did not sell as well as expected and only fifteen Type 638s were built, but one of these was completed as a special order for Mr Douglas and the Honourable Mrs Margaret Fairweather, who would both become famous for their contribution to the Air Transport Auxiliary during World War Two. This aeroplane, the Club Cadet Special, was exclusive to the Fairweathers as it had a 140 hp Cirrus Hermes in place of the Genet Major engine. The idea of an enclosed cabin biplane had intrigued Chadwick for some time and he was given approval to commence the design of an aeroplane based on the Cadet. Designated the Avro 639 Cabin Cadet, the aeroplane had a square section fuselage with

---

Surplus R.A.F. Ansons were an excellent source of revenue after the war as machines refurbished by Avro were exported in large numbers. This aircraft was bound for Portugal in June 1947.

accommodation for pilot and passenger in the normal tandem arrangement. Once again, sales of the Cabin Cadet did not materialise although it was flown and demonstrated to a number of interested parties at both Woodford and Hamble during 1933–34. Chadwick looked at developments to the aeroplane including a float version, but none were destined to proceed and the aeroplane stood engineless at Woodford for six months before being scrapped in 1936.

The principle of the Avro Cadet continued in the Avro 640 which was a three-seat development of the Type 638 with the pilot situated in the front cockpit with two passengers side-by-side in the rear. This machine was designed specifically for joy-riding work with the first four aircraft being ordered by the Scottish Motor Traction Company Limited for pleasure flying over the Highlands and Islands. These initial aircraft were fitted with the 140 hp Cirrus Hermes, but later Cadet Three-Seaters had the 135 hp Genet Major as powerplant.

Of the seventeen Club Cadets built, four were shipped overseas during June 1941 and are believed to have been lost at sea. The remaining Avro 638 was allocated to Saunders-Roe Limited as a communications aircraft and operated from Cowes and Eastleigh for the duration of the war. It is known that Sir Alliott himself used the aeroplane on a number of occasions and was proud of the fact that the machine bore the name of the company he had founded. This aircraft was struck off charge (SOC) in 1945, but was completely restored by Saunders-Roe and fitted

with a D.H. Gipsy Major engine. It was last owned by the Vintage Aeroplane Club, but the machine was completely destroyed in a crash at Denham Aerodrome on New Year's Day 1956.

The requirements of the smaller air forces with budget restrictions was never far from the thinking of the Avro team and from the designers came a handsome little biplane in the shape of the Avro 636. This dual purpose aeroplane was a two-seater, but could be flown as a single-seat fighter with the second cockpit faired over, or operated as an advanced trainer. Once again the Irish Air Corps were the first customers and, again, the aeroplane was ordered straight from the drawing board. The Irish, in fact, ordered six aircraft, but the budget restrictions brought the number down to four 636s and even these had to be fitted with refurbished 460 hp Armstrong Siddeley Jaguar engines retrieved from Vickers Vespa aircraft which had been scrapped by the Air Corps. The Avro 636A fighter version powered by a 680 hp Armstrong Siddeley Panther engine could have proved to be an excellent fighter, but with a multitude of projects underway development remained static. The 636 was designed by Roy Chadwick, but this time he had the co-operation of Armstrong Whitworth's John Lloyd who had designed the A.W. 35 Scimitar, an attractive fighter aircraft which had been ordered by the Norwegian Army Air Service. The Avro 636 had the now standard Avro-Fokker type welded tube frame while the wings were manufactured by Armstrong Whitworth at Coventry and the advanced single strut undercarriage was designed by George Dowty, a young man who joined Avro in 1921 and left some years later to join Gloucestershire (later Gloster) Aircraft Company, before going on eventually to form the famous company which bears his name today. The name Acrobat was the name put forward for the 636, but Dobson and Chadwick

disliked it with 'Dobbie' remarking, 'It sounds like something out of a bloody circus!' As Dobson usually got his way, the name was dropped.

The four Avro 636s were delivered to Baldonnel Aerodrome near Dublin on 16 October 1935 and although the performance was adequate with the reconditioned engines, the aircraft was never able to live up to its full potential. It provided the Irish Air Corps with excellent advanced training for its pilots, but two were written-off in landing accidents through failure of the tired engines, luckily without fatalities. The other two machines stayed in front-line service as fighters serving alongside the four Gloster Gladiators, purchased some time later, until the 636s were retired in 1941.

*Flight* for 31 May 1934 told potential customers:

'Car comfort, an ultra-reliable engine, a modest power expenditure and a performance which should satisfy a very large number of purchasers, are the main features of the very latest Avro machine.'

The magazine was reporting on the latest aeroplane to come from the Avro stable and it looked every inch a thoroughbred. It was the Avro 641 Commodore, a beautiful cabin biplane which came out of the experience gained from the Avro 639 Cabin Cadet. It was powered by the 215 hp Armstrong Siddeley Lynx, which was proving itself to be one of the most reliable aero-engines produced at that time. An additional feature was that the Commodore's engine was fitted with an electric self-starter and the cabin had accommodation for five people. With such an advanced design it remains a mystery why only six of this type were ever sold, the first being delivered on 24 May 1934 and it was this aeroplane which was the subject of *Flight*'s report. The most famous owner of a Commodore was the Maharajah of Vizianagram with his aeroplane being delivered to India in October 1934. Two aeroplanes served on communications duties during the war, but both did not survive it, as one Commodore supplied to the Air Transport Auxiliary crashed at White Waltham on 10 August 1941 while attempting to land in a thirty degrees cross-wind while the other machine served until 17 August 1942 when it was retired and became an instructional airframe.

---

OPPOSITE TOP:
De Havilland test pilot John Cunningham flew this Avro Lancastrian test-bed with D.H. Ghost jet engines in the outboard nacelles in July 1947. The photograph shows the aircraft with Walter rocket engines under the fuselage during take-off trials at Hatfield.

---

OPPOSITE BOTTOM:
Great things were expected of the Tudor as can be seen from the number of fuselages at Chadderton in August 1947.

The tragedy to the Tudor at Woodford on August 23 1947 was a bitter blow to Avro and a great loss to the aviation world. With Roy Chadwick, Bill Thorn and the other crew members died a wealth of irreplaceable experience.

BELOW:
Shattered dreams! The broken fuselage and tail assembly being loaded for transportation to Woodford flight sheds for detailed examination.

ABOVE:
An aerial view of the crash site with the Tudor's tail just visible on the left edge of the trees., It was a cruel twist of fate that the aircraft had to hit the only trees in that area causing the disintegration.

# CHAPTER 9

## The Anson is Born

On 18 May 1933 a meeting took place in London which was to lead to the design and manufacture of an aeroplane which would have the largest production total of any Avro aircraft — the Anson! Sir John Siddeley, knighted in the June 1932 Birthday Honours, met with G.E. Woods-Humphrey, managing director of Imperial Airways, to discuss the airline's requirements for a high speed, four passenger monoplane specifically for charter work. It was obvious that a number of advanced features would have to be incorporated, with the number one priority being for the machine to have a retractable undercarriage. The prospects of designing such an aircraft delighted Roy Chadwick and after many meetings with Major R.H. Mayo, technical adviser to Imperial Airways, who later achieved fame as the originator of the Short Mayo Composite flying-boat, their ideas formed the basis for the design of the Avro 652. The Type 652 design study was presented to the airline in August 1933 and outlined an attractive twin-engined low wing monoplane with accommodation for two pilots and four passengers. The machine, powered by two 270 hp Armstrong Siddeley Cheetah engines would have a cruising speed of 150 mph and a still air range of 600 miles. After considerable evaluation by the airline, a contract for two Avro 652s was signed by Imperial Airways at Avro Headquarters in Newton Heath on 16 April 1934. It was while the Type 652 was in the design stage that the Air Ministry invited companies to submit studies for an aircraft to fill a new role of general reconnaissance and the service requirement was so close to the 652 specification that it was a relatively simple task to prepare a military version, the Avro 652A.

The first Avro 652 took to the air for its maiden flight on 7 January 1935 flown by Frank Tomkins and the aircraft was found to have the usual excellent 'Avro' handling qualities. The second aeroplane was not far behind in production and the Type received its Certificate of Airworthiness on 1 March 1935. Delivery of both aircraft to Imperial Airways at Croydon was on 11 March, but a slight problem arose with the name which the airline had bestowed upon one of the machines. The first 652 was named *Avalon* and the second *Avatar*, but this was quickly shortened to *Ava* when someone pointed out that it meant something quite unmentionable in a certain European language!

Both the 652s gave the airline excellent service over the next three years mainly acting as mail carriers; but the operator outgrew them and the two aircraft were bought by Air Service Training in 1938. AST used the aeroplanes as navigation trainers at Hamble until outbreak of war when they were impressed into military service. Both the 652s were used by the Royal Navy at Lee-on-Solent in Hampshire, but were regarded as Ansons in line with many of the type in service by then.

Chadwick's design for the military version was completed by 19 May 1934, but competition for the service contract was fierce with both Airspeed and de Havilland bidding to supply an aeroplane for the general reconnaissance task. The Avro 652A was powered by the 295 hp version of the Cheetah which added ten miles-per-hour to the earlier cruising speed despite the addition of a gun turret on the fuselage. The turret contained a single Lewis gun and a Vickers gun was fitted to the port side of the nose for use by the pilot. A 360 lb bomb load could also be carried in the centre section. After service evaluation the Air Ministry team whittled the competition down to the Avro 652A and the de Havilland D.H. 89M which was the military version of the excellent Rapide. Orders were placed with both companies to supply one prototype each for the trials.

The prototype 652A flew for the first time from

The R.A.F. Lincoln *Aries II* was fitted with Lancastrian nose and tail fairings. This aircraft, operated by the Empire Air Navigation School, made a number of long distance flights including one to Australia in October 1947 where it carried out research into the earth's magnetic field.

Woodford on 24 March 1935 in the capable hands of Bill Thorn. Thorn, assisted by 'Tommy' Tomkins, flew the aeroplane for twenty-five minutes. Early trials showed longitudinal instability which was cured by increasing the tailplane span to give a twenty per cent greater area, with corresponding reduction in elevator area which had been a full fifty per cent of the total tailplane area.

The service trials at the Coast Defence Development Unit at Gosport covered both of the competitors and were held from 11–17 May 1935, strongly favouring the Avro machine. The RAF were more than happy with the results as it was getting them away from the biplane image. Great interest was shown when the Avro 652A appeared in the New Types Park at the RAF Display at Hendon on 29 June 1935. The aeroplane demonstrated its excellent range and endurance during fleet exercises held over the North Sea. The Air Staff Requirement No 23 was issued on 27 August 1935 for full development of the Avro 652A under the name Anson.

Back at Newton Heath the Avro employees were overjoyed to learn that Production Specification No 18/35 had been issued and a contract was awarded for 174 aircraft.

Further service trials at Martlesham showed a number of problems with the Centre of Gravity having to be changed to solve the problem of constant trim changes as crew members moved about inside the aircraft. Improvements in take-off and landing performance were made and various changes in engine position, trimming and weight distribution made the Anson a delight to fly. The aeroplane could be flown for long periods without undue strain and this would prove to be one of the features of the type during its long career.

The order for the Anson had taken longer than anticipated. Indeed it was uncertain if the aircraft had been selected at all and the result was that a number of redundancies had to be made. One of the redundant was a shop steward who called a meeting in Newton Heath's canteen to initiate strike action, but Roy Dobson, Teddy Fielding and Frank Greenhalgh, who later became Labour Superintendent, attended the gathering to assess the situation. As a walk-out seemed imminent Dobbie jumped up on one of the tables and, in his usual way, told them how 'bloody daft' they were as things were certainly about to improve and any strike could only cause harm to the company's prospects. Happily, the decision to strike was reversed and the employees stayed at work.

On 25 June 1935 the senior management of the Armstrong Siddeley Development Company Limited were shocked when Sir John Siddeley sold out his interest in the company. A new company called Hawker Siddeley Aircraft was formed to purchase the whole of the share capital of the Armstrong Siddeley Development Company and fifty per cent of the ordinary share capital of Hawker Aircraft Limited. The directors of the new company would be T.O.M. Sopwith, Fred Sigrist and Frank Spriggs and, although Sir John Siddeley was not included his name remained in the title. Sir John retired completely in June 1936 after staying as chairman of the Development Company.

There was uncertainty again at Avro, but all was well as the Manchester company was untouched by the changes which took place.

The expansion programme of the RAF brought excellent news for Avro as it was awarded a contract to licence-build 287 Hawker Audax advanced trainers to be issued to a number of new Flying Training Schools. The Hawker Company's production lines were fully extended at that time and with the prospects of the exciting new Hawker Hurricane moving into production stage, it was necessary to build the Audax elsewhere. In fact, Avro manufactured more Audaxes than even the parent company and went on to design a Panther-engined version in place of the RAF's Rolls-Royce Kestrel powered machine. The Armstrong Siddeley Panther version was known as the Avro 674 and twenty-four of this type were sold to the Egyptian Army Air Force, being delivered between March 1937 and May 1938.

There was a great deal of sadness amongst the

---

Woodford new assembly in July 1948 showing the production lines of Ansons for export to Afghanistan and for the R.A.F., Tudors are in the background.

Avro old-timers when they learned of the death of John Lord on 26 January 1936. Few people in the aircraft industry will have been as sincerely mourned and his death came as a great shock by coming soon after what was described as a mild stroke.

The Hawker Siddeley Aircraft Company Limited was expanding in all areas of the business and Roy Dobson was delighted when he was able to convince Frank (later Sir Frank) Spriggs of a similar requirement for the Newton Heath works as agreement was given for a 250,000 square feet extension to the plant. Two more flight sheds were built at Woodford and the foundations were being built for a third.

Work on the Anson was well underway with the first production machine making its first flight at Woodford on 31 December 1935 piloted by

Geoffrey Tyson. The first of the type to enter service with the RAF arrived at Manston, Kent on 6 March 1936 for No 48 (General Reconnaissance) Squadron. Interest in the aircraft was growing and in order to satisfy a Royal Australian Air Force requirement the Air Ministry agreed that twelve Ansons could be diverted from the RAF production and these aeroplanes were delivered to Melbourne on board the SS *Orani* on 19 November 1936 and a further twenty-one were sold to Australia the following year. Other orders for the Anson came in 1936 from Estonia and Finland.

During 1936 the company was still delivering its training aeroplanes with examples of the 621, 626, and 643 going all over the world. Countries flying Avro trainers at that time included Argentina, Brazil, Belgium, Canada, Chile, China, Czechoslovakia, Egypt, Estonia, Greece, Irish Free State, Lithuania, New Zealand, Portugal, South Africa and with ever increasing orders, Australia. Aircraft production was certainly in full swing

Athenas being built at Chadderton. The nearest aircraft already has its Rolls-Royce Merlin engine in place.

RIGHT:
The interior of this Tudor 5 of British South American Airways has comfortable seats and a wide aisle, but just thirty seats in such a large aircraft would be unacceptable today!

BELOW:
The Avro Tudor 8 was Britain's first four jet transport aeroplane and the aircraft was piloted by Jimmy Orrell on its maiden flight on 6 September 1948.

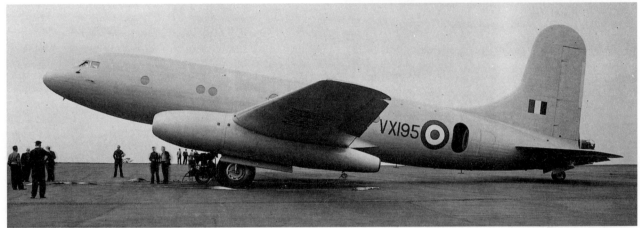

with the days of billiard tables and bassinets being well behind.

Anson deliveries to the RAF more than met expectations and the service amazed the foreign air attachés when five squadrons of the type flew over in mass formation during the Hendon Display on 26 June 1937.

In May 1938 Avro received a wonderful boost when they were asked if they could take on the production of the Bristol Blenheim light bomber and as the Audax programme was ending it did not take Roy Dobson, now General Manager and also a board member of Hawker Siddeley to confirm that they could.

The Blenheim Mk 1 was a sleek twin-engined light bomber already in full production at Filton, Bristol, but with a higher build rate needed, contracts were awarded to Rootes Securities and A.V. Roe & Company Limited with the latter being for 250 aircraft. It was the first aircraft built by

Avro in light alloy with stressed skin construction. The first production problem was to establish the class of labour to use as some of the skilled unions were ready to stake their claim. It was decided to build the structure with semi-skilled labour with the first move being to take over some new factory space and the Ivy Mill at Failsworth was selected to make the Blenheim components, with assembly of the main sections to be done at Newton Heath. The whole process slipped into gear with Avro eventually producing the 250 Blenheim Mk 1s before being awarded a further contract to manufacture 750 Mk IVs with production of this type ending in November 1941. However, that did not present a problem as bigger things were on the cards!

The Air Ministry Specification P.13/36 was issued for a new generation of twin-engined medium bomber and of the number of tenders received only the Handley Page H.P.56 and the Avro 679, designed by Roy Chadwick specifically to meet the requirement, were selected for construction of two prototypes each. The engines selected were the same for each aircraft being the new Rolls-Royce Vulture, a water-cooled engine of 1,760 hp. However, the Manchester, as the new Avro machine was named, won the competition, as the Handley Page aircraft was withdrawn in 1937. This aircraft was to emerge later powered by four Rolls-Royce Merlin engines as the Halifax.

The Manchester was ordered into production under the Specification 19/37 with advanced production methods being used wherever possible. The new bomber was all-metal construction with a retractable undercarriage and defensive gun positions in the nose, tail and midships. The crew would be seven with the aeroplane weighing some twenty tons, but carrying a bomb load of an average of five tons, which was a revelation for that time.

During the study and design of the Manchester more sad news reached Avro with the death of Reg Parrott only a few months after his retirement. A second blow came on 9 December 1936 when it was learned that Juan de la Cierva, the autogiro pioneer, had been killed the previous day in the crash of a KLM Douglas DC-2 which had flown into houses after take-off in the fog at Croydon. Both of these losses were deeply felt by all who knew them, but especially by Dobson, Chadwick and Sir Alliott. Roy Chadwick was hit by another death on 11 June 1937 when he was informed that his friend and fellow designer Reginald Mitchell had died. Mitchell's name, of course, was to live on forever as designer of the famous Spitfire.

An aircraft hangar at night is quite magical! This photograph taken at Woodford in October 1948 captures some of the magic with Tudors, Ansons and a Lincoln setting the scene.

# CHAPTER 10

# The New Giant Factory

The war clouds were gathering when, on 16 August 1938 Sir Kingsley Wood, Secretary of State for Air, announced that the government had decided to entrust the erection of a £1 Million aircraft factory to A.V. Roe & Company Limited of Newton Heath, Manchester. Sir Kingsley had flown into Woodford for a visit to the Avro works both there and at Newton Heath. He was greeted by Roy Dobson who escorted him on a tour of the facilities.

After an inspection of the production line at Newton Heath, Sir Kingsley met many departmental heads including Roy Chadwick, now a board member of Avro. It was during this time that the announcement of the new factory was made. Referring to the building Sir Kingsley stated,

'I have the greatest confidence that the firm of Avro under the management of Mr Dobson will fulfil all our expectations.... The site has not been definitely decided upon, but I hope that building will begin in the next few months.'

It certainly did because in a little over six months the first employees, transferring from Newton Heath, began to take up residence in the new plant.

After the announcement it did not take the planners long to put down the first stakes in the fields running alongside Greengate in Chadderton near Oldham and bulldozers began clearing the site almost immediately. The sceptics were already writing-off the programme as a White Elephant for where would all the orders come from to fill a site of that size? It would be a large site, but Roy Dobson had given instructions to the Avro chief engineer, John Green, who was in charge of the construction, 'Take the size of a normal aircraft factory and make it twice as big!'

It looked as though the sceptics were right when, on 30 September 1938, Adolph Hitler and Prime Minister Neville Chamberlain signed a document in Munich which proclaimed 'Peace in our Time'.

Fortunately, work on the Chadderton factory proceeded at a fast pace and in March 1939 employees began to move in. Office staff, personnel from the tool room, plating shop and the machine shop were among the first to arrive. Many of them would be working at their bench when there would be a tap on the shoulder to inform them to 'Get your coat on' which would signify a transfer to the new factory. If they used a vice for their work they would be allowed to travel on one of the flat-bed lorries which were busy moving material from Newton Heath to Chadderton. If they did not, they had to travel by bus to Gardeners Arms at New Moston and then walk the next quarter of a mile as no bus route went past the factory at that time.

Even with the new lacquered benches, fresh equipment and even their own storage space, the early days at Chadderton were grim for the new residents as it was cold and damp during the spring of 1939. With no heating or canteen facilities and large tarpaulin sheets over the roof structure to keep out the rain while the building work continued, the days seemed twice as long.

As with Newton Heath works, the Chadderton factory would manufacture the main aircraft components and these would be transported by road to Woodford for final assembly, test flying and delivery. It seemed strange that the first aircraft jigs going into Chadderton were not for Avro aeroplanes, but for Bristol Blenheims!

On 31 March 1939 King George VI visited the Ivy Mill where 1,500 employees were engaged in manufacturing components for Blenheims and then moved on to Newton Heath to see Ansons and Blenheims on the production line. His Majesty

ABOVE:
A Tudor 2 in military markings is a rare sight with the aircraft being allocated to the Ministry of Supply. Some records state that the aeroplane went to that organisation in 1951, but the date on this photograph was June 1949.

LEFT:
Jimmy Orrell, one of test flyings all-time greats. During a career spanning over thirty years he flew more than one hundred different types of aircraft and from 1942 to 1945 he personally tested more than 900 different Lancasters!

BELOW:
Following Sir Roy's forceful directive, all of the Tudors under construction at Chadderton were destroyed in August 1949. This is the first time a photograph of the demolition has ever been published.

had lunch at Newton Heath with Sir Frank Spriggs, Dobson, Chadwick and Fielding and showed much interest in the new factory although the visit was not scheduled to see Chadderton. The workers there expressed great disappointment at not being able to see the King.

Production of Blenheims and Ansons at Chadderton began as soon as practical, but the company was pinning its hopes for the future on the new bomber.

The Avro 679 Manchester made its maiden flight at Ringway on 25 July 1939 piloted by Sam Brown. The prototype was built at Newton Heath with the main sections being taken to Ringway for assembly during May. The Avro experimental flight department had been established at Ringway, originally in Hangar No 1 which adjoined the airport lounge and cafe. Stuart Davies, who had joined Avro in January 1938 as assistant designer, was put in charge of the liaison between Chadwick and the experimental department. On the day of the first flight the aircraft was pulled out of the hangar at daybreak and as there were no tractors available the airport fire engine towed the machine out.

As the runways were being laid on Woodford's grass airfield on 3 September 1939 when war broke out, it was decided to keep the experimental flight department at Ringway for the duration.

A contact for 200 Avro Manchester Mk 1s was placed with the company with the first delivery being made on 5 August 1940. Construction also commenced at the Metropolitan-Vickers plant at Trafford Park, Manchester. Unfortunately, on 23 December 1940 German bombs destroyed their first Manchester together with twelve other airframes in various stages of construction.

After the second prototype had flown, the twin-finned aircraft had a central fin added after its trials at Boscombe Down. The ventral turret was replaced by a more familiar-type dorsal one and modified wing tips increased the span. The Air Ministry was concerned about the cost of extending airfield runways to cater for large bomber aircraft or the possibility of an airfield being put out of action by bomb craters. Because of these concerns, the Manchester's airframe was strengthened so that aircraft could be launched by catapult. Trials were carried out with the prototype Manchester being successfully launched, but the whole project was soon to be cancelled.

An Athena 2 awaits delivery to the R.A.F.'s Central Flying School in October 1949.

The Avro Manchester entered service with No 207 Squadron at Waddington, Lincolnshire during November 1940. Their first operation was a raid on Brest on the night of 24–25 February 1941 when six aircraft took part. The Manchester was a delight to fly when the engines worked well, but the Vulture power plant was insufficiently developed and there were frequent engine failures.

The famous 1,000 bomber raid on Cologne on the night of 30–31 May 1942 saw forty-six Manchesters taking part with the loss of six of their number. The most famous exploit of an Avro Manchester was during this raid when Flying Officer Leslie Thomas Manser of No 50 Squadron was awarded the Victoria Cross for bravery. His aircraft was badly damaged over the target area, but he held the aircraft steady while the bombs were released. Despite further damage he set course for England, but the Manchester steadily lost height and as there was no hope of reaching safety, Manser ordered his crew to bale out and he held the bomber steady until the last man parachuted from the aircraft. He then lost control and was killed when the machine crashed in Belgium. His posthumous award was confirmed on 23 October 1942.

The last operational raid by Avro Manchesters was against Bremen during the night of 25–26 June 1942 but out of this aircraft's failure came the greatest bomber of World War Two — the Avro Lancaster.

With Anson and Manchester production well underway many employees were working on that fateful Sunday 3 September 1939 when Britain declared war on Germany and it was with mixed feelings that they went about their tasks. Peacetime standards had already been abandoned as the factories had quickly settled down to the business of mass production.

Once again more production floor space was required and early in 1939 the Air Ministry had approached Avro to expand their premises to cope with the build-up of the RAF. The site chosen was the Leeds and Bradford aerodrome at Yeadon in Yorkshire. By December 1939 work had already started on the building of a factory which was to be one and a half million square feet and half again as big as the Chadderton plant. At the time it would be the largest factory in Europe to be under one roof. The factory was completed in February 1941 and the task of trying to camouflage it was immense, but it was done most effectively. Earth was banked in ramps around the factory walls and the flat roof was laid out to merge with the surrounding countryside. The roof had a farm house, walled fields, dummy cattle and even a duck pond! The work cost £20,000, but it was generally regarded as one of the finest camouflage schemes in World War Two. The Yeadon factory had a production record second to none, but more of that later.

When Rolls-Royce cancelled any further manufacture of its ill-fated Vulture engine, Avro was left with an excellent airframe, but no engines to equip it. The Rolls-Royce Merlin engine in Spitfire and Hurricane fighters was proving to be everything the Vulture was not and, in particular, reliable! However, two Merlins were not powerful enough to equip an Avro Manchester, but four of them would be another matter! Roy Chadwick quickly modified drawings of the aircraft to take four engines and he and Roy Dobson visited the Ministry of Aircraft Production in London to outline their plans. Polite interest was shown, but the request for Merlin engines was refused as fighters were badly needed at that time and they would have priority.

Never one to be denied, Roy Dobson contacted his friend Mr E.W. Hives (later Lord Hives) at Rolls-Royce and it was through his good offices and a little of the 'old pals act' that four Merlins were forthcoming.

On 18 April 1940 the first general arrangement drawing was available after Roy Dobson had been visited by a representative from Rolls-Royce.

Stuart Davies had been in charge of the experimental department since 1 April and he was to supervise any new development without disturbing work on the current Avro Manchester. By 1 May 1940 the four-engined version, known at that time as the Manchester Mk III, was going ahead. The engines promised to Avro were the Merlins which had been subject of a study for the Bristol Beaufighter as one of the possible alternatives to its Hercules engines.

On 25 July 1940 Dobson received a letter from William (later Sir William) S. Farren of the Ministry of Aircraft Production stating that as much Manchester tooling as possible must be used on the four-engined version in order to maximise the number of heavy bombers available to the RAF at the earliest date.

Dobson was shocked when he received a letter from Air Member for Production, Air Chief Marshal Sir Wilfred Freeman dated 29 July which stated that Avro were to drop plans for the Manchester III as they were to build the Handley Page Halifax instead. Less than a day later both Dobson and Chadwick were at the Ministry of Aircraft Production with the full details and performance estimates for the Avro 683 four-engined bomber. Once again Dobbie, ably assisted by Roy Chadwick put up a good case and, again, was not to be denied as the programme was approved with the duo agreeing to produce two prototypes by July 1941.

The first aeroplane was built at Chadderton and then had been dismantled on 5–6 December 1940 for transporting to Ringway, but bombs were dropped on the aerodrome during that night and, after a slight delay, the approval was given to move the aircraft. The machine was to be ready for a first flight on 31 December, but changes to the hydraulic system prevented this.

The big day came on 9 January 1941 when Sam Brown with Bill Thorn as his assistant flew the prototype for the first time. The aircraft was still called a Manchester III, but the Clearance to Fly signed by Roy Chadwick on 5 January, clearly shows the aeroplane's name as 'Lancaster'. The performance and handling were 'marvellous' to quote Brown and its reliability was proved by nine rigorous test flights in the next twelve days. Before the aircraft left for service trials at Boscombe Down in Wiltshire, the name Lancaster was officially approved.

ABOVE:
The Shackleton assembly line at Woodford was in its early stages in March 1950. Further down the line are four Lancasters and a Tudor.

RIGHT:
The first prototype Shackleton on its maiden flight. The tail turret, which was soon to be deleted, is clearly shown in this photograph.

The second 'productionised' prototype was flown by Sam Brown on 13 May 1941 and it was as this machine was being prepared for the flight that Roy Chadwick received a letter from the Ministry of Aircraft Production which made him absolutely furious. The letter invited British chief designers to inspect a recently arrived B-17 Flying Fortress and other American types 'to see what a modern bomber should look like'. Chadwick immediately cancelled the proposed test flight, sped into Chadderton's design office, selected twenty-three draughtsmen and ordered them to Ringway. Teddy Fielding remembered that Chadwick placed his people, complete with drawing boards, around the aircraft and then he personally went over the aeroplane examining even the smallest detail. He completely rearranged many items and threw out others with accessibility and servicing being his main priorities. Easy fitment of components received great attention and the whole operation contributed greatly in the reduction of man hours during construction. The aeroplane took-off at two-thirty in the afternoon of 13 May and just twenty minutes in the air convinced Brown that the Lancaster was, indeed, a winner.

The Lancaster was proving to be the aircraft which the RAF wanted, but there was still bitterness within the senior ranks of the Air Ministry that Dobson and Chadwick had 'gone behind their backs to get what they wanted'.

Dobbie, of course, could not have cared less as the aeroplane was undoubtedly the finest heavy bomber in production and his faith in the aeroplane was rewarded when Avro received an order for 450 Lancasters in June 1941.

Chadwick was already familiar with American designs as Avro had been converting Douglas DB-7s taken over by the British from Belgian contracts, into Bostons and Havocs for the RAF. The work, at both Woodford and Ringway, commenced in July 1940 and continued until November 1940.

The Lancaster's fuselage was constructed in five sections and each one was fully equipped before they were joined together. This method proved to be a winner, not only in production, but during operations when battle damaged sections could easily be replaced. Roy Dobson and Teddy Fielding decided that the high production targets forecast could be achieved by using semi-skilled labour and large numbers of both male and female workers were recruited for this important task. As the effort built up to twelve hours a day, with seven-days working being normal, but sixty-six hours per week was average. Workers were given halibut oil capsules to keep them fit.

Average earnings in the early stages of the war were about £2-10s-0d (£2.50) per week and one bright young man was nominated by his colleagues to ask Mr Dobson for a rise. After listening to the young man's case about long hours, low pay and the stress involved, the fearsome Roy Dobson opened the door to an adjoining office, pointed to a single bed and said, 'See that? I am here twenty-four hours a bloody day, so don't talk to me about stress!' After that the young man left hurriedly and the workers never did get a rise!

Some Avro workers were also required to join the Home Guard to help protect the factories, so besides the long hours at work they were expected to don a uniform and take their turn at guard and picket duties. In charge of the Woodford Home Guard was test pilot Bill Thorn who received the rank of Major and was often referred to as 'Major' by his colleagues. Chief test pilot Sam Brown answered to the nickname 'Cappo', short for Captain as he had often used that title in his earlier career.

Besides the long hours and demanding work there was always the threat of enemy air raids and warnings constantly interrupted production. On one night early in the war the Chadderton workers became totally frustrated as the sirens sounded no fewer than twenty-seven times! Later, sirens were ignored and work continued and it was not unusual for workers to have to walk home after a long shift because all public transport had stopped owing to air raids.

Protection from bombs was vital and thick walls were built in many areas of the factories to prevent blast damage. Despite the importance of the work only one attack was ever made on the massive production plant at Chadderton and, miraculously, no-one was injured as the workers were on holiday. The date was 23 April 1941, Easter Monday and, by a great stroke of good fortune, the work force had voted to have that day as a holiday instead of the Good Friday. The management had offered one day

---

OPPOSITE TOP:
The Avro Ashton high-altitude research aircraft arrives at Farnborough for its first public appearance at the 1950 S.B.A.C. Show.

---

OPPOSITE BOTTOM:
Another debutant at the 1950 Farnborough Show was the Avro 707B seen here landing back at Boscombe Down after its first flight, 6 September 1950.

---

RIGHT:
Roly Falk, who was always immaculately dressed and carried out his test flying while wearing a lounge suit, in the cockpit of an Avro 707A.

off, but working on Good Friday was double time while, for some reason, Easter Monday was only time and a half. It was just after three o'clock in the afternoon when the German raider flew in just above roof-top height — some sources reported that the aircraft was a Dornier, but observers trained in aircraft recognition at first thought that it was a Blenheim. However, it was soon established that the aircraft was a Junkers 88, but only one of the guns in the area opened fire as the German machine was flying below the minimum elevation of the other Bofors guns. The Junkers flew low over the factory, banked sharply to avoid some power cables and then dropped four bombs. The factory's Home Guard unit manned a small calibre machine gun on the roof of the building, but reports vary on whether they actually fired on the bomber. The aircraft climbed away and disappeared into cloud. It was later reported that the Junkers 88 was shot down over the North Sea by a Lockheed Hudson of RAF Coastal Command, but this was never confirmed in post-war records. Some damage was caused to assembly bays, but one bomb hit the rivet stores sending millions of these metal fasteners of various sizes in every direction. This created a massive problem until, by a stroke of genius, someone suggested that the company enlist the help of blind people from the local Henshaw's School for the Blind. Everyone there volunteered to help and they did a magnificent job in sorting out the rivets purely by feel.

The last Anson to be built poses for Paul Cullerne's photograph before the aeroplane was handed over in a ceremony at Woodford on 27 May 1952. Wing Commander H. Budden was on hand to do what thousands had done before — accept an Anson on behalf of the R.A.F.

Surprisingly, the aircraft assembly factory and airfield at Woodford were never attacked although the Luftwaffe aerial reconnaissance photographs of the airfield are known to exist. A few bombs fell in the surrounding area, but they were thought to be strays from a bombing raid on Manchester. The Trafford Park area of Manchester was heavily bombed on a number of occasions and aircraft production at Metropolitan-Vickers was disrupted for a short time as recorded in the previous chapter.

Later in 1941 it was realised that the seven-day working week and long hours were making it impossible for even the most ardent of churchgoers to attend any kind of service, so the Christian Fellowship was formed and that organisation continues to this day at both Chadderton and Woodford.

The Avro Anson had provided splendid service for Coastal Command, but was now being replaced by the more modern Lockheed Hudson. It was an Anson which recorded the RAF's first attack on a U-boat just three days after the war had started and a number of similar actions followed. One action which is worth recording was when three Ansons of No. 500 Squadron were attacked by nine Messerschmitt Bf.109 fighters while flying over the Straits of Dover on 5 June 1940. Amazingly, the Anson gunners shot down two 109s, damaged a third and drove off the others. They also added to their score a Dornier 18 flying-boat, a Heinkel III bomber, a Messerschmitt Bf.110 fighter and a Heinkel 115 seaplane. Not a bad total for an aeroplane which was already obsolescent at the outbreak of World War Two.

Even in the Anson's early days the possibility of a trainer version was an interesting prospect and with war looming the aircraft was ordered for that purpose. On 18 December 1939 an agreement was signed which became known as the British Commonwealth Air Training Plan which would eventually require training aircraft of all types. Multi-engined type training for pilots had taken place in the RAF from as early as 1936 with some Ansons being used by the Flying Training Schools, but the new plan would require large numbers of Ansons to be used mainly in Australia, Canada, New Zealand, South Africa and Southern Rhodesia. The largest number of Ansons went to Canada with a total of 1,528 machines being

This is the very last shot in the sequence of historic photographs of an aircraft which had almost 11,000 predecessors. Jimmy Orrell banks the Anson away from the camera aeroplane before landing back at Woodford.

shipped over. Of this number, 223 were sent without engines because of the shortage of Cheetahs in England and many were fitted with the American Wright Whirlwind or Jacobs engines. A further 1,400 were built in Canada by five different companies and of these, fifty were delivered to the USAAF with the designation AT-20.

The 'Faithful Annie' as it became known to the thousands of aircrew who trained on the aeroplane all of whom, without exception, enjoyed flying in the Anson. The only real complaint against the aeroplane was that some poor chap had to turn a handle up to 174 times in order to wind up the undercarriage and many crew members were much relieved when later models were equipped with an hydraulic retraction system. However, one feature of the undercarriage which crews did like was that Chadwick had designed the aeroplane so that only half of the wheels went into the engine nacelle upon retraction and the occasional belly-landing usually only resulted in damage to the propellers as the machine would roll along on its still retracted wheels!

In all there were twenty-two different versions of the Anson with civil aircraft going into airline service after the war on some of the feeder routes. The Anson continued to be produced for the RAF until 1952 when, seventeen years after the start of production, the 10,996th of the type was signed off by test pilot Jimmy Orrell on 27 May 1952. The aircraft was quoted as being the 11,020th Anson and this figure has been widely used, but it was later found that in the final total one batch of twenty-four aircraft had been counted twice!

In February 1943, Roy Chadwick showed remarkable foresight when he was interviewed by the Air Correspondent of the *Manchester Evening News* regarding post-war aviation,

'I am convinced that this country should immediately devote some of its design and development staff to producing a very large civil aeroplane, capable of carrying passengers in comfort and security over great distance, such as London to New York.

'It is obvious that the world will be completely

---

The biggest event for Avro in 1952 was, of course, the first flight of the Type 698 which was soon to become known as the Vulcan.

covered by a network of civil airways and that these will play a most important part in the commerce and travel of the future.

'We shall be in severe competition with foreign countries in this connection and it behoves us to be prepared, as far as the concentration of our energies on the war effort permits.

'Fortunately, much of the work which has been done in developing war aeroplanes can be utilised in the design and construction of civil aircraft.'

Both Chadwick and Dobson went on to tell the newspaper that Great Britain must in future maintain a strong, well equipped and well trained Royal Air Force after the war rather than the poor attitude towards the services which prevailed between the two wars.

When this interview was published an aeroplane which was to play a part in civil air transport after the war, was already flying. This was the Avro York which Chadwick had started designing late in 1941 with the first drawings being passed to Chadderton's experimental department in February 1942. This aircraft had a new square section fuselage mated to Lancaster wings and tail with the York's first flight being made from Ringway with Sam Brown at the controls on 5 July, 1942.

# CHAPTER 11

# The Lancaster and its Derivatives

'Lancasters and more Lancasters' was the cry from the Air Ministry and with the required production rate being increased the 'Lancaster Group' was formed. The group consisted of Avro, Armstrong Whitworth, Austin Motors, Metropolitan-Vickers and Vickers at Castle Bromwich and Chester. With these factories in full swing, Rolls-Royce was having great difficulty in producing enough Merlin engines and Roy Chadwick came up with the design of the Lancaster Mk II which would use the Bristol Hercules radial engine. The original design of the Merlin-powered Lancaster proved to be the perfect combination, because although the four Hercules had 1,480 hp more than the Merlin engined machines, the maximum speed (loaded) of 260 mph was just the same with Lancaster Mk I having a greater range.

The magnificent Merlin began to be produced in the United States by Packard Motors Incorporated and the American-engined Lancasters became Mk IIIs. With British and American Merlins being fully interchangeable Lancasters Mk I and Mk. III were able to come off the same production line.

The Packard Merlins were also supplied to Victory Aircraft in Canada which was established to produce the Lancaster in Canada as the Mk X. The company had been formed at Malton, Toronto by the National Steel Corporation and manufacture had commenced under the guidance of Alfred Sewart, a young Manchester engineer who would eventually rise to works manager at Chadderton and, later, Production Director.

Lancaster production could not have continued without the contribution of many small firms who were involved in a great variety of component manufacture. In 1944 the total labour force involved in building Lancasters was over 40,000 and production was averaging 150 per month. By the war's end the Chadderton factory had turned out 3,050 Lancasters and Metropolitan-Vickers a further 1,051. Woodford completed the assembly of the combined total from the two factories of 4,101 aircraft. Production from other plants, including 430 from Canada, made a grand total of 7,377 Lancasters built.

The Lancaster was an outstanding aircraft and perhaps Roy Chadwick's greatest design achievement. It featured in some of the most daring raids of the war including the famous attack on the Ruhr Dams, the daylight attack on Augsburg and the sinking of the giant German battleship *Tirpitz*. The Lancaster was the first aircraft to carry an 8,000 lb bomb and the only aircraft ever to carry a 12,000 lb 'Tallboy' bomb. The fantastic load-carrying capability was further demonstrated when Lancasters delivered the massive 22,000 lb 'Grand Slam' and it was a tribute to the design that all of these loads were carried without major modifications to the airframe.

Lancasters delivered two-thirds of the total tonnage of bombs dropped by the Royal Air Force from mid-1942 with 608,612 tons of high explosive or enough to fill a freight train about 345 miles long. Lancasters also delivered 51,513,106 incendiary bombs! Averaging four tons of bombs per aircraft, this meant over 150,000 sorties consuming more than 228 million gallons of fuel. The Lancaster was indeed a legend!

On 26 March 1942 Avro had a Royal Visit when their Majesties King George VI and Queen Elizabeth toured the production lines at Yeadon. Anson manufacture was well under way and Lancaster production had commenced there just two months before. Their Majesties spent a great deal of the visit just chatting to the workers, but before leaving for another engagement, they saw the first two completed Lancasters from the new factory and christened them *George* and *Elizabeth*. After delivery to the RAF both of these aircraft

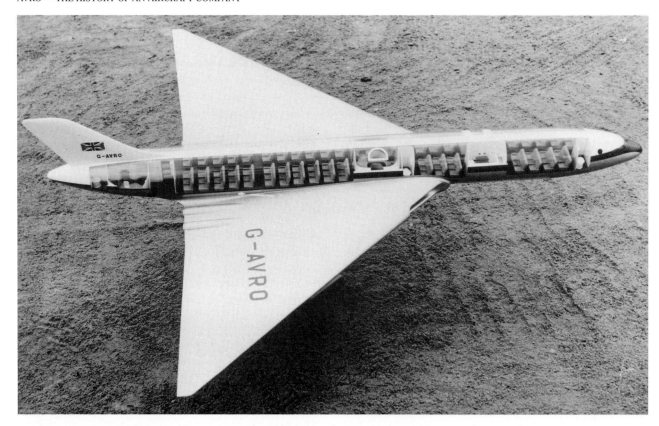

Details of the Avro Atlantic airliner were released in December 1952. Based on the 698 the aircraft was futuristic in appearance, but its economics were not good enough to tempt the airlines. The model in the photograph is still in existence and is preserved at Woodford.

took part in numerous attacks before, sadly, *George* was lost in a crash during a landing at Waddington in August 1942 while *Elizabeth* was destroyed by fire on the ground at Woodhall Spa in the following December.

Dobson and Chadwick were again Royal guides when their Majesties visited Woodford during a tour of the North-West on 19 November 1942. It was then that the Queen said to the Avro chief designer, 'Tell me, Mr Chadwick, how do you manage to design such huge and complex aeroplanes such as these?' Chadwick, quick as a flash, replied, 'Well, Mam, you don't have to be crazy, but it helps!' With that, both the King and Queen laughed heartily.

In 1940 it was decided by Avro to establish a repair depot well away from the possible bombing of a site near the production facility in Manchester.

The development of the Avro Repair Organisation received great impetus as a result of the necessity to establish close links between units of the rapidly expanding Bomber Command and the Avro factories.

As the Avro Manchester went into service a central headquarters was established at Bracebridge Heath near Lincoln which, in actual fact, was only 500 yards from the RAF station at Waddington. When the Lancaster arrived the Repair Organisation expanded to Langar in Nottinghamshire and was opened in September 1942 to cope with the rebuilding of badly damaged aircraft.

As the factories developed so too did the outworking repair parties and an outworking organisation was set up covering the whole of the country. For long periods these parties, known as CWPs (Contractors Working Parties) were putting more than thirty aircraft back into operational service every week. The Avro CWP were called into action for No. 617 Squadron, the famous 'Dam Busters' as before the actual raid their Lancasters were being damaged in practice while the crews were learning to drop the weapon correctly. In the days leading up to the attack the Avro team worked night and day to complete certain modifications to the aircraft.

At the end of hostilities more than 4,000 repaired aircraft, including some which could have been written-off, returned to service.

In post-war years the Avro Repair Organisation continued in the repair task, although modifications to service aircraft became their main priority with many being converted to overseas customer's needs or adapted as 'Flying Test Beds'. The site at Langar closed just twenty-six years after it was established, but the Bracebridge Heath facility, continued well into the days of British Aerospace before it too was eventually closed.

The Avro York was now proving to be a reliable aeroplane with its directional problems being solved by Chadwick. This problem arose from using the Lancaster twin-finned tail arrangement on the first two prototypes. The designer flew with Sam Brown on the second flight to assess the problem which the chief test pilot had reported. The change in the fuselage area as compared with the Lancaster was at the root of the trouble and the addition of a central fin cured the fault.

The Ministry of Aircraft Production had informed Avro that four prototypes of the York were to be completed, but also specified that two of these should be powered by the Bristol Hercules as opposed to the original Merlin engines. The fitment would be the same as for the Lancaster Mk II.

On 29 May 1942 the MAP instructed Avro to fit each of the four prototypes in a different configuration, but with interchangeable equipment. The variants would be a freighter, paratroop aircraft, a passenger transport and a troop-carrier. Paratroop dropping trials proved to be unsuccessful, but in the other roles the York could be extremely useful.

TOP RIGHT:
The beautiful lines of the Avro 707A are evident in this shot from March 1953. This aircraft can still be seen in the Manchester Museum of Science and Industry.

RIGHT:
The second prototype Vulcan returns to the Woodford flight sheds after its maiden flight on 3 September 1953. The first aeroplane can be seen in the distance.

It was, however, in the VIP role that the aircraft won most of its wartime praise. The third prototype was converted for use of the King and the Prime Minister and it was with the latter that it achieved fame. Named *Ascalon* the York carried Winston Churchill and many of his cabinet ministers on numerous overseas trips for war conferences in Moscow, Yalta and Teheran. The King did use the aeroplane for his tour of North Africa during 1943.

Following the completion of service trials, Avro was awarded a contract for 200 Yorks and it was the third production aircraft which was also fitted with the VIP configuration, this time, for Lord Louis Mountbatten, who was Commander-in-Chief of the South East Asia Command. Lord Louis used the aeroplane extensively and sent a personal letter of thanks to 'the workers who built this splendid aeroplane'. Other war leaders who had a

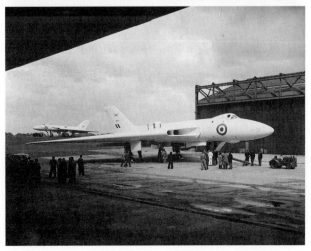

York at their disposal were the Duke of Gloucester, the Governor-General of Australia and also the famous South African, Field Marshal Smuts with the latter aircraft eventually seeing airline service in that country after being bought by Tropic Airways.

Eventually 250 Yorks were built and, in their true role as a freighter, they were probably best known for their outstanding contribution in the Berlin Air Lift when the Russians blockaded that city and the only supply route was by air. This extensive operation by both the Royal Air Force and the United States Air Force was an incredible feat of organisation and it was an Avro York which delivered the 100,000th ton of supplies to the city on 17 December 1948. Operation *Plainfare,* as the Berlin Air Lift was codenamed, brought welcome relief to the citizens with the forty Avro Yorks used by the RAF alone carrying a total of 230,000 tons in 29,000 return flights by the end of the operation. The blockade was officially lifted at one minute past midnight on 11 May 1949 after nearly eleven months, but the air lift continued until the following October in order to build up stocks in Berlin. Other Avro aircraft played an important part in the air lift including Tudors, Lancastrians and Lancasters, all flown by civil operators, but it was the RAF Yorks which carried the bulk of the British contribution.

Yorks remained in civilian service until the early 1960s providing the operators with an excellent freighting capability and, for the devotees of aviation, that wonderful sound of four Merlins!

With the arrival of the jet age Avro was called upon in the development of the gas turbine engine, assisting with the redesign and modifications to Lancasters to act as test-beds for this new type of engine. This concept had been pioneered in Britain by Group Captain Frank (later Sir Frank) Whittle and although other countries had their own jet propulsion designs, none were as efficient and reliable as Britain's. Jet engines were for military use, but Roy Chadwick showed great interest in such propulsion as it was obvious that post-war commercial aircraft would use this type of power.

The large companies soon realised the potential of the jet engine and early in the war Rolls-Royce, Rover, de Havilland and Metropolitan-Vickers were each developing their own designs based on Whittle's early work. Even by the end of 1942 a Wellington bomber was used as a test-bed with a Rover W.2B engine mounted in the tail.

The Lancaster, with its larger size and four reliable engines, was an obvious choice of aircraft to act as a test-bed for tail mounted jet engines. As new production Lancasters were being delivered urgently to squadrons, the only aeroplane which could be released for test work was the original prototype and it was with this machine which was flown to the Armstrong Whitworth airfield at Baginton near Coventry to be modified for the task. The Lancaster was fitted with a Metrovick F.2/1 turbojet mounted in the rear fuselage with the jet-pipe extending from where the rear gunner's turret would normally be.

The aircraft first flew in this configuration on 29 June 1943 piloted by Avro chief test pilot Sam Brown. It was with great resolution that Brown flew the Lancaster as only a few days before he had been informed that his son Alan had been killed in action. Alan, a pilot, had completed his tour of operations, but volunteered to stand in for an aircraft captain who had been taken ill and, sadly, the aeroplane was shot down with the whole crew being killed. Bill Thorn offered to make the test flight in Brown's place, but the latter was determined to continue with the planned flight.

At later stages of the war and in the early post-war years Lancasters did much valuable work acting as test-beds for a variety of jet and turboprop engines as well as many other areas of research including flight refuelling, glider towing, aerodynamics and arrested landings, to name but a few.

Britain was still at war when a plan was devised for an aircraft to do some pioneering of long distance air routes as a navigation exercise. The unit selected for this flight was, quite naturally, the Empire Air Navigation School based at Shawbury in Shropshire. A Lancaster was flown to the Avro repair depot at Waddington and with the Bracebridge Heath team working for nine full days, the aircraft was completely overhauled, its paint stripped off down to the natural metal and then highly polished. Faired-in nose and tail cones were fitted as was a strengthened undercarriage and extra fuel tanks. The machine was flown back to Shawbury and, after being given the name *Aries,* the Lancaster departed for its record flight. It was the first British service aeroplane to

Farnborough 1953 was dominated by Avro with the large crowds being delighted by the magnificent delta formation of the two Vulcan prototypes with four Avro 707s alongside.

circumnavigate the earth flying via Canada, United States, New Zealand, Australia, Ceylon, Aden, Egypt and Malta, before arriving back at its base on 14 December 1944 after a total of 41,454 miles. Its route, of course, had to be greatly extended to miss the war zones.

Morale was never a problem with the workers as the knowledge that they were building aeroplanes for the war effort, including the RAF's greatest bomber, was never far away. The factories were visited by a variety of VIPs with Royal tours always being the highlight and many of the workers were honoured by being introduced to their Majesties.

Among the famous RAF visitors were Wing Commander Guy Gibson, VC after the daring raid on the German dams; Squadron Leader John Nettleton, VC who led an equally daring attack on Augsburg and Flight Lieut Bill Reid, VC who, though badly wounded, had brought his crippled Lancaster back to England in order to save the lives of other wounded crew members. All of these officers were accompanied by their crews. The BBC's 'Worker's Playtime' was broadcast from the plants on a number of occasions and exhibitions of boxing and wrestling were always entertaining for the workers, especially when some of their own number took part. A visit by a Russian delegation is well remembered if only for the fact that one rather burly Russian lady proceeded to kiss everyone in sight!

Perhaps the one visitor who was remembered with most affection was the United States'

President Roosevelt's wife Eleanor. The American First Lady showed genuine interest in all aspects of the work and spoke at length to many of the workers. Mrs Roosevelt loved her apple pie dessert so much that she asked to see Woodford's canteen manageress for the recipe, carefully placing the piece of paper on which it was written into her notebook.

Even in 1943 Avro had begun planning a civil airliner capable of flying the North Atlantic, which would become known as the Tudor, but in the interim Chadwick had been adapting the Lancaster to become Britain's first post-war 'airliner' and this aeroplane was named the Lancastrian.

The end of the war would see a battle for air supremacy, this time in the field of air transport. The two major contestants would be Great Britain and the United States and it was the Americans who already had a distinct advantage. The USA had been able to develop a number of purpose designed transport aircraft and it would only be a short step to convert these into first class passenger aeroplanes. This proved to be the case when the Lockheed C-69 of the USAAF became the Constellation that was so familiar on the world's

air routes. The Douglas DC-4 evolved from the C-54 Skymaster and, the most famous of all, the pre-war DC-3 design was improved during wartime and produced in great numbers as the C-47, before it reverted to its civil role as the DC-3. The Dakota, as this aeroplane was known in Britain, did much fine work to re-establish civil flying around the globe.

The Avro Lancastrian design which came straight from the Lancaster as the first of the airliner types was a modification of the early production Lancaster which had flown to Canada to assist Victory Aircraft with the tooling for their own production line. This aircraft was

A Shackleton MR.2 equipped with an airborne lifeboat also took part in the 1953 Farnborough Show. The delta formation did not get all of the glory as Johnny Baker amazed the spectators by flying the Shackleton on just one engine.

Accidents will happen! There were a few red faces when this Lancaster, destined for the French Navy, rolled back down the notorious slope at Woodford's flight sheds and into a newly overhauled Anson in January 1954.

demilitarised with all gun turrets removed and with fairings over the nose and tail positions. The work was done at Victory Aircraft, but after a number of experimental flights across the Atlantic, the Lancaster was flown back to Avro's at Ringway where it was fully converted to the civil role. The first true Lancastrians were laid down by Avro in 1944. BOAC received their first Lancastrian on 18 February 1945 when it left Woodford for Croydon and completed a number of trials at Hurn near Bournemouth before making a record-breaking flight in April 1945 to Auckland, New Zealand in just three and a half days, piloted by Captain R.G. Buck. The Lancastrian was, at that time, the only British commercial aeroplane with the capability of flying the South Atlantic and the BOAC chief pilot, Captain O.P. Jones, the joyriding Avro 504 pilot of the 1920s, flew one to Buenos Aires on 5 October, 1945. The machine then went over the Andes to Santiago, Chile before flying on to Lima, Peru. This flight led to British South American Airways (BSAA) placing an order for six Lancastrians.

Besides civilian operators both home and

overseas, the Lancastrian equipped RAF Transport Command. One interesting customer was QANTAS, who had vowed never to buy anything again from the company after the Avro 547 fiasco twenty-five years earlier. However, it was pointed out by the Australians that they actually bought the aircraft from BOAC and not Avro! The Lancastrians had commenced scheduled service from England to Australia by BOAC on 31 May, 1945, but the airline declared them surplus as the Lockheed Constellations began to arrive from the United States for service with BOAC. Production of the Lancastrian ceased at the end of 1946 as the 82nd, and last of the type, left Woodford. Like the Lancaster, the Lancastrian was extensively used for testing and development of both jet and turboprop engines. Lancastrians also should not be forgotten for their fine contribution during the Berlin Air Lift.

The Lancastrian section would not be complete without a note on the loss of Jack Dobson in a BOAC aircraft which was lost without trace in the sea north of the Cocos Islands on 24 March 1946. Jack, eldest son of the Avro managing director, was on his way to Australia to organise production of the Avro Lincoln by the Government Aircraft Factory at Fisherman's Bend in Victoria and his death was a great blow to the Dobson family. It was also a blow to the company as Jack was a popular young man with great potential and an obvious candidate to eventually succeed his father.

In 1943 the Air Ministry had issued Specification B.14/43 for a long-range bomber which could replace the Lancaster. The Japanese war in the Far East had brought new problems and the development of a new bomber for the RAF to operate in the Pacific theatre was a pressing requirement. This larger machine designed by Avro was known in the factory as the Lancaster Mk IV with a considerable number of changes from the earlier machine. There was greater engine power, improved performance, modified fuselage and redesigned wings. Although it looked like a large Lancaster, it was a completely new type.

Sam Brown was on hand to fly the Avro Lincoln, as the new bomber had been named, from Ringway on 9 July 1944. The aircraft had all of the handling qualities of the Lancaster, but it came too late to see action and as World War Two ended orders for the Lincoln were cut drastically, but eventually over 600 were built in Britain and Australia and some saw service with the RAF until 1963.

The Lincoln served with Bomber Command making many overseas flights on goodwill tours, but the aircraft did see action in Malaya when both British and Australian versions attacked the Communist terrorists and RAF Lincolns were also used in anger against the Mau Mau in Kenya during 1953.

The Shackleton MR.3 was a departure from the earlier models as it had a tricycle undercarriage and wing tip fuel tanks. The long nose probe on the prototype was a yawmeter used on the aerodynamic flight tests.

The Empire Air Navigation School at Shawbury replaced its famous Lancaster *Aries* with a Lincoln which became *Aries II* being fitted with Lancastrian-type nose and tail fairings. The Lincoln *Aries III* was later added to the fleet to continue the EANS's excellent navigation development and mapping work.

As with the Lancaster and Lancastrian, the Avro Lincoln was found to be an excellent aircraft for the flight testing of new engines. Lincolns were also used for aerodynamic and de-icing research.

In the early days of the Lincoln flight testing the work of piloting the machine was being shared between Sam Brown, Bill Thorn and Jimmy Orrell, the latter was an ex-RAF pilot who joined Avro in 1934 as a draughtsman, but then qualified as a test pilot. However, in February 1935 he joined Imperial Airways, flying as a Captain on a variety of types. In April 1941 he was posted to BOAC and piloted Lockheed Hudsons on a number of daring flights to neutral Sweden. Orrell's contract with Imperial Airways ended in March 1942 and it was Sam Brown who persuaded him to return to Avro, which he did in April 1942. As Lancasters were coming off the Woodford assembly line at the rate of seven per day there was plenty of test flying for all the pilots and Jimmy Orrell alone tested 900 different Lancasters!

The team of test pilots and flight engineers were a very close knit group who worked extremely hard with the sheer volume of aircraft being produced. The situation was eased when a number of Bomber Command pilots were allowed to assist the Avro team.

The team was hit hard in the afternoon of 11 September 1944 when Woodford received a

telephone call stating that a four-engined bomber had crashed near the village of Siddington, which was about nine miles south-west of the airfield. The only Lancaster on test at that time was a Mk III being flown by Syd Gleave with his engineer Harry Barnes. Upon hearing this news, Woodford Air Traffic Control tried to contact Gleave without success and Sam Brown and group chief inspector, 'Sandy' Jack, drove to the scene of the accident. The sight that met them was incredible as the aircraft had crashed into the top of a small hill in what must have been a vertical dive as the crater made was practically the front view of the bomber. One exercise in the Lancaster flight test programme was that every tenth aeroplane would be dived at 375 mph and as this aeroplane was that number, Gleave would be carrying out that test. Chadwick, quite naturally, was upset and concerned, putting the trusty Harold Rogerson in full charge of the company's investigation team. Because of the great impact there were very few clues to the cause of the accident, but it was obvious that the elevators were in some way to blame. Just one week later some small children playing a mile away from the crash site found a piece of the aeroplane which proved to be a fuel-jettison pipe. It was established that during the pull-out from the dive the pipe could have detached from the wing and stripped the covering from the elevator. Whatever the cause, Woodford had lost two popular members of the flight test team in the only accident involving a Lancaster in over 4,000 test flights of the type from the airfield.

The nearest thing to an accident at Woodford came when Squadron Leader Ken Cook's Lancaster was taking off for a test flight. Travelling down the runway with the tail wheel just off the ground, Cook saw a Manchester Corporation double-decker bus driving across the runway having completely ignore the red light controlling the traffic flow across the airfield. There was no way in which the Lancaster could miss the bus, but Cook pulled back as hard as he could and then chopped the throttles. The aeroplane hopped over the vehicle and landed on the other side of it and looking back he could see that Manchester Corporation had just gained a single deck bus as one of the Lancaster's main wheels had taken the roof off! Luckily, the bus was empty and the driver only shocked, but it took quite a while to calm

In 1955 a Rolls-Royce Avon engine was fitted under the centre fuselage of this Ashton 3. Forward of the engine can be seen water spray equipment to test intake icing for the Avon.

down the conductress. Cook praised his engineer Don Wilson for closing the throttles slowly allowing the Lancaster to jump the bus and then settle gently on the ground afterwards!

Ken Cook had joined the Avro flight test team to assist with Lancaster testing after completing a tour of operations with Bomber Command. After completing his RAF service Ken Cook joined Avro permanently, test flying Lancasters, Yorks and Tudors before retiring from flying and taking up the post of Air Traffic Control Manager, a position he held until his retirement from the company in 1962.

The great shadow factory at Yeadon was on the north side of the airfield with some of the facility being underground. The first production task was to be the Armstrong Whitworth Albemarle twin-engined transport, but before manufacture could commence the programme was withdrawn because of a major modification to the wing. In October 1940 the factory began work on the Hawker Tornado, a new fighter powered by a Rolls-Royce Vulture engine. One aircraft was completed and flown at Woodford on 29 August, 1941, but the failure of the Vulture engine, as in the

Avro Manchester, forced the fighter to be cancelled. Four other Tornados were in various stages of completion at Yeadon, but these were dismantled and sent to Hawker where they were used in early production models of the Hawker Typhoon.

The first Anson built at Yeadon was flown in June 1941 and by January 1942 twelve Ansons were rolling of the production lines every week. Work on the Avro Lancaster started in January 1942 and continued until after the war's end with a peak month for production being in January 1945 when forty-four of these great four-engined bombers were delivered. Published figures for Yeadon production has varied, but the Avro statistics from commencement of production in June 1941 until the surrender of the Japanese on 14 August 1945 state that production was; 3,881 Ansons, 608 Lancasters, five Tornadoes and two Lincolns. Peak deliveries for the Anson were in the months of October and November 1943 and January, February and March 1944 when 135 of the type were delivered in each of those months. Lancasters, Ansons, Lincolns and Yorks continued to be produced after the war ended, albeit at a slower rate and the build programme was gradually run down until the Yeadon factory closed in November 1946. The staff from Chadderton and Woodford seconded to Yeadon returned to their respective sites and some Yeadon design staff relocated to Chadderton.

RIGHT:
The sleek Avro 720 mixed jet and rocket powered interceptor fighter in Chadderton's experimental department in 1956. The aircraft was in an advanced stage of completion when development was cancelled in government economy cuts.

BELOW:
Chadderton's massive design office in 1957. The 450 draughtsmen moved to Woodford in the mid 1960s with this large area now been partitioned into a number of sections including the site's excellent computer room.

# CHAPTER 12

# The Tudor

The aircraft designed specifically for the North Atlantic route, the Avro Tudor, was ordered in prototype form by the Air Ministry to their Specification 29/43 in September 1944. The first machine, of the two prototypes ordered, made its initial flight from Ringway on 14 June 1945 piloted by Bill Thorn and Jimmy Orrell.

Sam Brown had been looking forward to flying this new airliner on its maiden trip, but a regular medical check a week earlier had showed that he had high blood pressure and medical officer Doctor George Taylor prevented him from flying. Brown was 'grounded' and given the position of flight test manager while Bill Thorn was appointed chief test pilot. Not being able to fly was a great disappointment to Brown and he soon retired to live in Kent. In April 1953 Sam Brown collapsed and died soon afterwards. Jimmy Orrell and Dobson's assistant Jimmy Kay represented the company at Brown's funeral, but it was also attended by many of his test pilot friends and others in British aviation. Jimmy Kay was a bright young man who eventually succeeded Roy Dobson as managing director of A.V. Roe & Company Limited.

In the New Year's Honours for 1945, Roy Dobson received a knighthood, but much to everyone's surprise there was no mention of Roy Chadwick! Chadwick had received the CBE in 1943 for his contribution to the Dam Buster's attack and many in the aviation world felt and expected, that Chadwick should have been knighted. He certainly deserved it and as the other partner in the Lancaster duo it was thought to be a certainty!

The prototype Tudor was awaiting flight tests on 7 May 1945 when Germany signed unconditional surrender and on the following day in the House of Commons, the Prime Minister Winston Churchill announced the surrender and proclaimed it Victory in Europe (VE) Day.

Avro received an order from BOAC initially for fourteen Tudors and this was increased to twenty as an additional six were required by BSAA. The second prototype Tudor 1 made its first flight when it took off from Woodford with Bill Thorn at the controls. Thorn and Orrell shared the flying of the Tudors and when the first production aeroplane joined the test programme it was Orrell who was pilot on its maiden flight on 12 January, 1946.

The Ministry of Supply's brief to Chadwick was for the aircraft to have Transatlantic range, but to utilise as many Lincoln components as possible. This severely restricted the designer and BOAC also resented the restrictions placed upon the Tudor. The aeroplane had a number of innovations including fully pressurised fuselage and it was the first machine built in Britain with such comfort for its passengers.

The flight testing was not going well with the aeroplane being directionally unstable and having longitudinal problems in fast level flight. There was bad buffeting in the stall followed by a nasty nose drop and the general performance of the

A model of the Avro 739 low level strike aircraft for Woodford's wind tunnel. The type did not proceed beyond the project stage.

Tudor 1 was well below estimates in a number of areas. To the public the aircraft was performing well and credence was given to this by the old adage, 'If it looks right it is right'. Well, the Tudor was a beautiful machine and certainly looked right, but the test pilot's results were telling a different story.

The BOAC observers were not satisfied and the airline ignored the Ministry altogether and demanded more than 300 modifications to the Tudor. Chadwick was a constant visitor to Woodford flight sheds and at the end of a long tiring day there, he would still drive the sixteen miles back to his office at Chadderton to work out the problems and re-check his calculations. He solved the stability problems by adding to the fin area and shielding the rudder, with the tailplane span being increased to forty feet.

During the final design conference held on 12–13 March 1946 this list of modifications required by BOAC was steadily growing as the airline tabled 343 changes. Some of these seemed impossible to incorporate while others were small and niggling as the airline seemed determined to find fault with the Tudor. As the airline team got around to what appeared to be needless alterations to the decor, the normally placid Chadwick thumped the table and demanded, 'Why the hell couldn't you specify what you want in the first place?'

The Tudor production programme was in total disorder with Avro trying to incorporate the airline's changes and endless disagreements, delays and disruptions made the whole thing a fiasco. The performance was still a source of anxiety for Avro with trials at Boscombe Down and tropical tests in Nairobi, Kenya in December 1946 proving unsatisfactory.

The fourth production Tudor 1 was officially handed over to BOAC at a ceremony at London Airport when the then Princess Elizabeth christened the aircraft *Elizabeth of England*. The date of the ceremony was 21 January 1947, but less than three months later the airline decided that even the much modified aircraft would not be suitable for their requirements and the order for the Tudors was cancelled on 11 April 1947.

Four Tudor 1s for BSAA were converted to Mk 4s with Arabic style of mark numbers replacing the Roman-type. The Mk 4 had the forward fuselage lengthened by six feet and the passenger capacity increased from twenty-eight to thirty-two. This airline eventually had six Tudor 4s and two Tudor 1s, but the aeroplane's reputation suffered again when BSAA lost *Star Tiger* north east of Bermuda on 30 January 1948 followed by *Star Ariel* somewhere between Bermuda and Jamaica on 17 January 1949 with both losses remaining a mystery. The first of these was on a flight from Santa Maria in the Azores to Bermuda carrying a crew of six and twenty-five passengers including Air Marshal Sir Arthur Coningham. A message from *Star Tiger* to Bermuda asked for a bearing and this was given and acknowledged by the aircraft. Nothing further was ever seen or heard from the Tudor. No abnormal weather conditions were reported. On 2 February 1948 all Tudor 4s were grounded pending investigation, but the aircraft were cleared and flying resumed. The second accident was similar to the first as *Star Ariel* was carrying seven crew members and thirteen passengers when the machine disappeared. The aircraft had sent a radio message early in the afternoon on a flight from Bermuda to Jamaica, but was not heard from again. Once again there were no abnormal weather conditions.

On 1 March 1949 it was announced in the House of Commons that the Minister of Civil Aviation had decided the Tudor 4s should not continue to be used for passenger carrying but, subject to certain modifications, it would be possible to use them for freight carrying.

Tudors in the freighter role had proved their worth in the Berlin Air Lift and the aircraft received a new lease of life when a number were bought by Aviation Traders Limited of Stansted and Southend who converted them into excellent cargo aircraft. The aircraft was renamed the Avro Super Trader and continued in service until 1959.

When the original Tudor specification was issued a further requirement was outlined, this time for a sixty-seat airliner for BOAC. This aircraft would be similar to the Tudor 1, but have a shorter range. Chadwick's answer was the Tudor 2 which used all the main components of the Mk 1, but had a fuselage which was over forty feet longer in order to accommodate the extra passengers.

Once again, two prototypes were ordered with the first of these being flown from Woodford on 10 March 1946 by Bill Thorn and Jimmy Orrell for just thirty minutes before they returned to the airfield.

Another project under development was the Avro 730 supersonic bomber. The Type 731 was a three-eighths scale aircraft designed to test canard configuration of the 730. A test rig was in use at Woodford during 1957, but once again, economy measures caused both projects to be abandoned.

Thorn reported to Chadwick that the aeroplane was not up to scratch.

The airlines showed a great deal of interest with BOAC, QANTAS and South African Airways (SAA) ordering a total of seventy-nine of this version. The old handling problems still remained and the performance suffered badly through the great increase in weight and the orders were reduced drastically.

The first production Mk 2 appeared with Bristol Hercules radial engines replacing the Merlins and was redesignated the Mk 7. Bill Thorn took it on its first flight on 17 April 1947, but was not greatly impressed.

Probably the greatest tragedy to hit Avro occurred on 23 August 1947. The prototype Tudor 2 had been due to fly on the previous evening, but a snag had developed and the flight was postponed until the following morning. The night shift worked on the aircraft and found that the problem entailed the disconnecting of the ailerons. After the fault was rectified the ailerons were reconnected and the aeroplane cleared for flight. The flying controls had been checked, but no one noticed that they were incorrect!

In the afternoon of 22 August, Jimmy Orrell was flight testing a production Tudor 1 and was over the Lake District when Bill Thorn called him on the radio to check if he could fly the Tudor 2 the next morning. The 23rd was Saturday and Orrell was to take part in a golf match, but said to Thorn that he would toss him for it. Bill Thorn must have tossed a coin immediately, because he came back on the radio to say that he had lost the gamble and that he (Thorn) would fly the aeroplane.

As the delay had put the flight to a Saturday, Bill Thorn had slight difficulty in getting a crew together as his staff were either already scheduled to fly in other machines or they were off for the weekend. Thorn's co-pilot was David Wilson, an ex-RAF Squadron Leader who had joined the team and Eddie Talbot, the engineer who was on the flight because he lived locally and was called out to join the flight. The radio operator was John Webster, who was the senior operator and due to fly on the aircraft on the previous afternoon.

As it was the weekend Roy Dobson and Roy Chadwick, who was now technical director, asked if they could join the flight. Also going along for a 'jolly' was Stuart Davies who had succeeded Chadwick as chief designer.

All were on board and Bill Thorn was preparing to start engines as someone ran out of the offices to inform Sir Roy that there was an urgent telephone call for him. The call was long and it was decided that the aeroplane should go without him.

The giant Tudor taxied out and after his checks Thorn began his take-off run towards the Poynton end of the runway. As the aircraft began to lift off and bank to starboard the wing-tip hit the ground causing the aircraft to cartwheel over and over before coming to rest in a pond near Shirfold Farm with its back broken and the front of the Tudor completely demolished. Rescuers quickly ran to the scene, but it was too late for Roy Chadwick, arguably the world's greatest aircraft designer, who was thrown out as the fuselage split, fracturing his skull on a tree.

Lost too were Avro's great chief test pilot Bill Thorn and his colleague David Wilson, who had survived more than seventy operations during the war. It was with great sadness that it was discovered that both of these pilots were only stunned in the actual crash, but drowned in the pond while still strapped in their seats. Radio operator John Webster also died from a fractured skull.

Thankfully, Stuart Davies did survive and climbed out of the shattered fuselage with a badly gashed head and other cuts. Amazingly, Eddie Talbot was rescued from the pond by his own father, who was a supervisor at the Woodford Flight Sheds and he was ably assisted by Jack Beatty, an Avro flight engineer who was off that day and was buying eggs at a nearby farm when

Woodford's new assembly area is over one million square feet with three production lines each a quarter of a mile long after addition in 1957. A Vulcan and Valiant can be seen on the airfield.

he saw the crash in graphic detail.

The crash investigation found that the ailerons had been connected wrongly so that a sideways movement of the controls would have the complete opposite effect on the aeroplane. As Bill Thorn tried to correct the starboard wing drop he only made the situation worse as the aircraft was so near the ground he would only have a split second to assess the situation before the aircraft veered off the runway. He had chopped the throttles, but the take-off momentum carried the machine forward hitting some trees which wrecked the aeroplane before it came to rest in the pond.

It is known that Thorn tried the 'free and easy' movement of the controls before take-off, but from the flight deck he could not see the ailerons due to the long fuselage of the Tudor 2. He shouted,

Vulcan nose sections under construction in Chadderton's Bay 2 in 1958. This area is now used for the manufacture of rear fuselage units for the RJ Avroliner.

'ailerons' during the control wheel movement and a crew member in the back of the aeroplane confirmed their movement. What they could not know is which way he was moving the control column at the time.

Had the Tudor taken off straight and level for the climb and got to a reasonable height before starting to turn Bill Thorn would have certainly corrected the situation and, no doubt, would have landed safely. It was a cruel twist of fate that caused the accident, robbing the aviation world of some of its greatest talent.

Roy Chadwick's lifetime in aviation had produced some of the world's great aeroplanes and his death, at the age of fifty-four, cut short a career which could have produced even greater designs. He did, however, leave behind early

drawings and calculations for a delta-wing bomber which would become famous all over the world — the mighty Avro Vulcan.

Chadwick's death cast a great shadow over Avro and nowhere more so than in the drawing office at Chadderton where his team of designers were stunned to lose their leader. His office in the front corridor remained empty for many months and his internal telephone extension – 213 – was not used for even longer. (Note; thirty years later, in a telephone reshuffle at Chadderton, the author tried to get this number for himself, but to no avail!)

Luckily for Avro, a late telephone call saved Sir Roy from possible death and both he and survivor Stuart Davies were left to continue with the work in hand and take over designs Chadwick had initiated. Eddie Talbot spent two years recovering from his injuries, but did return to Avro.

In the years immediately after the war the one field in which Britain was supreme was the design and production of the gas turbine engine. During the war an open blueprint of the jet engine was passed to the United States together with assistance and advice from British scientists and, as recorded earlier, Avro assisted with such development by the use of Lancasters, Lancastrians and Lincolns for use as flying test-beds. Many years later an Avro Vulcan would be used as the test aircraft for the development of the Olympus engine for the supersonic Concorde.

The failure of the Tudor in its intended role was a great set-back and the tragedy at Woodford did not endear the aeroplane to many people. A number of Tudors on the production line at Chadderton were disposed of to R.J. Coley of Dunkinfield, Cheshire who was the local scrap metal merchant. It may be apocryphal, but it is said that Sir Roy went to the Tudor line and said, 'Scrap the bloody lot!'

The Tudor, however, did achieve fame when it became Britain's first four-jet transport aeroplane. The second prototype Tudor 1 had been converted to the longer Mk 4 and later still it was decided to fit the machine with four Rolls-Royce Nene jet engines paired in streamline nacelles. Flying for the first time on 6 September 1948 with Jimmy Orrell, now chief test pilot, at the controls the aircraft was designated Tudor Mk 8. It wore military markings and was displayed to the public at the Farnborough Show later that week. The aircraft was later used for various tests at Boscombe Down and Farnborough.

In the other versions of the Tudor design, two Mk 3s were built from Mk 1 airframes while the larger Mk 2 was used to produce six Tudor 5s with five of them serving with BSAA for some years. The Mk 6 was also based on the on the Tudor Mk 2 and the company received an order for six from Argentina, but they were never built. A freighter version designated the Avro 711A Trader was also a Mk 2 development, but was never built.

One person who always had faith in the Avro Tudor was Air Vice-Marshal D.C.T. Bennett, 'Pathfinder' Bennett as he was know to friends and colleagues after his wartime exploits with Bomber Command. As chief executive of BSAA, he fought long and hard against grounding the Tudor after the loss of *Star Tiger*, arguing that a number of new American airliners had also crashed and he felt that the Ministry of Civil Aviation was being over emotional about the loss and the almost

unanimous condemnation of the airliner. In later years he reflected that the de Havilland Comet airliner suffered as badly as the Tudor, but went on to become an excellent aircraft. After leaving BSAA Bennett was unemployed, but as the Berlin Air Lift was underway he raised money through the City of London and purchased a Tudor Mk 2 and also a Mk 5 to form the company Airflight Limited. With Don Bennett doing much of the flying work himself, the Tudors performed well and with others operated by BSAA they did great work on the Air Lift and much to vindicate Chadwick's design.

Don Bennett's flying skill and faith in the Tudor were severely tested in August 1948 while he was taking off from Wunstorf with the aircraft fully loaded with diesel oil. After checking the controls for free movement he began the take-off run, but he found the elevator was locked solid and only by his quick thinking was he able to get the aeroplane airborne, preventing a disaster by going off the end of the runway. He found that longitudinal control was obtained solely by the trim tabs. After four circuits of the airfield to get the feel of the aeroplane Bennett found the runway lights in the rain and mist of a gloomy night and made a perfect landing. It was later found that his flight engineer had not completely removed the elevator control locks and as the aircraft began to take-off they snapped back in position. Chadwick would have been delighted to know that his Tudor design had such a great champion.

After Roy Chadwick's death the Avro technical organisation received a new leader in William (later Sir William) Farren as technical director while Stuart Davies remained chief designer. Jimmy Orrell was confirmed as chief test pilot and Alex 'Sandy' Jack took over the technical services department. The experimental department which included construction at Chadderton and assembly and flight testing at Woodford was the responsibility of Alf Sewart. Under Davies in the design office were two old stagers in the shape of Harold Rogerson as chief technician and Jimmy Turner who was chief draughtsman. The former, of course, had joined Avro before World War One and he stayed with Avro at Manchester until 1953, when he was promoted to technical liaison manager for the Hawker Siddeley Group in London. He retired from there in 1956.

# CHAPTER 13

## The Mighty Vulcan

With the dawning of the atomic age in August 1945 it was obvious to military strategists that any future bomber capable of delivering a nuclear weapon would, ideally, be jet powered and of advanced design. The Royal Air Force requirement for such an aircraft was outlined in Specification B.35/46 which was issued to industry on New Year's Day 1947. Six companies including Avro were invited to tender.

The Avro design team under Roy Chadwick started initially with a conventional layout with swept wings, but by progressively shortening the fuselage and then removing the tailplane a delta-wing planform emerged. This was a bold step by Avro as little was known about delta aerodynamics at that time and the concept of developing a 'flying triangle' of such large proportions was a daunting prospect. However, by March 1947 Chadwick had made a firm decision to go ahead with this configuration.

Some of the early designs bore little resemblance to the aircraft which became familiar the world over, but by the time the tender, known as the Avro 698, was submitted to the Air Staff in May 1947 the triangle design had grown a nose with large engine intakes at each side.

Such were the advanced requirements of the specification, that the Air Staff wisely decided on an insurance design for an aeroplane of a more conventional nature. This aircraft became the Vickers Valiant which was the first generation V-Bomber.

The summer of 1947 saw the tender for the Avro 698 firmly in the hands of the Ministry of Supply, but the grievous loss of Roy Chadwick put the project in doubt. Avro felt that the Ministry might lose confidence in the design, but all was well with the proposal being accepted. Stuart Davies, who had now recovered from the accident took over the design leadership of the delta programme.

Research into delta-wing aircraft had also been conducted by the Royal Aircraft Establishment (RAE) at Farnborough and the combined results of this programme and those of the Avro team brought about a number of changes in the 698 design. The wing became thinner with the engines buried inside and the intakes built into the wing roots. The proposed wing-tip fins were deleted in favour of a large central fin with the whole aeroplane beginning to take the appearance which is so well known.

Avro received an order for two prototype 698s in January 1948 and work commenced immediately. To investigate the characteristics of the delta

In January 1959 Jimmy Kay, Avro general manager, was appointed to the board of Hawker Siddeley Aviation at the age of forty-four. The youngest ever accepted at that time.

design it was decided that a series of one third scale research aircraft would be built and the design for the Avro 707s started in May 1948.

The first Avro 707 was a fairly simple aeroplane with an unusual engine air intake built into the top of the fuselage behind the cockpit. To speed construction the first aircraft utilised the cockpit and nose-wheel leg of a Meteor and the main undercarriage of an Avro Athena trainer. The 707 was flown for the first time on 4 September 1949 by Avro test pilot S.E. 'Red' Esler. Esler was an RAF Flight Lieutenant who had come to Woodford in 1944 to assist with the test flying of Lancasters, but he had returned to his unit to complete another tour of operations before leaving the service with

the rank of Squadron Leader. At the war's end he returned to Woodford as a test pilot. After the maiden flight Esler flew the aeroplane a number of times on the following day as a sufficient number of flying hours had to be completed in order to qualify for inclusion in the Farnborough Air Show. He flew the little 707 to Farnborough on 6 September where it was exhibited in the Show's static aircraft park. Unfortunately, on 30

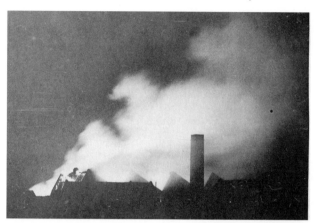

RIGHT:
The Chadderton factory at the height of the blaze in October 1959.

BELOW:
A massive clearance of the debris commenced almost immediately and the scale of the task is well illustrated here.

September 1949 the 707 crashed near Blackbushe in Hampshire during a test flight and Esler was killed.

Avro 707s of varying designs were flown and had contributed valuable research to the 698 programme before the bomber prototype took to the air on 30 August 1952 with R.J. 'Roly' Falk at the controls. Falk was an ex-Wing Commander and a very experienced RAF test pilot who had joined the Avro team in 1950 as superintendent of flying under Jimmy Orrell. Falk already had a tenuous connection with the company as he married Leysa Thorn, daughter of the late Bill Thorn.

Falk flew the Avro 698 to the SBAC Show at Farnborough on 2 September 1952 and the aircraft was without doubt the star of the Show. During the display he brought the aircraft in for a low pass with an orange-coloured Avro 707A off one wing while on the other flank was a blue Avro 707B and it was hard to realise that Falk was flying the big delta solo! After this show-stopping appearance the aircraft settled down to handling trials at Boscombe Down.

In December 1952 the name Vulcan had been chosen for the aircraft and Sir Roy Dobson announced it to the work force in his Christmas message. The name completed the trio of the RAF V-Bombers with the Vulcan joining the Handley Page Victor and the Vickers Valiant. The Victor had been one of the Vulcan's competitors for the Specification B.35/46 while the Valiant was the interim aircraft designed to a less demanding specification.

In the early years of the Vulcan a number of changes were incorporated including the addition of a 'crank' in the aircraft's straight wing leading edge and following a trial installation on an Avro 707, the second prototype Vulcan was similarly modified in the summer of 1955.

Once again, the SBAC Air Show at Farnborough proved to be a fine show-case for the Vulcan as, during the 1955 Show, Falk eclipsed previous successes by slow-rolling the second production aircraft, to the delight and amazement of the spectators. Apparently, Sir Roy was not well pleased!

Operational reliability trials for the RAF proved to be a great success and on 9 September 1956 the first Vulcan B.1 to fly overseas left Boscombe Down and flew to Melbourne, Australia in just over twenty-three hours. The aircraft visited New Zealand before returning to England and on board, acting as second pilot, was Bomber Command's C-in-C Air Marshal Sir Harry Broadhurst. After what had been a magnificent start to the Vulcan's service career, disaster struck when the aircraft crashed in bad visibility at Heathrow Airport , London upon its return on 1 October 1956. Sir Harry ejected from the machine and survived the tragic accident as did the aircraft captain Squadron Leader D.R. Howard. Sadly, Avro's chief technical service representative Fred Bassett lost his life as did three RAF officers. Sir Harry went on to champion the Vulcan's cause and later, on 1 March 1961, he was appointed managing director of A.V.Roe & Company Limited.

An extensive modification programme produced the Vulcan B.2 with the most noticeable change from the early aircraft being the addition of twelve feet to the B.1's ninety-nine feet wingspan. The new design first flew on 31 August 1957, with Roly Falk at the controls and, once again, just in time to take part in that year's SBAC Show.

Vulcan B.2s joined the B.1s in service with the Royal Air Force with the latter being upgraded to a higher standard. One of the Squadrons flying the B.2 was No 617, the famous 'Dam Busters' who, in February 1963, were declared fully operational with the Avro W.100 Blue Steel, a stand-off missile developed by the company for use by the V-Force.

The Vulcans gave excellent service to the RAF having a variety of role changes along the way. The main task was to act as a nuclear deterrent which the Vulcan did admirably.

The only time the Vulcan was used in anger came at the very end of its career. The aircraft's retirement programme had already begun, but that scheme was put on hold when the Falklands War started. On 1 May 1982 a Vulcan flew the 3,400 miles from Ascension Island to the Falklands to drop twenty-one 1,000 lb bombs on the airfield at Port Stanley. The aircraft was refuelled en route by Victor K.2 tankers which, incidentally, had been converted to that role from bombers at Woodford. A second Vulcan attack on the night of 3–4 May 1982 also caused damage while on other occasions Vulcans equipped with Shrike missiles attacked Argentinian radar stations. These operations code-named 'Black Buck' showed the services the importance of air-to-air refuelling and the tanker fleet later received a boost with the addition of six Vulcan K.2s which had been converted to tankers at Woodford. Although the damage done to the airfield was not great it was a bitter blow to Argentine morale as further attacks could come at any time.

The last bomber squadron to fly the Vulcan, No. 44 (Rhodesia) was disbanded on 31 December, 1982 while No. 50 Squadron which operated the K.2 tankers flew on until early 1984.

The Avro Vulcan remained in front-line service with the Royal Air Force for nearly twenty-eight years ably performing its many and varied tasks and was a superb example of the ultimate peak of subsonic bomber design. The last Vulcan was withdrawn from operation in 1993 after nearly eight years of thrilling air show crowds while being flown by the Vulcan Display Flight. This aeroplane and its dedicated air and ground crews gave great pleasure to untold thousands during its display period but despite a massive campaign to keep the aircraft flying, the machine was grounded and sold to a private owner for static display. At the Ministry of Defence and at the Chadderton factory of British Aerospace the record card for this aircraft reads, 'Struck off Charge 23.3.93'. It will be a long time before Chadwick's 'flying triangle' will be erased from the minds of aviation enthusiasts everywhere.

The elder statesmen of the aviation industry were greatly saddened to learn of the death of Humphrey Verdon Roe on 25 July 1949 at the age of seventy-one. His injuries sustained in the night bomber crash in World War One affected him for the rest of his life as he suffered frequent black-outs and falls. Besides his pioneering days in aviation, H.V. and his wife Dr Marie Stopes founded the world's first birth control clinic in 1921. Fortunately, he lived long enough to see this work acclaimed in the Royal Commission on Population. As Alliott had fought bigotry and criticism in aviation, H.V. had to endure similar derision with his birth control ideals.

With his experience on the four-jet Tudor 8, Jimmy Orrell was asked to go to Canada to test fly the Avro Canada C102 Jetliner. The aircraft had been designed and built by Avro Canada which had become a subsidiary of the parent company in 1945 when, as Victory Aircraft at Malton, it had been involved in the wartime production of Avro

aircraft, completing 1,168 aeroplanes. The Jetliner was of similar design to the Mk 8 Tudor and was a fifty-seat medium-range airliner powered by four Rolls-Royce Derwents. Orrell flew the first prototype on 10 August 1949 and, six days later, he had to land the airliner on its belly after an undercarriage failure. The landing was a text book tribute to Jimmy Orrell's flying skills and, incredibly, the machine was repaired and completed ten more hours of flying before it was displayed to the public on 5 October 1949. The Jetliner made a number of notable flights between cities in Canada and the United States, but no orders for the aircraft were ever received and the production of a second prototype was cancelled. The one and only Jetliner remained in operation as a trials aircraft until 1956.

Orrell returned to Woodford on 1 November, 1949 to take up the reins and continue the test flying of a wide variety of aircraft being produced by Avro at that time. He had already made the initial flights on the Athena advanced trainer with the Mamba-powered version flying on 12 June 1948 and the Merlin version on 1 August 1948. The Athena was Avro's response to the Specification T.7/45 for an advanced training aircraft to replace the Harvard. Both Avro and Boulton Paul proposed designs and three prototypes were ordered from each company with the latter putting their Balliol aircraft into the air first. The Athena, powered by an Armstrong Siddeley Mamba turboprop engine, was the first Avro version to fly while the more conventional Merlin-powered Mk 2 followed two months later. The aircraft was adapted to carry guns and bombs as an armed trainer, but the Athena never satisfied the service requirements with only fifteen production Mk 2s being delivered to the RAF Flying College at Manby in Lincolnshire. After a number of changes an Athena Mk 2 was civilianised for a demonstration tour of India in February 1950, but this did not result in any orders.

Earlier in 1949 Orrell had completed the maiden flight of an aeroplane which was to stay in service for the next forty-two years! It was on 9 March when he flew the prototype Avro Shackleton for just thirty-three minutes and upon landing back at Woodford he reported that the aeroplane 'flew extremely well and had that comfortable feel of its predecessors the Lancaster and Lincoln'. After a

A Vulcan formates with a B-52 of the U.S.A.F. during exercises in the United States. Vulcans were great favourites there and five of these aeroplanes are preserved at various air bases in the U.S.A.

few minor adjustments he made a second flight, this time of forty-five minutes. It was the first four-engined British aircraft to have contra-rotating propellers and was also the largest British aircraft to fly at that time.

Roy Chadwick named the aeroplane in honour of the famous British explorer Sir Ernest Shackleton who, as the leader of the South Polar Expedition of 1921 had become firm friends with the designer after Chadwick had proposed the Avro 554 for the Antarctic trip. Sadly, Roy Chadwick did not live to see the Shackleton fly nor his other creation, the Avro 698, which became the mighty Vulcan.

The RAF's need for a long-range reconnaissance aircraft was becoming acute and Roy Chadwick had looked at a Lincoln version to meet the Specification R.5/46, but he rejected the idea as unsatisfactory in terms of performance, equipment and crew conditions. The new aircraft would have a redesigned wider fuselage mated to Lincoln wings, but powered by four Rolls-Royce Griffon engines each driving six blade contra-rotating airscrews.

The Shackletons eventually replaced Lancasters,

which had been used as interim aircraft, in Coastal Command and service experience fed into the Avro team brought about the introduction of the Shackleton MR2 which was first flown by Jimmy Orrell on 17 June 1952 with the first examples entering service with the RAF both at home and in Malta later that year.

A Shackleton MR2 was fitted with an airborne lifeboat for the Air-Sea Rescue role, and equipped with a Saro Mk 3 boat, the aeroplane appeared at the 1953 SBAC Air Show at Farnborough. During the Show, Avro test pilot Johnny Baker thrilled the crowds by ending his display with a fly-past on just one engine. In fact, that year, Avro completely stole the Show as the company also displayed a formation of the two gleaming white prototype Vulcans flanked by red, orange, blue and silver Avro 707s. This was a sight never to be forgotten!

It was Johnny Baker who made the first flight of the Avro Shackleton MR3 on 2 September 1955. The MR3 was an advancement on the Shackleton theme as it was fitted with a nose-wheel undercarriage and wing-tip fuel tanks for extended range. During the early flight tests the prototype MR3 was fitted with a twelve feet long yawmeter probe in the nose and it was on an aerodynamic trials flight, so the story goes, that Johnny Baker succeeded in getting his 'own back' on Avro chief photographer Paul Cullerne. Cullerne was flying in the rear gunner's position of a Lancaster which

Stuart Davies assumed responsibility for the design of the Vulcan after the death of Roy Chadwick and made the aircraft into the magnificent machine it was.

had the turret removed to accommodate the photographer and in the photo session he kept calling to Baker, 'Come closer. Come closer'. Finally, the exasperated Baker carefully inched the Shackleton closer to the Lancaster until the nose probe was practically touching Cullerne. 'Is that close enough?' Baker called!

Test flying, by its very nature, can be most dangerous as pilots have to take aeroplanes into new regimes where the unexpected can happen and sometimes does. No matter how experienced the pilot, a situation can develop from which there is little chance of escape and one such incident brought tragedy to Woodford once more.

After some modifications the prototype Shackleton MR3 was on a test flight on 7 December 1956 under the command of Squadron Leader Jack Wales, a pilot of great experience, when the aeroplane crashed near Foolow in Derbyshire killing Wales and his three Avro crew members R.A. Greenhalgh, C. O'Neill who were observers and G.A. Blake, flight engineer. The investigation revealed that the aircraft went into a spin after turning with bomb doors open and the radome extended. This manoeuvre was simulating the attack configuration which was one of the exercises

to be completed that day. After entering the spin the Shackleton then became inverted followed by all four engines stopping. Wales brought the aircraft out of the spin, but could not start the engines again and the machine crashed at slow forward speed and a high rate of descent resulting in complete destruction. Wales had been awarded the OBE in the 1952 New Year's Honours and was CO of No. 613 Squadron, R Aux AF.

The Shackleton MR3 did eventually go into RAF service in 1957 as contracts had been delayed through military budget restrictions. Eight MR3s were also sold to the South African Air Force and remained in service for nearly twenty-seven years.

The MR2s of the RAF eventually outlasted the newer MR3s! The addition of two Bristol Siddeley Viper jet engines, one behind the Griffon engine in each of the outboard engine nacelles, brought aircraft to what is called Phase 3 standard. The actual installation, which was meant to improve performance, just impaired it and had speeded up the MR3's fatigue life.

The MR2 did outlive the later version as it was this type which, in 1971, was selected to fill Britain's requirement for an Airborne Early

The last portrait of Roy Chadwick taken just before his tragic death in August 1947. Together with Sir Roy Dobson, Chadwick's name is synonymous with the Avro Company.

Warning (AEW) aircraft to counter the mounting number of intruders then entering British airspace. Twelve aircraft were converted at Woodford and Bitteswell with the Shackleton AEW.2, as it was designated, making its first flight from the former on 30 September 1971. The aircraft equipped No. 8 Squadron, a fighter squadron that was reformed at Kinloss on 1 January 1972 specifically for the AEW role. The unit moved to Lossiemouth on 14 August 1972 and stayed there until the Shackleton AEW.2s were retired from service on 1 July 1991, over forty-two years after the type made its first flight!

The Avro Shackleton was called upon for a multitude of roles from anti-submarine to search and rescue, maritime reconnaissance to colonial policing, supply dropping to bombing, troop carrying to airborne early warning and many other tasks too numerous to mention. All of these roles have been carried out to the very highest standards by a fine aeroplane and the professionalism of its crews. The Shackleton crews complained about the noise on their long missions, but like the aviation enthusiast many of them would give anything to hear the unique sound of 'The Old Growler' just once more!

The test flights with the Tudor 8 jet transport showed the need for a nose-wheel type undercarriage to keep the jet blast clear of the ground. Designs were underway for a Tudor Mk 9 when Avro was asked by the Ministry of Supply to submit plans for a high altitude research aircraft and after study of their requirements the Avro Ashton emerged. The production of six machines which had been ordered by the Ministry utilised Tudor 2 airframes which were given thicker gauge skins with the fuselage being shortened to the Mk 1 length. The Ashton made its first flight on 1 September 1950 piloted by Jimmy Orrell and he flew it directly to Boscombe Down in just one hour. Of course, it was Farnborough Show time again and Orrell made five flights at Boscombe before flying the Ashton to Farnborough on 5 September. The aircraft was demonstrated by him every day before it was flown back to Woodford by Johnny Baker as Jimmy Orrell had to return to Boscombe Down for some Shackleton test flying.

The six Ashtons flew for a number of years and provided a great contribution to the advancement of aviation research.

With the success of the Vulcan the Avro sales team under J.A.R. Kay published plans for a delta-wing airliner which aroused interest among the world's airlines. The design group led by Stuart Davies with project leader Harry King and Geoff Monk as his assistant had been working on a number of configurations from the end of 1952 with a finalised design being shown in June 1953. It was thought that if interest was shown and advanced orders received such an airliner could be in service by the end of the 1950s. The big difficulty at that time was that it was not possible to make a complete survey of the jet transport market and the Americans had not yet made public their plans for forthcoming jet airliners. Britain with BOAC held the undisputed lead in jet transport operations with the de Havilland Comet and the airline supplied information to Avro on their future requirements.

The outcome of the design studies was the Avro 722 Atlantic which was based on the Vulcan and would be able to carry 113 passengers from London to New York at a cruising speed of 600 mph. Sir Miles Thomas, chairman of BOAC, commented that if the airline completed their studies and decided to order the Atlantic they would expect to receive the first one by 1958. In the following year BOAC would examine four types of jet airliner, but it was not until 25 February 1955 that the airline announced that it would be buying Bristol Britannias for the North Atlantic route and until the British airliner was available, BOAC would buy Douglas DC-7Cs as interim aircraft.

The jet studies would continue, but on 17 March 1955 it was stated that the airline would be ordering the long-range version of the Comet. The estimated performance and economics of the Atlantic were not up to the standard of the Comet and airlines around the world were now showing enthusiasm for the emerging Boeing 707. With a number of projects under way and others in the pipeline Avro decided to cease design work on the Atlantic.

With the Vulcan and Shackleton in full production in 1954 the Ministry of Supply encouraged companies to look at more advanced aircraft designs. One of their requirements was for a high altitude interceptor fighter with the final selection being between Avro and Saunders-Roe and both were asked to investigate the design. The factory at Chadderton had pioneered the development of light alloy honeycomb sandwich construction and was the first to make honeycomb which was capable of being formed into almost any shape and, at that time, had unrivalled knowledge of this type of construction. The first machine to use a considerable amount of honeycomb structure was the fighter which was designed to meet the MOS Specification 137 and the design put forward was the Avro 720. The sleek delta which came out of the design office was to have a mixed powerplant system consisting of an Armstrong Siddeley Screamer rocket engine and

While the 748 was in its early stages of flight testing, Avro-Canada was similarly engaged in assisting the United States with the Avrocar. The saucer failed to sustain itself in forward flight and despite modifications trials were terminated.

an Armstrong Siddeley Viper conventional turbojet. It would be armed with two de Havilland Firestreak infra-red homing missiles, but the prototype of the 720 only left Chadderton's experimental department on the lorries belonging to R.J. Coley as the project was cancelled during the government's 1956 economy drive. As someone commented, 'The scrap man gets everything in the end!'

The government of the day cancelled a number of advanced projects under way by British companies at that time and along with the Avro 720 went a design for a high altitude supersonic bomber known as the Type 730. The Avro team had designed this aeroplane much in advance of its time with an outer skin of stainless-steel which would be able to withstand the high temperatures generated by flight at over twice the speed of

sound. The 730 was designed to use a visor over the pilot's cockpit operative at high speeds with the view being by a periscope.

One of the pilots who was involved in monitoring the two projects was ex-Squadron Leader James Gordon Harrison. Jimmy Harrison was a pilot of great experience as, after wartime flying, he became a test pilot for the Royal Aircraft Establishment at Farnborough with a fine knowledge of delta flying. He joined Avro in January 1954 after a personal invitation from Sir Roy Dobson. Harrison did much of the development flying for the Vulcan and on New Year's Day 1958 he was appointed chief test pilot when Roly Falk, whose title was superintendent of flying, moved to Chadderton as special assistant to Sir Roy. Jimmy Harrison continued in the role until 1970 when he retired from flying to take up the position of product support manager. At that time he was succeeded as chief test pilot by Tony Blackman.

On 28 June 1954 members of Avro's 'old brigade' attended a ceremony at Brooklands when a plaque was unveiled by Sir Alliott Verdon-Roe to commemorate his early pioneering flights. Mounted on a granite plinth the plaque had been erected by Vickers-Armstrong Limited, the owners of the aerodrome. Engraved on the plaque is:

'From this area on various dates in 1907 - 8 A.V. Roe made a series of towing flights and flight trials with an aircraft of his own design and construction, powered in the later trials by an 18/24 Antoinette engine.

'These trials were made along the finishing straight of the motor-racing track on this site.

'A.V. Roe thus becomes the first of the long line of famous pioneers and pilots of many nations who made air history on this flying field of Brooklands.

'This tablet was placed here in June 1954 by Vickers-Armstrong Aircraft Division and it was unveiled by Sir Alliott Verdon-Roe in his 78th year.'

Sir Alliott told the large gathering of his early work at Brooklands and how he first studied the gliding flight of the albatross sea bird.

Avro were once again asked to manufacture aircraft which were not of their own design when the Ministry of Supply requested the company to build a batch of English Electric Canberra twin-jet medium bombers. An order of 150 of these was placed, but budget restrictions caused the contract to be reduced by one half with the seventy-five Canberras being produced at Chadderton and Woodford between March 1953 and March 1955.

During the mid-1950s Avro once again diversified with their development and production not restricted solely to aircraft. The company pioneered the development of stretch-forming techniques and their application to aircraft materials, but later they included many wider engineering applications and scope of stretch-forming was greatly extended with the introduction of the Avro 250-ton machine. It is believed that not one was built for other users, but one of these machines remained in service at Chadderton for nearly thirty years. Avro was also actively engaged in designing and building radar aerials with a number of these utilising the Avro honeycomb sandwich construction for the reflector face. A number of these were sold before the decision was made to concentrate solely on the production of aircraft. Also in this diversification Avro used the many talents of its research department at Chadderton with their experience in metals, carbon fibre and composites, plastics and many other projects and assistance was sought by the nuclear industry as well as a variety of companies.

On 30 June 1955 Stuart Davies relinquished his post as chief designer and resigned from the company. His place was taken by J.R. Ewans who had been deputy chief designer and chief aerodynamicist. Sir William Farren remained as technical director. Stuart Davies had been instrumental in continuing with the design of the Vulcan after the death of Roy Chadwick. Davies had finalised the design of the Vulcan B.1 before its entry into service with the Royal Air Force and his successor Roy Ewans developed the larger B.2 version.

The afternoon of 19 August 1955 was filled with great excitement at Woodford for Jimmy Orrell was to test fly an aeroplane. Nothing new about that, but this time he was to fly an Avro 504K! The aeroplane belonged to the Shuttleworth Collection at Old Warden in Bedfordshire and it was in the summer of 1954 that a very derelict Avro 504N was seen laying dismantled in the back of one of their hangars. A plan was devised to get the aircraft flying once more and after some consultations between the trustees and interested parties such as Sir Alan Cobham being contacted, it was decided to approach Avro to rebuild the 504. Sir Roy Dobson was extremely keen on the idea and the task was allocated to the apprentices with the assistance of some of the older employees who had experience of that type. It was agreed that the Avro 504N should be refurbished into one of the K series and on arrival at Woodford it was thoroughly examined by Arthur Ainsworth and Charles Broadhead, both veterans of the early days of Avro with the former joining the company early in 1915. Ainsworth, who was awarded the MBE in 1945 for his wartime role, was works manager of Woodford from 1925 to 1949 when he retired. He was more than pleased to come out of retirement to assist in the 504 rebuild, but sadly he died on 5 June 1955 just two months before the aeroplane flew again.

The Chadderton drawing stores provided drawings for both versions of the aircraft and it was found that the initial changes would have to be in the wings, ailerons and centre section. The apprentices were soon under way with stripping off the old fabric and rotting wood while others cleaned and reassembled the 110 hp Le Rhône rotary engine which would power the aeroplane. Luckily Shuttleworth had this engine in their collection. Dunlop's agreed to renovate the undercarriage wheels and supply suitable tyres and inner tubes. Accles & Pollock supplied a large amount of special tubing and the Airscrew & Jicwood Company constructed the propeller from seasoned mahogany. However, before the Airscrew Company could start work Avro had to supply them with the working drawing, but none could be found in the archives. An SOS was sent to Harold Rogerson, who was now with the Hawker Siddeley Group as he was the expert on early propeller design. Guided only by an outline view Rogerson drew out the detail including dimensions and pitch required and his memory was totally correct as the finished propeller was perfect.

The aircraft was rebuilt in the original RFC colours as an Avro 504K and the machine was immaculate as it was rolled out for Jimmy Orrell to fly. The engine started first time and the aeroplane was soon in the air over Woodford lazily circling around the aerodrome. After getting the feel of the 504 once again, Orrell, not content with flying straight and level, looped the aircraft twice and completed a 'falling leaf', which was a favourite manoeuvre of Avro 504 pilots in earlier times. In the front cockpit flying as a 'passenger' was test pilot Jimmy Baker who had never flown in a 504 and asked Jimmy Orrell for a ride. Baker enjoyed the flight, but commented, 'It felt as though we had an Anson tied on behind!'

The Avro 504K has graced the skies over Old Warden ever since and it has even been back to Woodford to take part in the RAFA Air Shows. The aeroplane also took part in the film *Reach for the Sky* which described the exploits of the legless fighter pilot the late Group Captain Douglas Bader. Bader, who learned to fly on a 504K, showed great interest in the Avro rebuild and he was Guest of Honour at the Avro 504 Club reunion dinner in 1961.

A Royal visit to the Avro factories took place on 8 November 1955 when the Duke of Edinburgh flew into Woodford and later toured Chadderton. Prince Philip showed great enthusiasm for aviation and he was enthralled by the Avro 720, then almost complete in Chadderton's experimental department and also the Avro 730 bomber which was in the design stage. The Vulcan also intrigued him and he expressed a desire to fly one, but it was not until 24 June 1958 that his wish was granted when he was able to co-pilot a Vulcan on a flight from Wyton, Huntingdon.

The Duke of Edinburgh followed a number of personalities who flew a Vulcan. On 6 September, 1955 the Prime Minister of the day, Sir Anthony Eden had a flight with Roly Falk during the Farnborough Air Show. Sir Anthony had expressed his delight at Falk's Vulcan display in the Show and Sir Roy Dobson asked if he would like to fly in the aeroplane. 'I would indeed', replied Sir Anthony, 'provided you don't roll it!' During the flight Roly Falk allowed Sir Anthony to take over the controls and at the end of the flight he said, 'Wonderful, it was smoother than any airliner I've been in.'

Early in 1956 the Ministry of Supply requested that Avro prepare one of the 707A baby deltas for loan to Australia. It was an interesting request which had the Woodford personnel a little sceptical about the whole thing. However, on 6 March 1956 Jimmy Harrison was strapped into the aeroplane for a flight to Renfrew Aerodrome near Glasgow where it was loaded onto the Australian aircraft carrier HMAS *Melbourne*. The aircraft had been loaned to the Australian Government for research work. The Avro 707 did much valuable work for the Australians, strangely, at low speeds although the 707A was the high speed version! It continued until 1965 when the aircraft was retired from flying, but it was saved from the scrap yard by an enterprising citizen who still keeps the machine in his garden at Williamstown, Melbourne.

As the design and manufacture of missiles was entering the aeronautical scene on an ever increasing basis, Avro formed the Weapons Research Division (WRD) at Woodford. Alfred Sewart was appointed assistant general manager (missiles) and R.H. Francis as chief engineer; both were to become directors of Avro in October 1960. Jimmy Orrell had become flight superintendent of the WRD in 1956 and was awarded the OBE for his services to aviation on 31 May 1956. He was already familiar with the Vulcan, but on 10 December 1956 he flight tested a Vickers Valiant which was based at Woodford as a WRD trials aircraft. After a number of trial flights at Woodford Orrell flew the Valiant to Australia to continue the test programme, leaving Woodford on 16 July 1957 and landing at Edinburgh Air Base in Australia just five days and six stops later. The total flying time was twenty-five hours and fifty-five minutes with, typically, Orrell flying the aeroplane the whole time!

The WRD soon spread its wings in other directions as it opened design offices in Harrow, Middlesex and Chertsey in Surrey.

Jimmy Orrell continued to test fly the two Valiants assigned to the WRD until August 1958 when he failed his flying medical with his last flight as a pilot for the company being on the 30th when he flew the company's hack Anson Aggie Paggie (G-AGPG) from Woodford to Blackbushe and back. The following day he was grounded for ever. With Roly Falk going to Chadderton on special duties Jimmy Harrison was given Jimmy Orrell's old title of chief test pilot. After the latter retired he retained his interest in aviation until he passed away on 3 August 1988.

On 15 October 1956 Teddy Fielding was Avro's representative at a ceremony held at St Mawgan in

A new face came to Avro in March 1961 with the appointment of Air Chief Marshal Sir Harry Broadhurst. Sir Harry succeeded Jimmy Kay as managing director with the latter moving to Hawker Siddeley Aviation in London.

Cornwall where the last Avro Lancaster was being retired from RAF service. The aircraft was the MR.3 version which had been used as an interim maritime reconnaissance aircraft until the arrival of the Avro Shackleton in squadron service.

The New Year of 1958 did not start happily for Avro as, on 4 January, it was with deep sorrow that they learned of the death of the founder Sir Alliott Verdon-Roe. He passed away in his eighty-first year and Lady Verdon-Roe wrote to Sir Roy in response to his telegram of condolence telling him of Sir Alliott's great pride in the company which bore his name and, until his death, wrote daily in his Avro pocket diary. He had also kept every edition of the company's house magazine the *Avro News*.

The development of the Avro sites and the introduction of new equipment was ongoing and in May 1958 the company unveiled giant mufflers at Woodford to subdue the roar of the Vulcan engines during engine running periods. The four Bristol Olympus engines gave a combined thrust of 40,000 lb and the new installations gave a significant reduction in noise by deflecting the sound upwards.

Another addition to Woodford's facilities was a supersonic wind tunnel which was made public in July 1958. The wind tunnel had an operating Mach number range from 1.6 to 3.5 and complemented the subsonic and transonic wind tunnels already operating at that time. Originally the supersonic tunnel was required for programmes such as the Avro 720 and 730, but when these contracts were cancelled the company was already committed to the development of a supersonic air-to-surface missile later named Blue Steel. This and other projects of the WRD and of other companies, who rented the tunnel, kept the facility occupied for many years to follow.

In 1957 Avro had a number of Lincoln bombers in storage at Langar when three of these aircraft were bought by Field Aircraft Services for conversion to freighters for the Argentine Government. The machines were to fly meat over the Andes, but the project hit a problem when it was found that the aircraft could not be granted a Certificate of Airworthiness as although the aircraft could take off easily with the required ten tons of meat it would have broken its back if it tried to land with it! One of the Lincolns was completely converted to the freighting configuration, but was later scrapped after the programme was discontinued.

At a meeting in March 1959 several new appointments were announced for the Board of Directors, consisting of Jimmy Kay as managing director; Stuart Joy, general manager; Teddy Fielding, works director; Sir William Farren, technical director; John Green, controller-general engineering with Alf Sewart, Roy Ewans and Rod Francis becoming executive directors.

During 1958 and the first quarter of 1959 the Hawker Siddeley Group saw a great amount of activity as changes would see the broadening of the group's industrial activities. In aviation the interests were controlled by Hawker Siddeley Aviation (HSA) Limited under the chairmanship of Sir Roy with Jimmy Kay and J.T. Lidbury of Hawker Aircraft Limited being joint managing directors. The aviation section of the group comprised Avro, Armstrong Whitworth, Gloster and Hawker and, at that time, HSA was considered as the strongest aircraft design, research and manufacturing unit in the British Commonwealth.

News reached Sir Roy that yet another of his colleagues from the early days of Avro had passed away. Harry Broadsmith died at his home on the Isle of Wight on 25 September 1959 where he had kept a home since he left Avro in 1928. Broadsmith had joined A.V. and John Lord when they took controlling interest in S.E. Saunders Limited and early in 1929 the company's name was changed to Saunders-Roe Limited. During World War Two he was appointed to organise facilities for the testing and modification of Catalina flying-boats as they arrived from the United States. He was joint managing director of Saunders-Roe from 1939 until he resigned in 1945 to be an aviation consultant before going to Australia, where he had established the Avro facilities. He later returned to the Isle of Wight where he ended his days.

Harry Broadsmith had contacted Sir Roy in January 1958 when he and a number of the early employees had been thrilled to hear that a section of wing and other aviation items were discovered in the roof at Brownsfield Mill! These items and others found in 1977 were preserved by the Manchester branch of the Royal Aeronuatical Society.

Teddy Fielding retired from Avro in September 1961 at the age of sixty-seven, but continued to be active as chairman of the North-West Region of the Air Training Corps and also as president of the Royal Aeronautical Society's Manchester Branch.

# CHAPTER 14

## The Last Avro

After the 1957 White Paper on Defence issued by Duncan Sandys stated that there would be no more manned bombers for the Royal Air Force, Avro decided that it would take an in-depth look at the civil market. It was a drastic turnabout for the management team since, after the disappointment of the Tudor all their designs and production had been for the military.

A world-wide review of the air transport industry was undertaken and there appeared to be a clear market for an aeroplane to replace the famous workhorse Dakota. Any new aircraft would have to operate from unpaved runways and go anywhere a Dakota could, but with twice the payload and with higher safety standards.

A number of designs were studied, the go-ahead was given in January 1959 for the construction of four airframes; two of these would be prototypes while the other two would be the structure test specimens. For one of the test specimens a 70,000 gallon water tank was erected at the Middleton end of Chadderton factory. The aircraft would be known as the Avro 748.

It was while the prototype 748s were under construction that the Chadderton factory was hit by a series of fires. The first of these occurred on 3 October 1959 when a massive blaze destroyed a large part of the plant. When the fire was finally brought under control the flames were licking at the design office. It had devastated the factory floor, affecting Vulcan production and many departments were completely destroyed, including central records containing historical information dating back to the very earliest days of Avro. Group inspection where records of aircraft production were contained disappeared and in the photographic department movie footage and over 47,000 negatives dating back to the pioneering days were lost. The technical library had been consumed with its thousands of reference books as

were the jig and tool drawing office, process, aircraft control, job cards, and the ratefixing department. Under the twisted heaps of girders lay many of the production departments including Avro's pioneering honeycomb section. The design office print room was damaged with the thousands of drawings being reduced to a soggy mess.

The aftermath did look like the 'Blitz' with roofless buildings, blackened walls or no walls at all, smoke and steam escaping from broken pipes and water everywhere.

A formidable task faced all at Chadderton, but everyone affected by the fire was moved to other parts of the factory or set to cleaning up their particular section if it was possible. Soggy drawings were hung out to dry like yesterday's laundry and soon large plastic sheets sealed off the damaged areas.

Almost immediately an army of workers descended on the piles of debris and bulldozers were soon at work clearing the site and as each area was cleared builders were on the scene. The piles of rubble started to disappear and stacks of new bricks, sand and cement appeared in their place.

The rebuilding seemed a daunting proposition, but the main production line was soon underway again but, luckily, the first prototype Avro 748 was in a different part of the factory and was not damaged.

However, in less than twelve months Chadderton was damaged by more fires with the largest of these destroying the experimental department where the second prototype 748 was nearing completion. The aircraft was badly damaged when a roof girder smashed into the top of the fuselage, but they built them good at Avro's and this aircraft operated in service for over twenty-eight years before being retired by Dan-Air in 1990.

With the fires behind them the Chadderton

Luckily, the Chadderton fire did not damage the prototype Avro 748 as it was in a different part of the factory. The aircraft flew for the first time on 24 June 1960.

workers settled down to serious production once more with the main aim being to get the prototype Avro 748 into the air. This was achieved on 24 June, 1960 when the 748 took off from Woodford for its first flight. In the cockpit was Jimmy Harrison with Colin Allen as the second pilot with Bob Dixon-Stubbs and Mike Turner on board as flight test observers. The aircraft had a fine start because it was later learnt that this flight of two hours, forty-one minutes was a record duration for the first flight of a civil airliner. The take-off of the prototype took place just seventeen months after the go-ahead had been given by the Hawker Siddeley Group and it was due to a fine team effort with chief designer Roy Ewans and chief aerodynamicist John Scott-Wilson leading the way, but with Joe Rimmington having overall responsibility for the production of

the prototype and project engineer Dick Conner having to ensure that hundreds of detail drawings were ready on time.

One of the first to show interest in the 748 was the Indian Government and even before the first aircraft had flown, a manufacturing agreement had been signed for the Avro 748 to be built in Kanpur by Hindustan Aeronautics Limited. That company went on to build eighty-nine 748s with many of them still in service today.

The 748 was designed as a regional airliner capable of carrying forty-four to sixty passengers or six tons of freight. The aeroplane was powered by two Rolls-Royce Dart turboprop engines which were extremely reliable and economical to operate.

As its reputation spread, orders began to come in for the 748 and this rugged aeroplane operated everywhere from jungle airstrips to desert runways and the frozen north. The 748 flew in many parts of the world from forty degrees centigrade in parts of Africa to minus twenty-five degrees centigrade in Northern Canada. With safety and reliability as its greatest features it is not surprising that it was chosen as the personal transport for no fewer than sixteen heads of state, including Her Majesty the Queen. The British VIP 748s are known in the Royal Air Force as the Andover C.C.2 and, although no longer serving in the Queen's Flight, these aircraft, which are thirty years old, are still giving excellent service to No. 32 Squadron, which is the RAF's VIP unit based at Northolt, Middlesex.

The 748 was continually developed throughout its career and the later versions, although similar in appearance to the earlier models, incorporated more than 6,000 modifications and improvements. The 748 still operates in every type of role from airliner to cargo aircraft and from navigation aid inspection to electronics and navigational trainers. A rear loading version of the 748 was built and serves with the RAF and the Royal New Zealand Air Force as the Andover C.1 with the former also operating the electronics version designated the Andover E.3.

The ubiquitous 748 continued in production until 1988 and with nearly 400 sold in fifty countries around the world the aeroplane has proved itself to be well suited to the many and varied tasks of large and small operators alike. The 748 has over five-and-a-half million flying hours to its credit; it has lived up to all expectations and still shows itself to be an excellent aircraft with a fine reputation for its robustness and reliability.

On 1 March 1961 Sir Harry Broadhurst, who had just retired from the RAF with the rank of Air Chief Marshal and Commander of Allied Air Forces, Central Europe, was appointed managing director of A.V. Roe & Company Limited, in succession to J.A.R. Kay. Sir Harry also joined the board of Hawker Siddeley Aviation Limited. Jimmy Kay, who felt it was impossible to give his best as managing director of Avro and also to his position in the Hawker Siddeley Group, took up the position of sales director with Hawker Siddeley Aviation which had wider responsibilities as he was in charge of sales for the whole aviation group.

In June 1961 Roy Ewans, the chief designer, also left Avro to take up a position in the United States and his post was filled by the arrival of M.J. Brennan with the title of chief engineer (aircraft). Maurice Brennan had been chief engineer with

Folland Aircraft Limited, a member company of the Hawker Siddeley Group and later became famous for designing the Saro SR.53, the mixed rocket-jet powered fighter similar to the Avro 720. He also designed the SR.177, a larger development of the SR.53, but as with most types at that time, it was cancelled as an unfortunate repercussion of the notorious 1957 White Paper on Defence.

More changes came in Avro's top management in September 1961 with the retirement of works director Teddy Fielding. However, his departure from the company did not see him disappear from the aviation scene altogether as he was retained as a production consultant to the Hawker Siddeley Group. He was awarded the OBE in 1944 for his part in the production of the Avro Lancaster when the factories under his responsibility were turning out 150 of this type every month. Fielding's position at Avro was taken over by Harry Dobson, Sir Roy's youngest son.

Another 'old timer' who left the company in 1961 was Aggie-Paggie, Avro's faithful old Anson after sixteen years in continual service. The aircraft was sold to Skyways Limited in July of that year and, after being sold to Ekco Electronics it continued flying until 1971. It was then presented to a museum and, after a few changes of owner, it

Chief test pilot Jimmy Harrison is clearly delighted with the 748 after an excellent maiden flight. Others in the team are, from the left, Tony Blackman, Dick Connor and Cyril Bethwaite. Following behind are Joe Rimmington, in spectacles and Prince Emmanual Galitzine, Avro sales manager.

is currently being restored to exhibition standard by a museum in Kent.

Another Anson currently being restored is at Woodford where retired British Aerospace employees devote some of their time to rebuilding the machine. A Vulcan B.2 is also cared for by retirees of 'The XM603 Club' which has been so named for the aircraft's serial number. The veterans have a wealth of experience and this, together with the dedication they have shown all of their working lives, is invaluable to the restoration of these great aircraft and for the preservation of Avro's fine heritage.

In 1963, with the retirement of Sir Thomas Sopwith, Sir Roy Dobson was appointed chairman of the Hawker Siddeley Group and Sir Roy's position of group managing director was taken over by Arnold (later Sir Arnold) Hall. Hall chose John Lidbury as his deputy and both of them began to plan changes in the ever growing Hawker Siddeley Group as with such a large number of companies each with different ideas and methods it was obvious that some form of rationalisation was required.

The major reorganisation of the companies came into effect on 1 July 1963 with Avro, Armstrong Whitworth, Blackburn, de Havilland, Folland, Gloster and Hawker becoming established into divisions of Hawker Siddeley Aviation Limited. Three divisions were formed and one of these was the Avro Whitworth Division which covered the work of Avro, Armstrong Whitworth and Gloster. The Avro 748 became the Hawker Siddeley 748 overnight!

Under a further streamlining the Hawker Siddeley Group merged the divisions into one organisation. The historic firms lost their identity forever as Sir Arnold Hall announced that the three divisions would cease operating to provide a greater degree of central control by Hawker Siddeley Aviation Limited. Sir Harry Broadhurst became deputy managing director of the new organisation.

So the famous name of Avro passed into history on 1 April 1965. In the 1963 changes the factories of A.V. Roe & Company Limited clung on to the Avro name, but now it was gone forever.

And what of the great personalities of Avro? Alliott, Humphrey, Roy Chadwick, Reg Parrott, Harry Broadsmith and half a score of others had all

gone. Sir Roy Dobson lived until 7 July 1968 when the aircraft industry lost one of its outstanding and most colourful figures. Teddy Fielding passed away on 19 June 1983 and is still remembered with affection and respect. Stuart Davies lives in retirement at Bognor Regis.

The great factories of Avro still exist, but in a variety of guises and a number of owners. Changes have taken place at both Chadderton and Woodford as, under British Aerospace, the two factories have taken different paths. However, both are still involved in the task for which they were originally built, the production of aeroplanes. Chadderton, now known as British Aerospace (Aerostructures) Limited, continues to manufacture major components for a number of aircraft with Airbus work and military support activities being extensive. The plant is now diversifying, with a number of specialised engineering programmes under review. Woodford has gone full circle as far as the name of the unit is concerned as, early in 1993, this British Aerospace site adopted the name Avro International as a tribute to its predecessor. Production of the BAe 146 was transferred from Hatfield and after the manufacture of this aircraft ceased it was replaced on the Woodford production line by the Regional Jet RJ Avroliner. This aircraft has enjoyed considerable success since its introduction in 1993 with orders from a number of operators and great interest being shown by potential customers. Avro International is already planning an entirely new design of airliner, currently known only as the RJX.

The Avro custom-built factory at Hamble is used by the Petter Works while the airfield is partly covered by Shell Oil storage tanks. The large factory at Newton Heath is now a storage depot for the Co-operative Society and sadly the last sign of the site's Avro heritage, the factory chimney which bore the name AVRO, was demolished in recent years. The Mather & Platt unit used by the company in World War One is still used for light engineering. The massive 'shadow factory' at Yeadon is the home of a container truck operator with a number of small companies using various areas. Bracebridge Heath is now used as a warehouse while Avro hangars at Langar are part of an industrial estate. The company's first workshop at Brownsfield Mill is still in use, but the Clifton Street works were demolished and the site now belongs to a scrap metal dealer.

Since A.V.'s first biplane nearly 35,000 aircraft of Avro design have been built throughout the world. The 748 was the last aeroplane to bear the famous name and is still known in Latin America as 'El Avro'.

As the company name has been revived by British Aerospace and the factories at Chadderton and Woodford, both proud of their history, are striving to continue the great traditions established by Alliott Verdon-Roe and his dedicated followers, the name Avro will be preserved for future generations.

Sir Roy Dobson retired in July 1967 at the age of seventy-five! He was the driving force behind Avro and, later, Hawker Siddeley Aviation with his energy and vitality being famous throughout the industry. He died in July 1968 just one year after retiring.

BELOW:
The Avro Vulcan was a show stopper wherever it went and, sadly, the R.A.F.'s last flying example was retired in 1993 despite a concerted campaign to keep it in the air. It was grounded, of course, as an economy measure!

# APPENDIX A

## Avro Canada

Avro Canada arose from the ashes of the government-owned Victory Aircraft and became a wholly-owned subsidiary of the Hawker Siddeley Group on 1 December 1945. It was Sir Roy Dobson who became interested in purchasing Victory when, after the war was over, he realised that there were many capable aircraft technicians who were going to be unemployed despite being located in what was considered one of the most modern engineering units in the world.

It is reported that after a tour of inspection just after the war's end, Sir Roy in typical fashion, staggered fellow directors with, 'I've been and bought the bloody lot!' He certainly had with a staff of 500 growing to a peak of 14,000 under the H.S. Group banner. The deal was signed between the Right Honourable C.D. Howe, Minister for Munitions and Supply for the Canadian Government and Sir Roy for Hawker Siddeley with the whole arrangement being made by Fred T. Smye who was director of aircraft production for the Canadian Government.

The financial backing came from Hawker Siddeley, but Avro Canada was fully managed by Canadians with the exception of Sir Roy, who took great pride in the company's achievements and it was he who requested that the name of A.V. Roe & Company Limited be used for the Canadian venture.

During the war Victory Aircraft had an excellent production record completing 736 Ansons, 430 Lancasters, one Lincoln and one York and afterwards, as Avro Canada, the company built the CF-100 jet fighter which was used in large numbers by the Royal Canadian Airforce and exported to Belgium. The company also produced the C-102 Jetliner which is covered elsewhere in this book and the very advanced CF-105 Arrow jet fighter.

The company also designed and built the Avro Model 1 Avrocar which was a disc-shaped test vehicle for VTOL research. 'The Saucer' was powered by three small turbojets which drove a central fan to create an air cushion with a projected performance being a 1,000 miles range and a maximum speed of 300 mph. The programme was taken over by the United States Department of Defense in 1955 and was given the US Army designation VZ-9V. However, during tests the performance was poor and a second version flown by NASA lifted off for the first time on 17 May, 1961, but once again the trials were a failure with the vehicle only lifting a few feet and it was unable to move forward with any speed. Both were retired and placed in museums, one with the US Army and the other in the National Air and Space Museum, Washington DC.

Avro Canada owned a Gas Turbine Division which later became Orenda Engines who designed and manufactured the first jet engine to be built in Canada and which first ran on 17 March 1948.

The futuristic-looking Avro Arrow was a twin-turbojet all-weather fighter designed to a 1952 requirement by the RCAF. Powered by Avro Orenda Iroquois engines, the Arrow was first flown on 25 March 1958 and later exceeded 1,000 mph in level flight. With trials going extremely well an order for thirty-seven aircraft was placed by the RCAF in June 1958, but after a total of five aircraft was completed a change of government in Canada saw the programme completely cancelled in February 1959.

The Hawker Siddeley Group had invested much in Canada with heavy industry under its control besides Avro Canada and the cancellation of the Arrow had grave consequences for the HSG and the whole Canadian work force had to be laid off.

It was the end for Avro Canada with the loss of the Arrow depriving the country of an irreplaceable part of its aircraft industry.

# APPENDIX B
## Avro Project Numbers

**T**he Avro aeroplane designation system which was used until the company was absorbed into Hawker Siddeley Aviation in 1963, commenced in 1912 with the Avro 500. Before that time the aircraft built had the various number and letter designations as described in the main text. Type numbers were allocated to every project undertaken by the company, but less than one third of the designs were actually built. The following list represents the projects which were seriously studied, but did not reach the development stage.

| Type Number | Remarks | Date |
|---|---|---|
| 505 | Not used | |
| 506 | 160 hp or 200 hp Gnome-powered seaplane gun carrier. | June 1913 |
| 507 | Not used for aircraft, but allocated to wings designed for an aeroplane to be built by Mr H.G. Leigh. | July 1913 |
| 509 | Originally for components designed and supplied to the Walsh Brothers of New Zealand for a flying-boat. The use of type numbers for components was dispensed with and Type 509 was reallocated to a seaplane design to be powered by two 120 hp Astro-Daimler engines. | Nov. 1913 |
| 512 | A biplane powered by a 65 hp Astro-Daimler engine. | Dec. 1913 |
| 513 | Twin-float bomber seaplane with two 80 hp Gnome engines. | Mar. 1914 |
| 515 | 150 hp Sunbeam-powered biplane. | Sep. 1914 |
| 516 | 80 hp Gnome-powered monoplane. | Jan. 1915 |
| 517 | Biplane version of the Type 516. | Feb. 1915 |
| 518 | Single-seat fighter using a 150 hp Sunbeam engine. | May 1915 |
| 520 | Single-seat landplane for the Royal Navy. 150 hp Sunbeam engine. | May 1915 |
| 524 | Single-seat scout aircraft powered by 80 hp Gnome. | June 1915 |

| Type Number | Remarks | Date |
|---|---|---|
| 525 | Single-seat ground attack aeroplane to R.A.F. Class 2 specification. | Nov. 1915 |
| 526 | As for Type 525, but with redesigned tail unit of monoplane structure. | Nov. 1915 |
| 532 | Short-range reconnaissance aircraft with two-man crew. Powered by an A.B.C. Dragonfly radial engine of 330 hp. | Apr. 1918 |
| 535 | Single Rolls-Royce Falcon 280 hp engine was to power this Transatlantic aircraft. | Apr. 1919 |
| 537 | Ten passenger twin-engined biplane with 300 hp Puma powerplants. | Mar. 1919 |
| 541 | Shipboard reconnaissance seaplane with folding wings stowage. Powered by one 450 hp Napier Lion, it was designed to Specification R.A.F. Class 21. | Sept. 1919 |
| 542 | Civil passenger version of 541. | Oct. 1919 |
| 550 | Not used, but reserved for reconnaissance triplane to Specification 37/22. | Oct. 1922 |
| 551 | Civil version of Type 550 with accommodation for fifteen passengers. Power was to be three Rolls-Royce Condor 600 hp engines. | Jan. 1923 |
| 553 | Training version of the Avro 548. | Feb. 1921 |
| 556 | Coastal Defence torpedo bomber which was cancelled in favour of Avro 557 Ava. | Nov. 1921 |
| 559 | An uncompleted light monoplane designed for the 1923 Lympne Trials. | Jun. 1923 |
| 564 | Two-seat monoplane fighter powered by 650 hp version of R-R Condor. | Jul. 1924 |
| 565 | 450 hp Napier Lion version of Type 564. | Jul. 1924 |
| 568 | Single-seat fighter of all metal construction. | Nov. 1925 |
| 569 | Large wing aeroplane with R.A.F. 30 wing section. A version of the Avro 566 Avenger. | Nov. 1925 |
| 570 | Single-seat seaplane version of Avro 566 Avenger. | Nov. 1925 |

| Type Number | Remarks | Date |
|---|---|---|
| 573 | Scaled-up version of Avro 563 Andover to be powered by three Bristol Jupiter 425 hp engines. To be equipped with folding wings and large freight door. | Jan. 1926 |
| 577 | General purpose aeroplane. | Jan 1926 |
| 578 | Seaplane version of Type 577. | Jan. 1926 |
| 579 | Avro 562 Avis with R.A.F. 15 wing section. | Feb. 1926 |
| 580 | Four-engined heavy bomber with the 450 hp version of the Bristol Jupiter as powerplant. | Feb. 1926 |
| 583 | A geared Napier Lion version of the Avro 566 Avenger. Engine power 570 hp. | Mar. 1926 |
| 588 | A monoplane version of the Avro 581 Avian prototype. Powered by 70 hp, A.S. Genet. | Jul. 1926 |
| 589 | Seaplane version of 588. | Aug. 1927 |
| 590 | Together with Types 591 and 592 were designed as Army Co-operation biplanes to the Australian Specification AC. 35, 36 and 37. To be powered by one 450 hp Bristol Jupiter engine, but were not accepted for production in Australia. | Oct. 1927 |
| 593 | Seaplane version of Type 590, but with 450 hp Armstrong Siddeley Jaguar engine. | Oct. 1927 |
| 595 | Two-seat land or seaplane reconnaissance aircraft to Specification 0. 22/26. | Feb. 1927 |
| 596 | Three-seat bomber version of Type 595. | Feb 1927 |
| 597 | Landplane bomber version of Avro 571 Buffalo. | Feb. 1927 |
| 598 | And Type 599 were designed to an Australian trainer specification and given the names Warregull Mk. 1 and Mk. 2 even though the designs were never built. | Mar. 1927 |
| 600 | Avro 594 Avian with R.A.F. 15 wing section. | Apr.1927 |
| 601 | 450 hp Napier Lion powered reconnaissance aeroplane. | Apr. 1927 |
| 602 | Much modified version of the Avro 566 Avenger. Offered as fighter to the R.A.F. | May 1927 |

| Type Number | Remarks | Date |
|---|---|---|
| 603 | Three-engined aeroplane with accommodation for eight passengers. Designed to a requirement of West Australian Airways, but the airline chose the Vickers Viastra. | May 1927 |
| 606 | Three-engined flying-boat to Imperial Airways specification. Monoplane design with square hull. | Oct. 1927 |
| 607 | As Type 606, but with semi-circular hull. | Oct. 1927 |
| 608 | Two-seat biplane fighter to be known as the Hawk, but construction was abandoned and airframe was later used in the development of the Type 622 and finally the Avro 627 Mailplane. | Dec. 1927 |
| 609 | 450 hp Bristol Jupiter powered three-seat general purpose seaplane. | Dec. 1927 |
| 610 | High-wing monoplane with accommodation for a pilot and four passengers. Could be powered by any of the 200 hp engines available at that time. | Jan. 1928 |
| 613 | A twin-engined night bomber to Specification B. 19/27. Jaguar engine proposed. | May 1928 |
| 614 | Three 180 hp Armstrong Siddeley Lynx engines were to power this high-wing commercial monoplane, but the licence-build agreement for the Avro 618 Ten forced plans for the 614 to be dropped. | Jun. 1928 |
| 615 | Seaplane version of Type 614. | Jun. 1928 |
| 622 | A fighter-bomber version of the Type 608 Hawk powered by a 540 hp Armstrong Siddeley Panther. Converted to Avro 627 Mailplane before completion as Type 622. | Apr. 1930 |
| 623 | Two-seat high-wing survey aeroplane powered by either Armstrong Siddeley Lynx or Cheetah engine. | Apr. 1930 |
| 628 | Mail-carrying version of Avro 619 Five. | Aug. 1930 |
| 629 | Single-engined mailplane. | Aug. 1930 |
| 630 | Bomber development of the Avro 627 Mailplane. | Sep. 1931 |
| 632 | Carrier-borne torpedo bomber/reconnaissance aircraft to Specification S. 9/30. | Dec. 1932 |

| Type Number | Remarks | Date |
|---|---|---|
| 633 | Single-seat fighter version of Avro 631 Cadet. | Mar. 1931 |
| 634 | Two-seat low-wing training monoplane. | May 1932 |
| 635 | Low-wing cabin monoplane powered by a single Armstrong Siddeley Lynx of 215 hp. | Jul. 1932 |
| 644 | The proposed engine for this two-seat reconnaissance bomber was a 420 hp Armstrong Siddeley Jaguar. | Apr. 1933 |
| 645 | A six-seater monoplane powered by two Armstrong Siddeley Double Mongoose engines each of 340 hp. | May 1933 |
| 647 | Also Type 648 were slightly differing designs for twin A.S. Genet Major engines of 140 hp to power these six-seat low-wing cabin monoplanes. | Jun. 1933 |
| 649 | A four-engined seventeen-seat passenger seaplane with the power provided by 240 hp Armstrong Siddeley Lynx engines. | Jul. 1933 |
| 650 | Eight-seat monoplane with four 140 hp A.S. Genet Major radial engines. | Jul. 1933 |
| 651 | A three-engined monoplane powered by two 240 hp A.S. Lynx engines on the wings and with a single A.S. Jaguar 420 hp radial in the nose of the aeroplane. | Aug. 1933 |
| 653 | Long-range seaplane with four A.S. Cheetah IIA engines. | Oct. 1933 |
| 655 | Also Type 656 were twin-engine low-wing bombers of different design, but both having the Armstrong Siddeley Jaguar for power. | Nov. 1933 |
| 657 | High performance military aircraft. | Dec. 1933 |
| 658 | Three-seat low-wing monoplane powered by a geared A.S. Genet Major giving 140 hp. | Jan. 1934 |
| 659 | Also Type 660. Low-wing twins similar, but smaller than the Avro 652 transport aircraft. Engines were A.S. Genet Majors and the machines had fixed faired-in undercarriages. | Jan. 1934 |
| 662 | A.S.Lynx-powered Avro 621 Tutor. Updated to Type 669. | Feb. 1934 |
| 663 | Cadet trainer powered by 135 hp A.S. Genet Major engine. | Feb. 1934 |

| Type Number | Remarks | Date |
|---|---|---|
| 664 | Low-wing twin abandoned in favour of the Avro 652A Anson. | May 1934 |
| 665 | A cabin autogiro utilising the fuselage of an Avro 641 Commodore fitted with the rotor system of a Cierva C. 33. | Jun. 1934 |
| 666 | Dive bomber biplane powered by 790 hp Armstrong Siddeley Tiger radial engine. Designed to Specification 0. 27/34 with one version having a gun turret behind the pilot's glazed canopy. Competition for the Specification was eventually won by the Blackburn Skua. | Oct. 1934 |
| 668 | The Type Number was given to the Cierva C.37, a twin-engined cabin autogiro project with an Avro-designed fuselage. | Feb. 1935 |
| 669 | Tutor Special powered by the 310 hp version of the Armstrong Siddeley Cheetah. | Mar. 1935 |
| 670 | Army Co-operation aircraft designed to the Specification A.39/34. This competition was won by the Westland Lysander. | Apr. 1935 |
| 672 | A twin-engined reconnaissance aircraft to the double Specification of G.24/35 and M.15/35. Powered by A.S. Terrier engines. | Oct. 1935 |
| 673 | Twin-engined training aircraft with 200 hp D.H. Gipsy Six engines. | Oct. 1935 |
| 675 | As Type 672, but power supplied by up-rated Terrier engines. Smaller overall dimensions than 672. | May 1936 |
| 676 | Also Type 677 both submitted for Specification T.6/36, but Miles Master selected for service. Rolls-Royce Kestrel powered. | May 1936 |
| 678 | Single-seat shoulder-wing fighter with one Rolls-Royce Merlin driving two propellers. | Aug. 1936 |
| 680 | Four-engined heavy bomber to Specification B.1/39. | Apr. 1939 |
| 681 | Also Type 682 were heavy bomber projects. | Jan. 1940 |
| 684 | 'Stratosphere' bomber powered by four Rolls-Royce Merlins. Lancaster airframe with Wellington pressure cabin. Supercharged engines. | Sep. 1941 |

| Type Number | Remarks | Date |
|---|---|---|
| 686 | High-altitude bomber. Lancaster replacement. | Oct. 1944 |
| 690 | Avro 22 transport with six R-R Merlin engines. | Aug. 1944 |
| 692 | Avro 23 transport. Six R-R Merlins. | Sep. 1944 |
| 693 | Designed to Brabazon Specification 3A for high speed transport. Originally turbo-prop, but eventually to be equipped with Rolls-Royce Avon jet engines. Project continued until February 1947 when it was finally cancelled. | Jan. 1945 |
| 697 | Medium range transport aircraft. | Jun. 1947 |
| 700 | Transport aeroplane with accommodation for twelve passengers. Power provided by two Armstrong Siddeley Cheetahs each giving 475 hp. | Jan. 1945 |
| 702 | Aircrew trainer for Royal Canadian Air Force Specification 4/10. | Dec. 1945 |
| 703 | Thirty-six passenger jet transport for Trans Canada Airlines. | Sep. 1947 |
| 704 | Two-seat jet trainer powered by Rolls-Royce Derwent engines. | Nov. 1947 |
| 705 | Tricycle undercarriage four-jet transport. Rolls-Royce Nenes provided the power. | Nov. 1947 |
| 708 | Long-range transport to Empire Specification. | Nov. 1949 |
| 709 | Long-range version of the Avro 689 Tudor 2. | Jun. 1948 |
| 710 | Half-scale version of the Avro 698. | Feb. 1949 |
| 711 | Version of the Avro 688 Tudor 4. Work commenced on Type 711A Trader, but discontinued. Tricycle undercarriage. | Oct. 1948 |
| 712 | Meteorological version of Avro 694 Lincoln. | Feb. 1950 |
| 713 | Avro 696 Shackleton meteorological version. | Apr. 1950 |
| 714 | Jet-powered basic trainer. | Apr. 1950 |
| 715 | Eight-ten seater jet transport. | Jun. 1950 |

| Type Number | Remarks | Date |
|---|---|---|
| 716 | Development of the Avro Shackleton MR.3. | May 1951 |
| 717 | Avro 694 Lincoln aircraft test-bed for two Napier Nomad engines. | Jun. 1951 |
| 718 | A four-jet military transport powered by Bristol Olympus engines. | Jun. 1951 |
| 719 | Avro 696 Shackleton, a Mk. 4 version powered by four Napier Nomad engines. | Nov. 1951 |
| 721 | Low-level strike bomber of four-jet design. | Oct. 1952 |
| 722 | Avro Atlantic four-jet delta airliner based on the Avro 698 Vulcan and designed to carry 113 passengers from London to New York in under seven hours. | Dec. 1952 |
| 723 | A replacement for the Douglas DC-3 type. Four Alvis Leonides engines. | May 1953 |
| 724 | Project 'Y' VTOL aircraft, alternative to Canadian Avrocar flying saucer. | Jun. 1953 |
| 725 | Trainer based on Avro 720. Proposed single jet power either by de Havilland PS.35 or Bristol BE.26. | Oct. 1953 |
| 726 | Light delta fighter with D.H. PS.35 or Armstrong Siddeley P1.51 jet engines. | Nov. 1953 |
| 727 | NATO Specification ground attack fighter using Type 720 wings, but redesigned fuselage to accommodate Bristol Orpheus engines. | Feb. 1954 |
| 728 | Naval interceptor developed from Avro 720. Powered by de Havilland Gyron Junior. | Mar 1955 |
| 729 | Gyron Junior powered all-weather fighter. | Jan. 1955 |
| 730 | Stainless-steel supersonic bomber with eight Armstrong Siddeley P.176 turbojets. Mock-up work commenced, but project cancelled. | Jun. 1955 |
| 731 | Three-eighth scale development aircraft for Type 730. Two Gyron Juniors as powerplants. | Oct. 1955 |
| 732 | Supersonic development of Avro 698 Vulcan. | Jul. 1956 |

| Type Number | Remarks | Date |
|---|---|---|
| 733 | Type number given to Shackleton wings for use on the Armstrong Whitworth Argosy. | Aug. 1956 |
| 734 | Decoy counter-measures aircraft. Single Armstrong Siddeley P.176 engine. | Nov. 1956 |
| 735 | Eight-jet supersonic Vulcan-type airliner. | Nov. 1956 |
| 736 | Turboprop transport aircraft powered by four Napier E.223 or A.S. P1.82 engines. | Nov. 1956 |
| 737 | STOL transport with similar power to Type 736. | Jan. 1957 |
| 738 | Projected weapons system. | May 1957 |
| 739 | Low level strike aircraft. | Jun. 1957 |
| 740 | Airliner to BEA spec. Three rear mounted jet engines and vee tail configuration. | Jul. 1957 |
| 741 | Exec. jet. Two Bristol Orpheus engines. | Jul. 1957 |
| 742 | Transport. Wing jet flaps. Three Bristol BE.53 turboprop engines. | Jul. 1957 |
| 743 | Military transport. Four Bristol Orion turboprop engines. | Jul. 1957 |
| 744 | Nuclear-powered aircraft project. | Aug. 1957 |
| 745 | Maritime patrol aircraft to NATO spec. Four Rolls-Royce turboprop engines. | Aug. 1957 |
| 746 | Jet flap research aircraft. Three Bristol BE.53 turboprop engines. | |
| 747 | Transport aircraft. Four Rolls-Royce Dart engines. | Oct. 1957 |
| 749 | VTOL transport to BEA requirement. | Feb. 1958 |
| 750 | Short range airliner (80 pax). Two Rolls-Royce RB.141/4 engines, rear mounted. | Feb. 1958 |
| 751 | Airliner. Three jet engines. | Mar. 1958 |
| 752 | VTOL assault aircraft. | Mar. 1958 |
| 753 | Freighter utilising Avro 745 wing. | May 1958 |

| Type Number | Remarks | Date |
|---|---|---|
| 754 | Civil transport utilising Avro 745 wing. | May 1958 |
| 755 | STOL aircraft using deflected slip-stream. | Jun. 1958 |
| 756 | Long range military transport. Four Rolls-Royce Tyne turboprop engines. | Jul. 1958 |
| 757 | Avro 748 to Indian spec. Large rear freight door. | Sep. 1958 |
| 758 | High wing version of 748 to Indian requirement. | Feb. 1959 |
| 759 | Narrow-delta research glider. | Oct. 1958 |
| 760 | Supersonic airliner. | Nov. 1958 |
| 761 | Airliner (77 pas). Two Rolls-Royce RB.163 turbofan engines, rear mounted. | Nov. 1958 |
| 762 | Advanced weapons system. | Nov. 1958 |
| 763 | VTOL vehicle-jeep. | Dec. 1958 |
| 764 | AW 650 VTOL military transport. | Feb. 1959 |
| 765 | VTOL lift-fan fighter. | Jan. 1959 |
| 766 | Four-jet long-range military transport. | Feb. 1959 |
| 767 | Joint project with Bristol Aeroplane Company for a four jet airliner. | Feb. 1959 |
| 768 | Early warning aircraft. | Mar. 1959 |
| 769 | VTOL weapons system version of Avro Vulcan. | Jun. 1959 |
| 770 | STOL assault transport. | Nov. 1959 |
| 771 | Twin-jet airliner. Smaller version of 761. | Mar.1960 |
| 772 | Car transporter aircraft. | Jan. 1960 |
| 773 | STOL military freighter. | Mar. 1960 |
| 774 | Long endurance weapons system. | Nov. 1960 |

| Type Number | Remarks | Date |
|---|---|---|
| 775 | Maritime reconnaissance with two Rolls-Royce Tyne turboprop engines and one rear-mounted RB.168 turbojet. | Nov. 1960 |
| 776 | To same spec. as Type 775. Three rear-mounted Rolls-Royce RB.178 turbofans. | Apr. 1961 |
| 777 | Type number not used. | |
| 778 | Twin-engined airliner with rear-mounted Rolls-Royce RB.161 engines. Originally Avro 748J. | Apr. 1960 |
| 779 | High wing STOL transport based on 748 components. | May 1961 |
| 780 | Avro 748M later designated 780 Andover C.1. | May 1961 |
| 781 | Twin-turbofan shortened version of Avro 748. | May 1962 |
| 782 | Shortened version of Avro 780. | Jun. 1962 |
| 783 | STOL version of Avro 780 for NATO. | Jan. 1963 |
| 784 | Maritime reconnaissance aircraft powered by four turboprop engines to same spec. as Avro 776. | Jun. 1963 |

The Avro numbering system was replaced by Hawker Siddeley Aviation on 12 July 1963.

# APPENDIX C
## Avro Prototypes First Flights Since 1935

| Date | Type | Aircraft | Reg. | Pilot | Location |
|------|------|----------|------|-------|----------|
| 7 Jan. 1935 | Avro 652 | Proto | G-ACRM | F.B. Tomkins | Woodford |
| 24 Mar. 1935 | Anson 1 | Proto | K4771 | S.A. Thorn | Woodford |
| 25 Jul. 1939 | Manchester 1 | Proto | L7426 | H.A. Brown | Ringway* |
| 26 May 1940 | Manchester 1 | 2nd Proto | L7247 | H.A. Brown | Ringway |
| 9 Jan. 1941 | Lancaster 1 | Proto | BT308 | H.A. Brown | Ringway |
| 13 May 1941 | Lancaster 1 | 2nd Proto | DG595 | H.A. Brown | Ringway |
| 26 Nov. 1941 | Lancaster 2 | Proto | DT810 | H.A. Brown | Ringway |
| 5 Jul. 1942 | York 1 | Proto | LV626 | H.A. Brown | Ringway |
| 4 Apr. 1943 | York 1 | 3rd Proto | LV633 | H.A. Brown | Ringway |
| 20 Feb. 1944 | York 1 | 2nd Proto | LV629 | S.A. Thorn | Ringway |
| 1 Mar. 1944 | York 2 | Proto | LV626 | H.V. Worrall | Ringway+ |
| 9 Jun. 1944 | Lincoln 1 | Proto | PW925 | H.A. Brown | Ringway |
| 9 Nov. 1944 | Lincoln 1 | 2nd Proto | PW929 | H.A. Brown | Ringway |
| 17 Jan. 1945 | Lancastrian 1 | Proto | G-AGLF | J.H. Orrell | Woodford |
| 15 Jun. 1945 | Tudor 1 | Proto | G-AGPF | S.A. Thorn | Ringway |
| 30 Dec. 1945 | Anson 19 | Proto | G-AGNI | H.V. Worrall | Yeadon++ |
| 10 Mar. 1946 | Tudor 2 | Proto | G-AGSU | S.A. Thorn | Woodford |
| 19 Jun. 1946 | Tudor 1 | 2nd Proto | G-AGST | S.A. Thorn | Woodford |
| 27 Sep.1946 | Tudor 3 | Proto | G-AIYA | J.B. Walker | Woodford |
| 9 Apr. 1947 | Tudor 4 | Proto | G-AHNJ | S.A. Thorn | Woodford |
| 17 Apr. 1947 | Tudor 7 | Proto | G-AGRX | S.A. Thorn | Woodford |
| 5 Aug. 1947 | Anson 20 | Proto | VM305 | A.K. Cook | Woodford |
| 12 Nov. 1947 | Tudor 2 | 2nd Proto | G-AGRY | J.H. Orrell | Woodford |
| 6 Feb. 1948 | Anson 21 | Proto | VS562 | J.H. Orrell | Woodford |
| 12 Jun. 1948 | Athena 1(Mamba) | Proto | VM125 | J.H. Orrell | Woodford |
| 1 Aug. 1948 | Athena 2 | Proto | VW890 | J.H. Orrell | Woodford |
| 6 Sep. 1948 | Tudor 8 | Proto | VX195 | J.H. Orrell | Woodford |
| 24 Sep. 1948 | Tudor 5 | Proto | G-AKBY | J.H. Orrell | Woodford |
| 8 Jan. 1949 | Athena 2 | 2nd Proto | VW891 | J.H. Orrell | Woodford |
| 17 Jan. 1949 | Anson 22 | Proto | VM306 | J.D. Baker | Woodford |
| 9 Mar. 1949 | Shackleton 1 | Proto | VW126 | J.H. Orrell | Woodford |
| 25 Aug. 1949 | Athena 2 | 3rd Proto | VW892 | S.E.Esler | Woodford |
| 2 Sep. 1949 | Shackleton 1 | 2nd Proto | VW131 | J.D. Baker | Woodford |
| 4 Sep. 1949 | Avro 707 | Proto | VX784 | S.E. Esler | Boscombe Down |
| 17 Sep. 1949 | Athena 1(Dart) | 2nd Proto | VM129 | S.E. Esler | Farnborough |
| 21 Dec. 1949 | Athena 1(Mamba) | 3rd Proto | VM132 | J.C. Nelson | Woodford |
| 29 Mar. 1950 | Shackleton 1 | 3rd Proto | VW135 | J.H. Orrell | Woodford |
| 1 Sep. 1950 | Ashton 1 | Proto | WB490 | J.H. Orrell | Woodford |

| Date | Type | Aircraft | Reg. | Pilot | Location |
|------|------|----------|------|-------|----------|
| 6 Sep. 1950 | Avro 707B | Proto | VX790 | R.J. Falk | Boscombe Down |
| 14 Jun. 1951 | Avro 707A | Proto | WD280 | R.J. Falk | Boscombe Down |
| 7 Jul. 1951 | Ashton 3 | 3rd A/c. | WB492 | J.H. Orrell | Woodford |
| 19 Jul. 1951 | Shackleton 2 | Proto | VW126 | J.H. Orrell | Woodford+++ |
| 2 Aug. 1951 | Ashton 2 | 2nd A/c. | WB491 | J.C. Nelson | Woodford |
| 18 Dec.1951 | Ashton 3 | 4th A/c. | WB493 | J.C. Nelson | Woodford |
| 9 Apr. 1952 | Ashton 3 | 6th A/c. | WE670 | J.C. Nelson | Woodford |
| 30 Aug. 1952 | Vulcan (698) | Proto | VX770 | R.J. Falk | Woodford |
| 18 Nov. 1952 | Ashton 4 | 5th A/c. | WB494 | J.C. Nelson | Woodford |
| 20 Feb. 1953 | Avro 707A | 2nd Proto | WZ736 | J.C. Nelson | Waddington |
| 1 Jul. 1953 | Avro 707C | Proto | WZ744 | J.B. Wales | Waddington |
| 3 Sep. 1953 | Vulcan 1 | 2nd Proto | VX777 | R.J. Falk | Woodford |
| 2 Sep. 1955 | Shackleton 3 | Proto | WR970 | J.D. Baker | Woodford |
| 31 Aug. 1957 | Vulcan 2 | Proto | VX777 | J.G. Harrison | Woodford++++ |
| 24 Jun. 1960 | Avro 748 | Proto | G-APZV | J.G. Harrison | Woodford |
| 10 Apr. 1961 | Avro 748 | 2nd Proto | G-ARAY | J.G. Harrison | Woodford |

| | |
|---|---|
| * | Now Manchester International Airport |
| + | Converted to Mk.2 from first prototype |
| ++ | Now Leeds Bradford Airport |
| +++ | Converted to Mk.2 from first prototype |
| ++++ | Converted to Mk.2 from second prototype |

# Avro Lancaster Production Group

## General History of the Group

The Lancaster Group was in being from September 1941 to September 1945, and its organisation was based on experiences from the early Manchester Group, which aircraft was the forerunner of the Lancaster, the Manchester having been in existence since 1937.

It is interesting to note that the nucleus of the Manchester Group consisted of A.V. Roe, the parent design firm, and Metropolitan-Vickers who were later joined by Armstrong Whitworth and the Fairy Aviation Company. The latter, however, left the Group owing to reduction in requirements.

In 1941 the Lancaster Group consisted of A.V. Roe Ltd, Metropolitan-Vickers Ltd., Sir W.G. Armstrong Whitworth and Vickers Armstrong Ltd, Castle Bromwich.

In March 1943 the Group was further expanded to meet increased Lancaster Bomber requirements and the following contractors became members of the Group — Vickers Armstrong Ltd, Chester and the Austin Motor Co. Ltd, Birmingham.

Messrs Short & Harland of Belfast were also intended to become members of the Group and received an order to build 200 aircraft. This was later cancelled as it was found that the whole of the Lancaster requirements could be satisfied from the capacity available in England.

The following table gives a broad picture of each firm's achievements in the way of total aircraft delivered:

| Contractor | Mark | Contract |
|---|---|---|
| A.V. Roe, Man./Yeadon | I | 896 |
| " " " | III | 2,774 |
| Austin Aero Ltd | I | 150 |
| " " " | VII | 180 |
| V.A., Castle Bromwich | I | 300 |
| Vickers, Chester | I | 235 |
| Metro.-Vickers | I | 944 |
| " " | III | 136 |
| Armstrong Whitworth | I | 919 |
| " " | II | 300 |
| " " | III | 110 |
| Victory Aircraft, Canada | X | 430 |
| | | 7,374 |

Plus three prototypes = 7,377 Total

# General Review of each Firm in the Group

## A.V. Roe & Co. Ltd

| | |
|---|---|
| Managing Director | Sir Roy Dobson |
| Assistant General Manager & Director | Mr C.E. Fielding |
| General Works Manager | Mr J. Green |
| Chief Superintendent | Mr J.A.R. Kay |
| | (Secretary of the Group) |

The firm produced their first Lancaster in October 1941 and their last in October 1945, during which period they reached a peak of 155 aircraft per month during August 1944.
During the above period the firm produced a total of:

896 Lancaster Mark I
2,774 Lancaster Mark III

making a total of 3,670 aircraft.

A.V. Roe produced and delivered aircraft from two factories — Manchester and Yeadon — the Yeadon factory contributing 608 aircraft towards the above total.

## Metropolitan-Vickers

| | |
|---|---|
| General Manager & Director | Mr T. Fraser |
| Works Manager | Mr A.J. Leslie |

The first aircraft was produced and delivered in January 1942 and the last in August 1945, during which period the firm reached a peak of 45 machines per month in August 1944.
During the above period the firm produced a total of:

915 Lancaster Mark I
136 Lancaster Mark III

making a total of 1,051 aircraft.

The assembly of the Metropolitan-Vickers Lancaster was carried out at Woodford by Messrs A.V. Roe who averaged, from this Assembly Unit alone, 150 per month. A really outstanding achievement.

## Armstrong Whitworth Aircraft Ltd

| | |
|---|---|
| General Manager & Director | Mr W. Woodhams |
| Assistant General Manager | Mr P.G. Crabbe |
| Works Manager | Mr E.L. Lockwood |

This firm produced their first Lancaster in August 1942 and the last in October 1945, during which period the firm reached 75 machines per month in October 1944, and delivered the following aircraft:

919 Lancaster Mark I
300 Lancaster Mark II
110 Lancaster Mark III

Making a total of 1,329 Lancasters of all types.

## Vickers, Chester

| | |
|---|---|
| Superintendent | Mr B.A. Duncan |
| Sub-Contracts Manager | Mr Lefevre |

At Vickers, Chester, most of the work was sub-contracted, final assembly being carried out at Chester.
The firm produced their first Lancaster in June 1944 and its last in September 1945, during which period the firm reached a peak of 36 aircraft per month in March 1945.
During the above period the firm delivered a total of:

235 Lancaster Mark 1

**Vickers Armstrongs, Castle Bromwich**

Resident Director during Lancaster production period, Mr W.A. Dixon

The firm produced their first Lancaster in November 1943 and their last in August 1945, during which period a peak of 25 machines per month was reached during December 1944.
The total number of aircraft produced by the factory was:

<u>300</u>

**Austin Aero Ltd**

| | |
|---|---|
| Manager | Mr F.V. Smith |
| Production Manager | Mr G.A. Durant |

This firm produced their first Lancaster in March 1944 and were still in production with 26 aircraft outstanding to be completed by the end of 1945, during which period a peak of 35 machines per month was reached in June 1945.
The total number of aircraft produced by the factory was:

150 Lancaster Mark I
180 Lancaster Mark VII

Making a total of <u>330</u> Lancasters of all types.

This total was not the original figure the firm had planned to produce but with the termination of the war their contract was cut. They had planned to continue production until June 1946.

# Development of the Lancaster

As Lancaster production was proceeding, the parent firm was actively engaged in the development and production of a super Lancaster, eventually known as the Lincoln and as the European War was drawing to a close this aircraft was commencing to come into production.
It had already been decided to reduce the Group to three firms and this necessitated —

Vickers Armstrongs, Castle Bromwich
Vickers, Chester
Austin Aero Ltd

completing their Lancaster production and leaving the Group.
This left —

A.V. Roe Ltd
Armstrong Whitworth
Metropolitan-Vickers

to continue with Lincoln production but with the conclusion of the Japanese War Metropolitan-Vickers left the Group at the end of 1945.

From the foregoing it will therefore be seen that the Group has a wartime record of which it can be extremely proud, having delivered a total of 7,374 Lancaster aircraft, plus three prototypes.

# APPENDIX E

## Avro Wartime Manufacturing Arrangements at Various Factories

*Chadderton Works*

Aircraft Design
Experimental
Preproduction Office
General Office
Tool Manufacture
Lancaster Fuselage Production
Lancaster Fuselage Floors
York Fuselage Production
Lancaster C/Section & Wing Spars*
York C/Section Spars
Machining of all details for above and also machining of all details for components at Ivy Works and Laurel Works.

*Newton Heath*

Lancaster C/Section
Lancaster C/Section Floors
Lancaster Mainplanes*
Lancaster Mainplane Tips*
Machining of all details for above, also machining of all details for Lancaster components (other than bomb gear) which are being assembled at Ashton Works.

*Ashton Works*

Lancaster C/Section Leading Edge
Lancaster Mainplane Flaps*
Lancaster Ailerons*
Lancaster Rudders*
Lancaster Fins*
Lancaster Engine Cowling*
Lancaster Bomb Slips & Carriers
York C/Section Leading Edge

*Ashton Works continued*

Anson Mainplane Flaps
Anson Bulkhead
Anson Cowling
Anson Canopies
Anson Exhaust Manifolds
Machining of details for Bomb Slips & Bomb Carriers.

*Ivy Works, Failsworth*

Lancaster C/Section D.T.E.
Lancaster C/Section Flaps
Lancaster Tailplanes
Lancaster Elevators*
Lancaster Engine Subframes*
Lancaster Bulkheads*
Lancaster Undercarriage Doors*
    Nacelles & Valances
Lancaster Canopies
York Centre Section D.T.E.
York Centre Section Flaps
York Tailplanes
Anson Mainplane D.T.E.
Anson Tailplanes
Anson Rudders
Anson Ailerons

*Laurel Works, Royton*

Lancaster Undercarriage Doors & Valances*
Lancaster Hydraulic Pipes
Lancaster Oxygen Pipes
York Hydraulic Pipes
York Oxygen Pipes
AV77 Marine Gun Turret

Note; Components marked * are common to Lancaster and York.

*Wythenshawe Works*
Lancaster Mainplane D.T.E.*
Lancaster C/Section Fuel Tanks
Lancaster Wing Fuel Tanks*
York C/Section Fuel Tanks
Machining for details above.

*Woodford Assembly Shops*
Assembly of Lancaster Aircraft

*Woodford Flight Sheds*
Erection and flight test of Lancaster aircraft.

*Empire Works, Failsworth*
Lancaster Oil & Cabin Heating Pipes
York Oil & Cabin Heating Pipes

*Yeadon Works*
Lancaster Fuselage
Lancaster Fuselage Floors
Lancaster C/Section
Lancaster C/Section Floors
Lancaster C/Section Leading Edge
Lancaster Engine Subframes*
Lancaster Bulkheads*
Lancaster Bomb Doors
Lancaster C/Section Fuel Tanks
Lancaster Wing Fuel Tanks*
Lancaster C/Section Spars
Anson Fuselage
Anson Wing
Anson Engine Mounting
Anson Undercarriage
Anson Engine Installation
Anson Fuselage Nose
Anson Engine Nacelles
Anson Cabin Sides(Electrical)
Lancaster aircraft erection and flight test
Anson aircraft erection and flight test
Machining of details for above and also machining
of details for Anson components being assembled
at Ivy Works and Ashton Works.

*Bracebridge Heath*
Repair Depot

*Langar*
Repair Depot

*Baytree Mill, Middleton*
Stores

*Dukinfield*
Stores

*Firwood Mill, Chadderton*
Stores

*Sun Mill, Oldham*
Stores

*Shepley Lighting Co.*
Dispersal Stores

*Ultralight Casket Co., Manchester*
Dispersal Stores

*U.C.Dairies, Failsworth*
Dispersal Stores

*B.D.A. Newlay Mills, Leeds*
Dispersal Stores

*Armstrong Siddeley Depot*
Collecting Depot

*Kennings Garage, Manchester*
Collecting Depot

*Packway Garage*
Repair Stores

# Avro Labour Force at Peak Production During the Second World War

| Location | Day Shift | Night Shift | Total |
|---|---|---|---|
| Chadderton | 7,887 | 3,380 | 11,267 |
| Newton Heath | 3,547 | 1,521 | 5,068 |
| Yeadon | 7,167 | 3,073 | 10,240 |
| Ashton | 143 | 612 | 755 |
| Laurel | 1,014 | 434 | 1,448 |
| Empire | 185 | 80 | 265 |
| Wythenshaw | 487 | 209 | 696 |
| Woodford Assembly | 1,770 | 759 | 2,529 |
| Croysdale | 308 | 132 | 440 |
| Ivy Mill | 1,393 | 598 | 1,991 |
| Woodford Flight | 336 | 144 | 480 |
| Yeadon Flight | 338 | 145 | 483 |
| Bracebridge (Repair) | 1,046 | 447 | 1,493 |
| Langar (Repair) | 584 | 250 | 834 |
| 10 Stores | 450 | 205 | 655 |
| | | | 38,644 |

# APPENDIX G

## Avro — Expansion of Floor Area
## 1934/1943

| Date | Factory | Area | Acc. Total |
|---|---|---|---|
| 1934 | Newton Heath | 250,000 sq ft | |
| " | Woodford Flight Sheds, Nos 1 & 2. | 30,000 sq ft | |
| | | | 280,000 sq ft |
| April 1936 | Ivy Works | 200,458 sq ft | |
| "    " | Woodford Flight Shed No 3 | 20,000 sq ft | |
| Sept. 1936 | Empire | 21,605 sq ft | |
| | | | 522,063 sq ft |
| Feb. 1937 | Collyhurst | 40,000 sq ft | |
| | | | 562,063 sq ft |
| 1938 | Woodford Flight Shed No 4 | 90,344 sq ft | |
| " | Newton Heath Extensions | 16,000 sq ft | |
| Dec. 1938 | Ashton | 211,178 sq ft | |
| | | | 879,585 sq ft |
| April 1939 | Chadderton | 750,000 sq ft | |
| Dec.1939 | Woodford Assembly | 689,484 sq ft | |
| Dec.1939 | Collyhurst (discontinued) 40,000 | | 2,279,069 sq ft |
| Dec. 1940 | Firwood | 39,000 sq ft | |
| " | Newton Heath Extensions | 20,000 sq ft | |
| " | Woodford Flight Shed No 5 | 70,000 sq ft | |
| " | Ringway Experimental | 24,500 sq ft | |
| " | Yeadon Assembly | 1,494,711 sq ft | |
| | | | 3,927,280 sq ft |
| Feb. 1941 | Laurel | 224,343 sq ft | |
| Mar. 1941 | Dukinfield | 50,344 sq ft | |
| May 1941 | Bracebridge | 86,909 sq ft | |
| June 1941 | Yeadon Flight | 209,910 sq ft | |
| Aug. 1941 | Sun Mill | 19,739 sq ft | |
| Nov. 1941 | Wythenshawe | 94,100 sq ft | |
| | | | 4,612,625 sq ft |
| Feb. 1942 | Audenshaw | 76,665 sq ft | |
| June 1942 | Baytree | 30,669 sq ft | |
| "   1942 | Langar | 176,302 sq ft | |
| | | | 4,896,261 sq ft |

| Date | Factory | Area | Acc. Total |
|---|---|---|---|
| Jan 1943 | Chadderton Extensions | 273,780 sq ft | |
| " | Newton Heath | 20,721 sq ft | |
| " | Ringway Assembly & Flight | 268,100 sq ft | |
| " | United Co-op Dairies | 6,240 sq ft | |
| Mar. 1943 | Stockport Manufacturing* | 114,200 sq ft | |
| June 1943 | Croysdale's | 60,000 sq ft | |
| " | Stanningley* | 140,000 sq ft | |
| July 1943 | Park Mill | 54,000 sq ft | |
| " | Newlay Mills | 92,500 sq ft | |
| " | Newton Heath Extensions | 40,000 sq ft | |
| " | Chadderton | 80,000 sq ft | |
| " | Yeadon | 50,000 sq ft | |
| " | Bracebridge Heath | 112,000 sq ft | |
| " | Langar | 9,000 sq ft | |
| " | Wythenshawe | 3,100 sq ft | |
| " | Woodford Assembly | 67,200 sq ft | |
| " | Ringway | 5,600 sq ft | |
| " | Dukinfield | 1,100 sq ft | |
| | | | 6,293,802 sq ft |

Less deductions for factories equipped but not controlled
by A.V. Roe, shown with an asterisk.                                254,200 sq ft

Net area controlled by A.V. Roe & Co. Limited                   6,039,602 sq ft

# APPENDIX H

## Avro at Ringway
## (Now Manchester International Airport)

| | |
|---|---|
| 1 May 1939 | Hangar No. 1 adjoining the original lounge and cafe was occupied by the Avro experimental flight department. The prototype Manchester was assembled in this hangar. |
| 25 July 1939 | First flight of prototype Avro Manchester. |
| 26 May 1940 | Second prototype Manchester makes its first flight. |
| 9 Jan. 1941 | Prototype Lancaster's maiden flight. |
| 13 May 1941 | Second prototype Lancaster Mk 1 first flight. |
| 26 Nov. 1941 | Lancaster Mk 2 prototype's maiden flight. |
| 11 Feb. 1942 | Douglas Boston, converted by Avro from Douglas D.B.7 makes its first flight. |
| 3 Mar. 1942 | Douglas Havoc night fighter's first flight. Converted by Avro from Douglas Boston bomber. |
| 25 Mar. 1942 | Possession of site on opposite side of the airfield taken by Kelvin Construction Company for erection of two assembly sheds and one flight shed. It was originally planned for Metropolitan-Vickers to use these premises for the assembly and flight testing of Lancasters, but that task remained at Woodford. The new site was leased by the Ministry of Aircraft Production from Manchester Corporation. |
| 5 July 1942 | Maiden flight of prototype York. |
| 16 Mar. 1943 | Avro take over new premises for assembly of Yorks. |
| 4 Apr. 1943 | Third prototype York flies for the first time. |
| 20 Feb. 1944 | Second prototype York's maiden flight. |
| 1 Mar. 1944 | Radial-engined York Mk 2's first flight. |
| 22 May 1944 | Avro signs agreement with Manchester Corporation to lease Hangar No. 1 first used by the company in May 1939. |
| 9 June 1944 | Prototype Lincoln, originally named Lancaster IV, makes its first flight. |
| 9 Nov. 1944 | Second prototype Lincoln Mk 1's maiden flight. |
| 15 June 1945 | Avro's first post-war civil airliner, the Tudor, flies for the first time. |
| 27 Oct. 1945 | Avro to operate new sheds as bonded store for Ministry of Aircraft Production. |
| 28 Jan. 1946 | Avro experimental flight department moved from Hangar No. 1 to Woodford. |
| 25 Mar. 1946 | Hangar No. 1 completely vacated by Avro. |
| 15 Nov. 1946 | Avro closes Ringway facility with all sections transferred to Woodford. The two assembly sheds and the flight shed operated as bonded store for Ministry of Aircraft Production were released for rental by British Overseas Airways Corporation (BOAC). |

# APPENDIX I

## Avro Aircraft Preserved in the United Kingdom

| Type | Reg. | Location | Status |
|------|------|----------|--------|
| Roe 1 Biplane | - | Brooklands Museum, Weybridge | Replica |
| Roe 1 Triplane | - | The Science Museum, London | Complete |
| Roe 1 Triplane | - | Museum of Science & Ind., Manchester | Replica |
| Roe IV Triplane | - | Shuttleworth Collection, Old Warden | Replica (F) |
| Avro 504J | C4451 | Southampton Hall of Aviation | Replica |
| Avro 504K | G-ABAA | Museum of Science & Ind., Manchester | Complete |
| Avro 504K | E449 | RAF Museum, Hendon | Complete |
| Avro 504 K | D7560 | The Science Museum, London | Complete |
| Avro 504 K | - | Royal Museum of Scotland, Edinburgh | Nose Only |
| Avro 504 K | G-AACA | Brooklands Museum, Weybridge | Restoration |
| Avro 504 K/N | H5199 | Shuttleworth Collection, Old Warden | Complete (F) |
| Avian IIIA | G-ABZM | Museum of Science & Ind., Manchester | Complete |
| Avro 618 Ten | G-ACGF | Royal Museum of Scotland, Edinburgh | Components |
| Tutor | K3215 | Shuttleworth Collection, Old Warden | Complete (F) |
| Anson 1 | N4877 | Imperial War Museum, Duxford | Complete |
| Anson C.19 | VP519 | The Aeroplane Collection, Warmingham | Nose Only |
| Anson C.19 | TX214 | Aerospace Museum, RAF Cosford | Complete |
| Anson C.19 | TX228 | City of Norwich Aviation Museum | Restoration |
| Anson C.19 | TX226 | Imperial War Museum, Duxford | Complete |
| Anson C.19 | VM325 | Midland Air Museum, Coventry | Complete |
| Anson C.19 | VL348 | Newark Air Museum, Winthorpe Airfield | Complete |
| Anson C.19 | VL349 | Norfolk & Suffolk Aviation Museum | Restoration |
| Anson C.19 | TX213 | North East Aircraft Museum, Sunderland | Restoration |
| Anson 19 Srs.2 | G-AHKX | Avro Aircraft Restoration, Woodford | Restoration |
| Anson 19 Srs.2 | G-AGPG | Brenzett Museum, Romney Marsh, Kent | Restoration |
| Anson T.21 | VS562 | RAF Llanbedr Museum, Llanbedr | Restoration |
| Anson T.21 | VV901 | Peninne Aviation Museum, Bacup | Restoration |
| Lancaster I | DV372 | Imperial War Museum, London | Nose Only |
| Lancaster I | W4964 | Newark Air Museum, Winthorpe | Rear Only |
| Lancaster I | PA474 | Battle of Britain Memorial Flight | Complete (F) |
| Lancaster I | R5868 | RAF Museum, Hendon | Complete |
| Lancaster VII | NX611 | Lincolnshire Aviation Heritage | Complete |
| Lancaster X | KB976 | Aces High Museum, North Weald | Restoration |
| Lancaster X | KB889 | Imperial War Museum, Duxford | Complete |
| York 1 | MW100 | Aerospace Museum, RAF Cosford | Complete |
| Lincoln 2 | RF342 | Aces High Museum, North Weald | Restoration |
| Lincoln 2 | RF398 | Aerospace Museum, RAF Cosford | Complete |
| Shackleton AEW.2 | WR960 | Museum of Science & Ind., Manchester | Complete |

| Type | Reg. | Location | Status |
|------|------|----------|--------|
| Shackleton AEW.2 | WL790 | Shackleton Preservation Trust, Ayton, Berwicks | Complete |
| Shackleton AEW.2 | WR963 | Shackleton Preservation Trust, Ayton, Berwicks | Complete |
| Shackleton MR.3/3 | XF708 | Imperial War Museum, Duxford | Restoration |
| Shackleton MR.3/3 | WR985 | Long Marston Aircraft Collection, Strat./Avon | Complete |
| Shackleton MR.3/3 | WR977 | Newark Air Museum, Winthorpe | Complete |
| Shackleton MR.3/3 | WR974 | Peter Vallance Collection, Charlwood, Gatwick | Complete |
| Shackleton MR.3/3 | WR982 | Peter Vallance Collection, Charlwood, Gatwick | Complete |
| Shackleton MR.3/3 | WR971 | Wellesley Aviation, Kings Lynn | Components |
| Shackleton T.4 | WG511 | Flambards Theme Park, Helston | Nose Only |
| Vulcan B.1 | XA893 | Aerospace Museum, RAF Cosford | Nose Only |
| Vulcan B.1 | XA903 | Wales Aircraft Museum, Cardiff | Nose Only |
| Vulcan B.2 | XM598 | Aerospace Museum, RAF Cosford | Complete |
| Vulcan B.2 | XM603 | Avro Aircraft Restoration, Woodford | Complete |
| Vulcan B.2 | XL391 | Blackpool Air Centre, Blackpool Airport | Complete |
| Vulcan B.2 | XL388 | Blyth Valley Aviation Collection,Walpole,Suff. | Nose Only |
| Vulcan B.2 | XL445 | Blyth Valley Aviation Collection,Walpole,Suff. | Nose Only |
| Vulcan B.2 | XM612 | City of Norwich Aviation Museum | Complete |
| Vulcan B.2 | XM575 | East Midlands International Airport | Complete |
| Vulcan B.2 | XJ824 | Imperial War Museum, Duxford | Complete |
| Vulcan B.2 | XL360 | Midland Air Museum, Coventry | Complete |
| Vulcan B.2 | XM594 | Newark Air Museum, Winthorpe | Complete |
| Vulcan B.2 | XL319 | North East Aircraft Museum, Sunderland | Complete |
| Vulcan B.2 | XL318 | RAF Museum, Hendon | Complete |
| Vulcan B.2 | XM607 | RAF Waddington | Complete |
| Vulcan B.2 | XJ823 | Solway Aviation Museum, Carlisle | Complete |
| Vulcan B.2 | XM597 | Royal Museum of Scotland, Edinburgh | Complete |
| Vulcan B.2 | XM569 | Wales Aircraft Museum, Cardiff | Complete |
| Vulcan B.2 | XH558 | C. Walton(Aviation)Ltd, Bruntingthorpe | Complete |
| Ashton 2 | WB491 | Wales Aircraft Museum, Cardiff | Nose Only |
| Avro 707A | WZ736 | Museum of Science & Ind., Manchester | Complete |
| Avro 707C | WZ744 | Aerospace Museum, RAF Cosford | Complete |
| Avro-Canada CF-100 | 18393 | Imperial War Museum, Duxford | Complete |

*Eire*

| | | | |
|------|------|----------|--------|
| Anson C.19 | 141 | Irish Aviation Museum, Dublin Airport | Complete |
| Avro 748 Srs.1 | EI-BSF | DC-7 Aero Museum, Waterford | Complete |

(F)  These aircraft fly on a regular basis

*Note*
A number of other Avro aircraft are preserved in various parts of the world, principally in Australia and Canada.

# APPENDIX J

## Avro 504 Club

On 19 August 1949, J.C.C. 'Joe' Taylor then aviation manager of Shell Mex & BP, who had been an apprentice with A.V. Roe & Company Limited in 1913, wrote to his old friend Sir Roy Dobson suggesting that old apprentices of Avro be rounded up for a reunion.

Sir Roy liked the idea and an extensive operation was put in hand to trace the whereabouts of all concerned. Enquiries were restricted to apprentices with the company prior to 1915 for, to have gone beyond 1915 would have made the task virtually impossible due to the vast increase in the number of employees as World War One continued. As it was, the enormity of the task can only be appreciated when it was realised that by September 1951 only thirty old apprentices had been traced.

The first reunion dinner was held at the Cafe Royal, London on 27 February 1952 with Sir Roy presiding. It was a unique gathering as many of those present had not seen each other for over thirty-seven years and during the occasion two important decisions were taken. Firstly, that those present should form themselves into a club and call it the Avro 504 Club and, secondly, to subscribe to the purchase of a trophy to be presented to the company for an annual competition to be awarded to the best apprentice on completion of training.

It was later decided that the winner of the trophy should attend the next dinner to receive the award from Sir Alliott Verdon-Roe and on the second dinner on 10 March 1953 it was presented to the top Avro apprentice. It was also decided that the winners of the trophy should be made life-members of the Avro 504 Club as it was considered

that this would keep the spirit and traditions of the Club alive when, with the passing of time, the original membership became depleted.

The Club's name had been chosen for obvious reasons. It was in 1913 that A.V. with Roy Chadwick's assistance had designed the Avro 504 and all the founder members of the club had been involved in its production.

Across the years from the first reunion in 1952 the annual dinners continued in unbroken succession. The list of guests provides a tapestry of aviation history, each having made a major contribution to the advancement of the science.

Just as members had foreseen, time did take its toll of the Founders, but at a higher rate than could be compensated for by the addition of just one new member every year. It was then arranged for a further infusion of 'old timers' by electing retired members of the Avro 40 Year Club.

Even with the addition of these old members the Club was losing rather faster than expected and, once again, it was voted that additional members could be forthcoming from the role of general manager of the Manchester factories of Chadderton and Woodford. A further category was established for historians who had furthered the name of Avro.

Currently there are just over fifty members with a similar number having passed on, but with British Aerospace still located in Manchester it continues the great traditions which A.V. established. The Avro 504 Club, described as the most exclusive aviation club in the world, is proud to continue as a tribute to the pioneering genius of Sir Alliott Verdon-Roe.

# INDEX

Referencers in italics refer to captions and/or photographs